MEMORIES OF MY LIFE

AMS PRESS
NEW YORK

Yours faithfully
Francis Galton

MEMORIES OF MY LIFE

BY

FRANCIS GALTON, F.R.S.

D.C.L., OXF.; HON. SC.D., CAMB.
HON. FELLOW TRINITY COLL., CAMBRIDGE

WITH SEVEN ILLUSTRATIONS

METHUEN & CO.
ESSEX STREET W.C.
LONDON
1908

Library of Congress Cataloging in Publication Data

Galton, Sir Francis, 1822-1911.
    Memories of my life.

      "Books and memoirs by the author": p. 325-331.
      1. Galton, Sir Francis, 1822-1911.
Q143.G3A3   1974   509'.2'4 [B] 72-1639
ISBN 0-404-08128-2

Reprinted from the edition of 1908, London
First AMS edition published in 1974
Manufactured in the United States of America

AMS PRESS INC.
NEW YORK, N.Y. 10003

PREFACE

THESE "Memories" are arranged under the subjects to which they refer, and only partially in chronological order. A copious list of my memoirs will be found in the Appendix with dates attached to them. These show what inquiries were going on at or about any specified year. The titles of books are printed in heavy letters. They summarise, as a rule, the best parts of the corresponding memoirs up to the dates of their publication. Nevertheless, a considerable quantity of matter remains in the memoirs as yet unused in that way.

It has been a difficulty throughout to determine how much to insert and how much to omit. I have done my best, but fear I have failed through over-omission.

The method of that most useful volume, the *Index and Epitome of the Dictionary of the National Biography*, has been adopted, of adding to each name the dates of birth and death. They serve for identification and for giving a correct idea of the age of each man as compared with those with whom he was associated. The dates are mostly taken from the *Dictionary*, so the reader will nearly always find in that work a biography of the person in question.

CONTENTS

LIST OF ILLUSTRATIONS

IN THE TEXT

MEMORIES OF MY LIFE

CHAPTER I

PARENTAGE

Birthplace—Grandparents—Dr. Erasmus Darwin—Lunar Society—
Captain Barclay Allardice—Mrs. Schimmelpenninck

JUST before the arrival of the letter in which my publisher asked me to write the memories of my life, I happened to be reading Shakespeare's *Henry IV.* and laughing over Falstaff's soliloquy after the gross exaggerations by Justice Shallow of his own youthful performances. It contained the sentence, "Lord, Lord, how subject we old men are to this vice of lying!" Feeling the truth of his ejaculation, I headed the first page of my memorandum-book with those words as a warning, knowing how difficult it is to be veracious about long-past events, threads of imagination insinuating themselves among those supplied by memory and becoming indistinguishable from them.

Many old notebooks and letters are, however, in my possession which have helped me; but my two latest surviving sisters, whose minds were sure store-houses of family events, and to whom I always referred whenever I wanted a date or particulars of a long-past fact, are now both dead, the one at the

I

age of ninety-three and the other at ninety-seven, each with a clear and vigorous mind to nearly the very end of her life. I have hardly any contemporary friends left who could aid in recalling the circumstances of my childhood and boyhood. With rare exceptions, "All, all are gone, the old familiar faces."

I was born on February 16, 1822, at the Larches, near Sparkbrook, Birmingham, with which town my father Samuel Tertius, my grandfather Samuel John, and my great-grandfather Samuel Galton, were all closely connected. Different members of the family had resided or were resident at various points beyond the circumference of the town, in houses then amidst green fields, but now overspread beyond recognition by its hideous outskirts.

My grandfather's place was at Duddeston, then commonly written "Dudson." Its gardens had been charmingly laid out by my great-grandfather and improved by my grandfather. The house, which was once a centre of refined entertainment, gradually lost its charm of isolation; later on, it wholly ceased to be attractive as a residence. It was then leased by my father to the proprietor of a lunatic asylum, because, as he remarked, no one in his senses would live in it. It is now turned into St. Anne's School, with its porticoes and other outer adornments shorn off, and with its once beautiful gardens changed into the sites of railway sidings and gasworks. I remember it distinctly in its beauty in the year 1830, which was two years before my grandfather's death.

The Larches, where I was born, had some three acres of garden and field attached to it, with other fields beyond; it was a paradise for my childhood. Its site is now covered with small houses. The two fine larches that flanked it gave me a love for that tree, which persists and is still recognisably associated with its origin.

My six nearest progenitors, namely the two parents and four grandparents, were markedly different in temperament and tastes, and they have bequeathed very different combinations of them to their descendants. I can only partly touch on these.

My grandfather, Samuel John Galton (1753–1832), was a scientific and statistical man of business. He was a Fellow of the provincially famous Lunar Society, whose members met at one another's houses on the day and night of the full moon, and which, though small in numbers, was so select as to include Priestley, Dr. Erasmus Darwin, Keir the chemist, Withering the botanist, Watt, and Boulton. Full particulars of the Lunar Society are to be found in Smiles' Life of Boulton, and elsewhere.

I may mention that the late Sir Rowland Hill, of penny-postage fame, told me that the event which first gave him a taste for science was the present of a small electrical machine made to him when a boy, by my grandfather.

Samuel John Galton was very fond of animals. He kept many bloodhounds; he loved birds, and wrote an unpretentious little book about them in three small volumes, with illustrations. He had a decidedly statistical bent, loving to arrange all kinds of data in parallel lines of corresponding lengths, and frequently using colour for distinction. My father, and others of Samuel John Galton's children, inherited this taste in a greater or less degree; it rose to an unreasoning instinct in one of his daughters. She must have been an acceptable customer to her bookbinder on that account, as the number of expensively bound volumes that she ordered from time to time, each neatly ruled in red, and stamped and assigned to some particular subject or year, is hardly credible. I begged for a bagful of them after her death, to keep as a psychological curiosity, and have it still; the rest were destroyed. She must have collected these costly books to satisfy a pure instinct, for she turned them to no useful account, and rarely filled more than a single page, often not so much of each of them. She habitually used a treble inkstand, with black, red, and blue inks, employing the distinctive colours with little reason, but rather with regard to their pictorial effect. She was perhaps not over-wise, yet she was by no means imbecile, and had many qualities that endeared her to her nephews and nieces.

Samuel John Galton was a successful man of business. He was a manufacturer, and became a contractor on a large scale for the supply of muskets to the army during the great war. Birmingham offered at that time a good field for the business of a contractor, because its manufactories were many and of moderate size, and central organisations were wanting. The Soho works of Boulton and Watt for steam-engines were almost the only large works at that time. My grandfather prospered in his business as a "Captain of Industry," to use the phrase applied to him in a book treating of Birmingham. He founded a Bank to help it, which was gradually brought to a close some few years after the war had ceased. He died in 1832, leaving a fortune of some £12,000 a year, of which about a quarter went to each of his three sons, of whom my father was the eldest, and the rest between his three daughters.

The Galton family had been Quakers for many generations. They came to Birmingham from Somersetshire, in the time of my great-grandfather, Samuel Galton (1720–1799). Some of its earlier members are buried at Yatton. There is a hamlet in Dorsetshire called Galton, adjacent to Owre Moigne, with which one at least of our name, and apparently a far back relative, was connected many generations ago.

My grandmother Galton (1757–1817) was also of Quaker stock, being daughter of Robert Barclay of Ury, a descendant of Robert Barclay (1648–1690) "the Apologist," as he used to be named from his work, Barclay's *Apology*, which, to quote the *Dictionary of National Biography*, is the standard exposition of the tenets of his sect, of which the essential principle is that "all true knowledge comes from divine revelation to the heart of the individual."

My grandmother's half-brother, Robert Barclay Allardice (1779–1854), commonly known as "Captain Barclay," was a noted athlete and pedestrian, and in later years an active agriculturist. When upwards of seventy years old he was dining at my father's house in Leamington, and on being asked, while sitting at dessert, whether he still performed any feats of strength, he asked my eldest brother, then a fully adult man of more than 12 stone in weight, to step on his hand, which he laid palm upwards on the floor by slightly bending his body. My brother was desired to steady himself by laying one finger on Captain Barclay's shoulder, who thereupon lifted and landed him on the table. I was not present at the feat, but heard it often described by word and gesture. However, the Captain rather strained his shoulder by performing it, as he confessed to my father afterwards. Captain Barclay's endurance of long continued fatigue was exceptional to a very high degree. The memoirs of his life are well worth reading.

My grandmother's half-sister was wife of Hudson Gurney (1775–1864), "antiquary and verse writer, friend of Lord Aberdeen," to again quote the Index to the *Dict. Nat. Biog.* He was a man of large fortune, and my two sisters, Bessy and Emma, paid long visits to his house in St. James's Square, where his wife was very kind to them, and where they saw much good London society.

My grandfather and grandmother Galton were practically Quakers all their lives, and so was one of their daughters, but the rest of their children fell off and joined the Established Church. Still, we saw not a little of our Quaker relations. A story was current in our family about myself, as a shy and naughty child, being quite subdued by the charm of Mrs. Fry (1780–1845). She did not even look at me, but merely held out her open hand with comfits in it, and went on speaking to others in her singularly sweet voice. I gradually worked my way nearer to her; then she quietly took me on her knees, where I sat for long in perfect content.

My grandparents on the other side were Darwins, my grandfather being Dr. Erasmus Darwin (1731–1802), physician, poet, and philosopher, and the very reverse of an ascetic or of a Quaker. He was grandfather to me by his second wife; and to Charles R. Darwin (1809–1882), the great naturalist, by his first wife. His hereditary influence seems to have been very strong. His son Charles, who died at the early age of twenty from a dissection wound, was a medical student of extraordinary promise; and the medical sagacity of another son, Dr. Robert Darwin of Shrewsbury, the father of Charles R. Darwin, is amply attested. I stayed for a night or two at the house of the latter while I was a boy and too young to form any opinion of him worth recording; besides, I was rather awe-stricken.

My grandmother Darwin (1747–1832), the second wife of Dr. Erasmus Darwin, was the widow of Colonel E. Sacheverel Chandos-Pole, and, judging from her portrait when young, a lady of remarkable grace and beauty. I saw her in her kindly old age when she lived at the Priory near Derby, but I know little with certainty of her early life and character. She died at the age of eighty-five, her mother at ninety-six. It is perhaps partly through her that the exceptional longevity of my mother and her sons and daughters has been derived. My mother died just short of ninety, my eldest brother at eighty-nine, two sisters, as already mentioned, at ninety-three and ninety-seven respectively; my surviving brother is ninety-three and in good health. My own age is now only eighty-six, but may possibly be prolonged another year or more. I find old age thus far to be a very happy time, on the condition of submitting frankly to its many limitations.

A half-sister of my mother married Captain,

afterwards Lord Byron, cousin and successor to the poet in the title. They were very kind to my sisters in their schooldays and after.

Now, as to my two parents and their brothers and sisters. My father, Samuel Tertius Galton (1783–1844), the third in descent of the name of Samuel, was one of the most honourable and kindly of men, and eminently statistical by disposition. He wrote a small book on currency, with tables, which testifies to his taste. He had a scientific bent, having about his house the simple gear appropriate to those days, of solar microscope, orrery, telescopes, mountain barometers without which he never travelled, and so forth. A sliding rule adapted to various uses was his constant companion. He was devoted to Shakespeare, and revelled in *Hudibras*; he read *Tom Jones* through every year, and was gifted with an abundance of humour. Nevertheless, he became a careful man of business, on whose shoulders the work of the Bank chiefly rested in troublous times. Its duties had cramped much of the joy and aspirations of his early youth and manhood, and narrowed the opportunity he always eagerly desired, of abundant leisure for systematic study. As one result of this drawback to his own development, he was earnestly desirous of giving me every opportunity of being educated that seemed feasible and right. He was the eldest son.

The second son, Hubert, married a sister of Robert Barclay, the banker. They had three daughters, who all died unmarried—two while young, the other in advanced age.

The youngest son, John Howard, married Isabella Strutt, a lady of considerable fortune, and built Hadzor, near Droitwich, a large house, with much artistic taste. He enjoyed varied society, and made Hadzor an important social centre.

My uncle Howard was father to Sir Douglas Galton, K.C.B. (1822–1899), an eminent authority on engineering, sanitation, and much else. Sir Douglas held a record position in the examination at Woolwich for entry into the Royal Engineers, being first in every subject (see *Dict. Nat. Biog.*). Curiously enough, though we cousins were both addicted to science, and belonged alike to many scientific societies, and were both Secretaries of the British Association, our paths rarely crossed, except socially, for we were interested in quite different branches of science.

My father's eldest sister, Mary Anne (1778–1856), was a lady of some note as Mrs. Schimmelpenninck, more briefly known to us by repute as "Aunt Skim." A most unhappy feud separated her from all the rest of the family. It is not my duty, and it would certainly give me no pleasure, to enter into what the older members of the family conceived to have been frequent and mischievous misrepresentations. I would rather dwell on the facts that she was highly accomplished and handsome, and that she acquired many fast friends, as shown in the Life of the Gurneys of Earlham and in her own Memoirs. Also that she lived in the reputation of much sterling piety at Bristol, and that three of my own friends, of totally different temperaments, who knew her well, and of whom I inquired particularly, all spoke in pleasant memory of her and her eccentric ways. They were

Prof. W. B. Carpenter (1813-1885) the physiologist, J. Gwyn Jeffreys (1809-1885), conchologist, etc., and Sir Lewis Pelly, K.C.B. (1825-1892), Indian soldier and diplomatist. She wrote a book on Port Royal, and left a valuable library of Port Royalist literature to Sion College, which Mrs. Romanes told me was of great service to her in writing her recent history of that establishment. For more, see *Dict. Nat. Biog.*

I wish I could have learnt more details than I possess of another brother of my father, Theodore Galton (1784–1810), who left England for the grand tour, picked up many curios in Spain and Greece, and, returning in health from the East, was placed in quarantine at Malta. The quarantine establishment was attacked by the plague; he caught it and it killed him. He had the highest reputation in the family for his natural gifts, mental and bodily. There is a touching notice of him in the *Annual Register*.

My mother was A. Violetta Darwin (1783–1874). I have heard from older friends, long since passed away, many charming stories of her as a young bride. She, as I understand, had nothing of the Quaker temperament, but was a joyous and unconventional girl. In her later life she formed the centre of our family during thirty years of widowhood, after my father's comparatively early death at the age of sixty. She was very methodical in her papers and accounts, and a most affectionate mother to myself. One curious faculty of hers deserves record. It was the ease with which she took in mentally, and afterwards reproduced in rough architectural drawing, the arrangement of any house she knew. Her method was to fold a strip of paper by doubling, quartering, and so on, into sixteen portions of equal lengths, and to use this strip of paper as a sixteen-foot scale wherewith to draw her rude but graphic plans. One of her children, my dear sister Lucy Harriot Moilliet (1809–1848), had an exceptional faculty for perspective drawing; she drew elaborate interiors with very little previous instruction.

As to my other brothers and sisters, they were most diverse in character, yet with a certain common resemblance which struck strangers. I shall have occasion to speak more of them later on in the course of my narrative.

The general result of the foregoing is that I acknowledge the debt to my progenitors of a considerable taste for science, for poetry, and for statistics; also that I seem to have received, partly through the Barclay blood, a rather unusual power of enduring physical fatigue without harmful results, of which there is much evidence when I was young. My father had this power in his early manhood, and it was well marked in my eldest brother and in others of the family. I suffer now from bronchitis with occasional asthma, which has been traced to my great-grandfather, Samuel Galton, and has descended in a greater or less degree through all his children who left issue. My father had a strong constitution otherwise, but he suffered terribly from hay asthma, which first attacked him as a youth. I escaped fairly well from any form of it until I was nearly eighty years old; and it is not hay that especially brings it on now, but warm carpeted rooms.

There are few apartments more pleasant to most persons to read in than the drawing-room of the Athenæum Club; I know of none that are now more apt to prove distressing to my throat and lungs.

CHAPTER II

CHILDHOOD AND BOYHOOD

Sisters and brothers—Sisterly teachings—Schools at Boulogne, Kenilworth, and Birmingham

I WAS born into a family of four sisters and two brothers, who were older than myself by ages ranging from seven to fourteen years, the brothers being all younger than the sisters. My third sister, Adele, was twelve years my senior. She had spinal curvature, and was obliged to lie all day on her back upon a board, and was thus cut off from the romps and companionship of her sisters, though all were greatly attached to her. She hailed my arrival into the world as a fairy gift, and begged hard to be allowed to consider me as her sole ward, and in her simple way educated herself as best she could, in order to be able to teach me. Her idea of education at that time was to teach the Bible as a verbally inspired book, to cultivate memory, to make me learn the merest rudiments of Latin, and above all a great deal of English verse. This she did effectually, and the result was that she believed, and succeeded in making others believe, that I was a sort of infant prodigy.

There exist numerous records of my early performances, and it is certain that I really knew at a very early age a great deal of Scott, of Milton, and of Pope's translation of the *Iliad* and *Odyssey*, and that I delighted in what the family nicknamed "spouting" verse. In middle life I feared that I had been an intolerable prig, and cross-questioned many old family friends about it, but was invariably assured that I was not at all a prig, but seemed to "spout" for pure enjoyment and without any affectation; that I often quoted very aptly on the spur of the moment, and that I was a nice little child. My memories become more or less continuous from about the age of five or six, when I was trotted off to live at a dame's school a mile away. During these and many subsequent years, my sister Adele had the greater share of my heart, and whenever I was at home I stayed by her sofa-side most of the day. My other sisters teased and petted me alternately; they were relatively too old to be really companions.

It is curious how unchangeable characters are: my eldest sister was just, my youngest was merciful. When my bread was buttered for me as a child, the former picked out the butter that filled the big holes, the latter did not. Consequently I respected the former, and loved the latter. A memory of this trifling occurrence remained inseparably connected in my mind with these dear sisters all my life, and I often amused them by referring to it.

My second sister, Lucy, married before I was ten years old. She was bright, lovable, and very original. Her house was like a second home to me during the four years of boyhood that I spent at Birmingham. I have indeed been fortunate in receiving the sisterly affection that has fallen to my lot.

But I must not stop at this period of my reminiscences to speak of other sisters than Adele, with whom my heart was then so intimately associated. I am enormously indebted to the influence of her pious, serene, and resolute disposition. Though she was compelled to pass the greater part of her life lying on her back, she was so energetic in other ways, and so capable of endurance, that she overcame difficulties that would have been insurmountable to most women who were equally handicapped. She was active in setting up schools and teaching the poor. She had a considerable correspondence, and exerted a wide influence among all classes during many years. Her natural capacity was of an unusually high order, and many who knew her well, and whose opinions deserve respect, thought that a slight betterment of opportunity and circumstances might have caused her name to be as widely loved and known as those of any of our English saints or heroines. She passed her life under an abiding sense of the presence of God and of duty to man, without which few persons have ever done great things. She was most unconventional in her ways, and her remarkable courage was recognised by all the family.

She married a clergyman, the Rev. Shirley Bunbury, shortly after my father's death in 1844, but was left a widow soon afterwards, with one little girl, on whom she lavished the same educational care that she had bestowed upon myself, but with fuller knowledge. That little girl is now in her turn a widow, with a large and grown-up family. She was married in 1866 to John C. Baron Lethbridge of Tregeare, in Cornwall, about six miles west of Launceston.

I think I can revive my principal feelings at that
early age with fair correctness, their change during
growth seeming to have been chiefly due to the
increased range of mental prospect.   The horizon of
a child is very narrow and his sky very near.   His
father is the supreme of beings.   He has to learn by
slow degrees that there are more and more appreciable
stages between the highest and the lowest, and the
number of such stages that he can discriminate affords
a good measure of his mental calibre at the time.
It was about the date of which I have been speaking
that my second brother, Erasmus, then a boy of twelve
or thirteen, entered the navy, and showed himself to
us in his uniform, with the dagger or "dirk" that
was part of it.   I, a child of five or so, fingered it
with awe, and with my little head full of Greeks and
Trojans looked upon him as a hero, like Achilles,
and can perfectly recall my sense of increased security
from knowing that England could henceforth avail
herself of his puissant arm and terrible weapon.

I lived and throve in what was practically the
country until the age of eight, when I was sent to a
school at Boulogne, whither my father escorted me.
It was erroneously supposed that I should learn
French there and acquire a good accent.   What I
did learn was the detestable and limited patois that
my eighty schoolfellows were compelled to speak
under penalty of a fine, and in this cruel way.   There
were transferable metal labels which were called
"marks," and the boys in whose possession these
marks remained after each playtime received a bad
record whose accumulation up to a certain point
entailed punishment.   I rebelled with my whole heart

against the treachery encouraged by this system. A boy with a "mark" in his pocket would sidle up and encourage you as he best could to say a word of English, then forthwith he clapped his "mark" into your hand, and went away rejoicing at the riddance.

The school was an old convent near to and within the Calais gate of the upper town; the playground was the paved square of the convent, in which we used the flat gravestones for playing marbles. It is now partly overbuilt by the large church whose dome is conspicuous from afar.

We were daily marched off in a long row of pairs, usually for a walk round the ramparts, sometimes to Napoleon's Column, then in process of building, and in the summer, not infrequently, to bathe by rocks near the old fort. We prepared ourselves for the latter grateful occasions by saving bread from breakfast; then, after having gathered mussels, we spread their delicious contents on it to eat. An opportunity was then afforded of inspecting with awe the marks of recent birchings, which were reckoned as glorious scars. The birchings were frequent and performed in a long room parallel to, and separated from, the schoolroom by large ill-fitting doors, through which each squeal of the victim was heard with hushed breaths. In that room was a wardrobe full of school-books ready for issue. It is some measure of the then naïveté of my mind that I wondered for long how the books could have been kept so fresh and clean for nearly two thousand years, thinking that the copies of Cæsar's Commentaries were contemporary with Cæsar himself.

An occasional walk was to a wet plantation on the

2

side of the little river Liane, that feeds the harbour,
at which one of our schoolfellows, a gaunt, dyspeptic-
looking boy, performed the following feat to our
terror and admiration, as we crowded round him to see
it. He took a frog by its hind feet, opened his wide
mouth and dropped the frog's fore-feet on his tongue.
The frog struggled to get free, and at the critical
moment the hind legs were let go, and down went the
frog, head foremost, into his gullet. He was our hero
for the time; none other dared to attempt the same
feat. He said that he felt the frog all the way as it
went down to his stomach, and in it.

The school was hateful to me in many ways, and
lovable in none, so I was heartily glad to be taken
away from it in 1832. I thence returned to my family
party, who were newly settled in Leamington. It
then consisted of my father, mother, and three sisters;
my brothers were away, and my other sister, Lucy,
who had married, was living near Birmingham.
My grandfather Galton had recently died, and the
consequent large accession to my father's income
justified his change of residence, whch gave him and
my sisters a wider social intercourse than they had at
the Larches. Leamington was at that time a little
place, attractive to many eminent invalids, who
drank the waters and consulted Dr. Jephson, then
becoming celebrated.

I was next sent to a small private school at
Kenilworth, consisting of some half-dozen pupils,
where I received much kindness, and breathed the
air of unconstraint during three happy years. It was
kept by Mr. Attwood, the clergyman of the parish
(a near relative of the inventor of "Attwood's

machine," by which the rate of falling bodies is measured), who, without any pretence of learning, showed so much sympathy with boyish tastes and aspirations that I began to develop freely. Two of my fellow-pupils, Matthew P. Watt and Hugh William Boulton, were brothers. They were grand-sons of my grandfather's friend of the original "Boulton and Watt" firm, and sons of my father's friend, who carried on the manufactory. Hugh William became an exceptionally handsome and socially favoured Life-Guardsman; he died young. Matthew was then, subsequently at Cambridge, and again for some years afterwards, an object of reverence to me. I have known few or any who seemed to me his natural superiors in breadth and penetration of intellect, but he was cursed with a fortune far in excess of his simple though cultured needs, which exacted duties from him that he hated. His large fortune also removed the stimulus which necessity gives for getting through work and having done with it, instead of lingering indefinitely. He consequently grew amateurish, wasting thought on ingenious para-doxes and literary trifles, and failed to check a natural tendency towards recluseness and some other oddities of disposition. He gained the University prizes for Greek and Latin Epigrams at Cambridge in 1841, but did not care to compete for other honours. His artistic sense was of a high and classical order. His ideal, like that of Goethe, was a uniform culture of all the higher faculties. There was nothing ignoble in his nature. Whenever I talked with him about my own occasional annoyances, they seemed to become petty through his broad way of looking at things, I may almost say under the mere influence of his presence. His photograph, which is near me as I write, testifies to a personality that accords with the grandeur of his character. I owe much to his influence, and still remain conscious of the void in my friendships caused by his death very many years ago.

When I was fourteen years old it became time for me to go to a bigger school. My father had a Quaker's repugnance to public schools of the usual type, and it was finally decided that I should be sent to King Edward's School in Birmingham, then commonly known as the "Free School," to which a headmaster of high attainments had been recently appointed. This was Dr. Jeune (1806–1868), afterwards Master of Pembroke College, Oxford, and Bishop of Peterborough. I lived as a pupil, together with a few others, at his house by the Five Ways, to which a considerable garden was attached, and whence we walked daily, through a mile or so of street, to and from the school. I retained Dr. Jeune's friendship until his death, and it was impossible not to recognise his exceptional ability and educational zeal, but the character of the education was altogether uncongenial to my temperament. I learnt nothing, and chafed at my limitations. I had craved for what was denied, namely, an abundance of good English reading, well-taught mathematics, and solid science. Grammar and the dry rudiments of Latin and Greek were abhorrent to me, for there seemed so little sense in them. I was a fool to have been recalcitrant, and not to have profited by what I could have had, because many of my schoolfellows prospered on the teaching.

Three of them, F. Rendal, H. Holden, and C. Evans, were the very first in classics of their respective years at Cambridge. The two first were bracketed as equally deserving the position of Senior Classic, and the third gained that honour unpaired. Still, the literary provender provided at Dr. Jeune's school disagreed wholly with my mental digestion. The time spent there was a period of stagnation to myself, which for many years I bitterly deplored, for I was very willing and eager to learn, and could have learnt much if a suitable teacher had been at hand to direct and encourage me.

CHAPTER III

MEDICAL STUDIES

First experience — Tour with Mr. Bowman — Birmingham Hospital — Accidents — Sense of pain — King's College — Professor R. Partridge and others — Escape from drowning

IT was strongly desired by both my parents, but especially by my mother, that my future profession should be medicine, like that of her famous father, Dr. Erasmus Darwin, F.R.S., and of her half-brother, Dr. Robert Darwin, F.R.S. As I had aptitudes for that kind of study, my father fell in with her views, and took great pains to give me the best educational advantages. He acted largely on the advice of Mr. Hodgson, who brought me as an infant into the world, and was a true and helpful friend to me all through his life.

Mr. Hodgson (1788–1869) had settled in Birmingham a few years before my birth, bringing with him a high medical reputation, especially for his treatise on arteries and veins, and he soon obtained an eminent status as a Warwickshire surgeon. He became President of the Medico-Chirurgical Society in 1851, and, subsequently retiring from general practice, left Birmingham and settled in London, where he held the office of President of the College of Surgeons in 1864. He and his wife died on the same day in 1869.

While I was still a young boy, my father contrived
that I should see something of a laboratory attached
to the shop of the principal chemist in Birmingham ;
again, during one of our summer visits to the seaside,
he discovered a needy foreign chemist who agreed to
take me in hand, at a rather high charge. All I
clearly recollect of him now was, that he seemed
obsessed with the idea of making some wonderful
compound out of succinic acid, which is derived from
amber, and that he spent all his spare shillings in
buying bits of amber and burning them. I learnt
nothing from his tuition ; on the other hand, certain
recollections of the chemist's laboratory still form part
of my stock of mental imagery.

The step most momentous to myself was taken by
my father in 1838, of removing me at the age of sixteen,
and in no ways against my will, from Dr. Jeune's school.

A little after, while I was at Leamington, my
father asked our medical attendant there, Mr. P., to
show me an example of the medical work I should be
engaged in before I was plunged wholly into it.
That first experience is very memorable to me. It
occurred on a night chilly out of doors, while indoors
our family party were assembled in cosy comfort at
dessert, after a good dinner, with a brightly burning
fire, shining mahogany table, wine, fruits, and all the
rest, when a servant brought a note from Mr. P.
awaiting an answer. It was to the effect that a
housemaid had suddenly died at Lord ——'s house,
and that he, Mr. P., was about to make a post-mortem
examination ; would I like to come ? Oh, the mixture
of revulsion, wonder, interest, and excitement ! I
changed clothes and went, entering the house by a

back door as directed, and treading softly up the back staircase to the cold garret where the poor girl lay. She was the first dead person I had seen, handsome in feature, but greatly swollen. She had been apparently in perfect health a few hours before, then she was suddenly seized with intense pain in the stomach, followed rapidly by peritonitis and death. I can easily reproduce in imagination all the ghastly horror of the scene and could describe it in detail, but it would be unfitted for these pages. The perforated portion of the stomach was such a small hole. Death "with a little pin, bores through the castle wall, and —farewell, King!" (*King Richard II.*). Mr. P. pricked his finger while sewing up the abdomen. A dissection wound when death has followed peritonitis is proverbially dangerous. It was so in this case, for Mr. P. nearly died of it. I returned home chilled, awed and sobered, and seemed for the time to have left boyhood behind me.

My father, ever thoughtful of securing for me the best education he could, had arranged through Mr. Hodgson that one of his most promising former pupils, who was going for a tour of a few weeks abroad, partly for vacation, partly to see certain medical institutions, should take me with him. He was William Bowman, in later years the great oculist, Sir William (1816–1892), who combined a most refined and artistic temperament with exceptional scientific ability. He obtained a European reputation for medical research long before he was thirty years of age. Thenceforward for many years he devoted himself almost entirely to professional work, and though keeping abreast of the information of the day, contributed little or nothing more of his own, in the way of research, to the great regret of many. He was in later years a much valued member of many scientific societies and an habitual frequenter of the Royal Institution, near which he lived. The cause of his death, as I heard of it, was pathetic. He had built and resided at a charming house in Surrey, near Holmbury St. Mary, but retained his house in Clifford Street for some years, where he occasionally made appointments with old patients. At last the time came for wholly abandoning it. He lingered about the cold house, visiting every part of it for the last time, for he had an affectionate nature, caught a severe chill in doing so, and died of pneumonia.

To go back to the year 1838. I greatly enjoyed the tour and the companionship of Bowman, from whom I doubtless imbibed and assimilated more than I can now distinguish. The only event of a medical character that I saw with him was a small operation, the first I ever witnessed. A comic experience next occurred. I accompanied Bowman to a lunatic asylum in Vienna. In those days I was particularly shy and sensitive, and a consciousness of even the least unconventionality made me blush to an absurd degree. In one of the female wards, a young, buxom, and uncommonly good-looking female lunatic dashed forward with a joyful scream, she clasped me tightly to her bosom with both her arms, calling me her long-lost Fritz! *Tableau*—Amusement of the others, myself pink to the ears.

I may as well here continue to talk about Bowman. He was a most accurate and gifted draughtsman of pathological subjects. One of his earliest discoveries related to the liver, and I was familiar with a drawing in colours that he had made in illustration, which was preserved with great respect at the Birmingham Hospital. In later years he told me that having no further use for his collection of drawings, he gave them to Dr. B. In time Dr. B. died, and Bowman then became desirous to get back his old drawings as mementoes of early work, but could hear nothing of them. By an extraordinary chance he was looking one day at prints in a second-hand and second-rate book-shop, when his eye caught sight of a corner of these very drawings. They were all there, and he bought them all back. He could not learn their intermediate history.

It was in the autumn of 1838 that I took up my abode, as indoor pupil, in the Birmingham General Hospital, then situated near Snow Hill. My immediate chief was the house surgeon, Mr. Baker, who ultimately gained considerable repute as a surgeon in Birmingham, but is now dead. My one fellow indoor pupil had a similarly successful career to that of Mr. Baker. There were also in the common dining-room two officials, the matron and the treasurer. Matters were very different then; I, a mere boy of sixteen, but with unquestionably an eager mind, was thrust without any previous experience into a post that I found in a few months' time to be one of much responsibility. At first I was set to work every morning to help in the dispensary. It was a room with a dresser and a service door at the side. I there learnt the difference between infusions, decoctions, tinctures, and extracts, and how to make them. Possibly the reader may not know the meanings of these words, so I venture to give them. Tea is an "infusion," made by pouring boiling water on the tea and allowing it to stand. Coffee is, or would be a "decoction" if made by boiling the mixture. Infusions and decoctions are cheap forms of medicine, suitable for hospitals where they are made daily, but they soon spoil when kept. "Tinctures" are made by pouring spirits of wine instead of water on the drugs; they keep indefinitely, but are more costly, and therefore rarely used in hospitals. "Extracts" are made by boiling down decoctions.

All this is easily done when the proper simple apparatus and means of heating are at hand. I once made an extract as an experiment that I recommend to the notice of students who may wish to taste the *ne plus ultra* of bitterness. It was from quassia, that curious tree of South America, of which the very chips are bitter. The once well-known "bitter cup" is made of quassia wood. When water is poured into the cup, it quickly becomes bitter. Quassia is a valuable tonic medicine, with perhaps the one fault of *cheapness*. An apothecary can hardly be expected to feel easy in conscience when he charges apothecary's prices for what every little chip of a timber tree affords when put into hot water. Anyhow, I made a large jugful of decoction of quassia and boiled it down until a sticky residue was left, which is, or might be, called "quassine." I put a piece of it about the size of a pin's head upon my tongue, and then—oh then! Try it, if you doubt its absolute bitterness.

It was amusing at first to make pills. The pill mass had to be brayed together in a mortar, occasionally adding water or I forget what other liquid, to render it of the proper consistency. Next a certain weight of the pill mass was rolled out by the help of a simple but ingeniously arranged slab, into a long worm of equal diameter and of standard length. Then the worm was cut simultaneously into equal segments, by the pressure of the grooved back of the same slab, by means of which the segments were also rolled into pills.

The other day I visited the great store and manufactory of chemical and other apparatus of Messrs. Griffiths, in or near Aldwych Street, and saw there a machine, occupying little more room than a moderately sized washing-stand, that claimed to turn out pills at the rate of *one million* in each twenty-four hours,—so if forty-five of these machines were kept continually at work day and night, it would enable a grandmotherly Socialist Government to supply to every man, woman, and child of the forty-five millions of inhabitants of the British Isles one free pill daily.

The out-patients clustered in the hall outside the service window of the dispensary, and were supplied in turn. Then the prescriptions of the in-patients were handed in and attended to. It was a busy time. I learnt to do most of my part pretty well in a very few weeks, after which I was promoted to higher things.

Having always the run of the dispensary, and being a boy, I found certain drugs, such as liquorice, much to my taste, but especially poppy seed. A large number of poppy capsules were kept in stock for making soothing lotions. They are full of seeds, which contain no opium at all. These are not used for the lotions, but are particularly pleasant to munch, and I ate them in abundance when the humour seized me. In later years I found poppy seeds in common use somewhere in Germany, for making a particular pudding; I think it was in Bonn.

The duties gradually imposed on me were to go with the surgeons on their morning rounds, always to attend in the accident room, where persons suffering from accidents were received whether in the night or day, and to help in dressing them, also to be present at all operations, and to take part at every post-mortem examination, of which there were perhaps two or three weekly. The times of which I am speaking were long before those of chloroform, and many long years before that of Pasteur and Sir Joseph Lister. The stethoscope was considered generally to be new-fangled; the older and naturally somewhat deaf practitioners pooh-poohed and never used it.

I cannot understand to this day why youths selected for their powers of sharp hearing should not be so far instructed as to be used by physicians, much as pointers and setters are used by sportsmen. They could be taught what to listen for, probably by means of some sound-emitting instruments more or less muffled, and how to describe what they heard. A patient during the incipient stage of his disease might be submitted to examination by one or more of these quick-hearing youths, who would report to the doctor, who thereupon would form and express his opinion. Similarly as regards touch, of which great delicacy is of the highest importance. Conceive what help might be given by them in discovering deeply seated tumours,

abscesses, and much else. The touch of a person far
less sensitive than that of the wandering Princess of the
well-known fairy tale might prove of vital importance.
It will be recollected that her Princess-ship was ac-
knowledged by all, through her discovering a pea
surreptitiously inserted as a test, below the bottom of
the pile of feather-beds on which she slept.

To return to my duties. Accidents occurred, of
course, at all hours of the day and night. It was
unpleasant to be summoned out of a warm bed to
attend upon these once on a cold night, but it was
not a hardship ; to be summoned twice was trying ;
but thrice, as sometimes happened, was more than
I could have endured had it frequently occurred.
Burns were the commonest of the accidents at night-
time. The sufferers were piteous to see. As a rule
they did not complain much of pain, but they shivered
from a sense of cold and were enfeebled almost to
prostration by the shock. There was nothing to be
done to them beyond cutting away all adherent
clothing and the like, packing them in cotton wool
and sending them to a ward. One particular ward
was allotted to that purpose. The contrast was great
between the neatly dressed patient of the first night
and the wretched creature two days after, when
suppuration had begun and the foul dressings had
to be carefully picked off and replaced by clean ones.

Broken heads from brawls were common accidents
at night ; then it was my part to shave the head, using
the blood as lather, which makes a far better preparation for shaving than soap. The wounds were stitched
together with a three-cornered "glove needle," which
cuts its way through the skin. Some riots connected

with the "Charter" occurred at this time, and many
people were hurt. It was curious to observe the
apparent cleanness of the cuts that were made
through the scalp by the blow of a policeman's
round truncheon.

It sometimes happened that a severe case was
brought at night-time, which required higher surgical
skill than could properly be expected in the house
surgeon, who, though professionally qualified, was
young, and therefore relatively unpractised. If the
treatment of any such accident admitted of no delay,
a messenger was dispatched to the house of the
surgeon himself, to wake and bring him. One of
these events made a great impression on me. It
was that of a man, a small piece of whose skull had
been depressed by something falling on his head and
stunning him. He was brought in utterly unconscious,
with the "stertorous" or snoring respiration characteristic of such cases. The man had to be trepanned, so
the surgeon was sent for. In the meantime everything
was prepared for his arrival. The trepan is a hollow
steel cylinder with teeth cut out of its lower rim, used
to saw a circular wad out of the sound bone nearest to
the fracture. A miniature steel crowbar is used to
raise the depressed fragment, and a rod to lay across
the sound bone as a fulcrum for the crowbar. I seem
to see it all before me as I write. The brightly lighted
room, the apparatus in order, the surgeon at work, the
eager faces of the bystanders, and the utterly unconscious patient. The wad was cut out, the crowbar
adjusted, and still the monotonous snore continued
unchanged. Then pressure was put on the free end
of the crowbar, the broken bit of skull was raised,

and instantly life rushed back. The man continued a sentence that he must have begun before the accident; then he stared wildly, and said, "Where am I?" The clock of life had stopped through a temporary obstruction, the obstruction was removed and the clock ticked on as before. He was soothed, a silver plate was inserted over the hole, the scalp was replaced and stitched together, and he was sent into the ward. In due time he wholly recovered, the scalp having grown over the plate.

I had the option of accompanying any of the surgeons or physicians on his morning round. Each had his clinical clerk, who made notes of the case and wrote the treatment prescribed from time to time, upon a paper affixed to a board at the bed-head. I appreciated from the very first the high importance of careful study and record of every case. My feeling is now fully developed which was then in embryo, that it is our duty to avail ourselves of the opportunities that arise from the apparently unmoral course of Nature, of rendering similar events less dangerous and painful in the future. Blind Nature seems to vivisect ruthlessly, let us as reasonable creatures elicit all the good we can from her vivisections, for which we ourselves are in no way responsible. I became a clinical clerk in time, but felt acutely my incompetence to act up to my own high ideals.

It was a surprise to me to notice so few signs of pain and distress in the wards, even among the mortally stricken. I met with no instances of terror at approaching death, while the ordinary interests of life seemed powerful up to the close of consciousness. But it must be terrible to a sensitive and stricken fellow-patient with all his senses still on the alert, when the death-hour of some one else in the ward arrives, and the curtains are drawn around the dying man's bed to hide the scene, and again when his remains are removed to the post-mortem room. All these things are, however, more hideous to the imagination than in reality. One piteous death-bed scene much impressed me. A girl was fast dying of typhus, and I had been instructed to apply a mustard plaister. When I came to her, she was fully sensible, and said in a faint but nicely mannered way, "Please leave me in peace. I know I am dying, and am not suffering." I had not the heart to distress her further.

The opinions held by the students about the several physicians and surgeons were curiously guided by a mixture of loyalty and irreverence. There was no doubt of the fact that M., one of the doctors, who never professed or had a claim to scientific acquirements, got his patients out of hospital more quickly than any of his colleagues. His treatment was as simple as that of Dr. Sangrado, though of quite another kind. It consisted of a strong purgative followed by low diet, and a subsequent feeding up as soon as all fever had gone. The composition of his drench never varied; a big bottle of it was made every morning in the dispensary, in readiness to be served out. It was so cheap that the overplus could be thrown away and a fresh infusion made the next day.

It is to be wished that some "index of curative skill" could be awarded to doctors, based on their respective hospital successes. I have often amused myself with imaginary schemes to this effect. If it

3

could be compiled truthfully, it would be an excellent guide to those who wanted a doctor but were doubtful whom to consult. A high index of curative skill would serve as a measure of merit, and the fee to the doctor might be regulated by its height.

I threw myself into my duties with zeal, and loved neat bandaging and neat plaistering. Each clinical clerk had a dressing board, supported against his body by a strong band passed over his neck : its ends were fixed to the board. Lint, plaister, scissors, forceps, probe, and a few other simple surgical instruments completed the outfit. There was much bleeding from the arm, especially of out-patients ; there were also cuppings and insertion of issues and of setons. All these I could soon do creditably ; I was fairly good even at tooth-drawing. I set broken limbs, at first under strict supervision, but was latterly allowed much freedom. I had also occasionally to reduce dislocations of the arm, and once at least of the thigh. The mechanism of the body began to appear very simple in its elementary features. At one time no less than sixteen fractures, dislocations, or other injuries to the arms, or parts of them, were practically under my sole care all at the same time. Of course my proceedings were carefully watched.

The following incident in those pre-chloroform days set me thinking. A powerful drayman was brought in dead drunk, with both of his thighs crushed and mangled by a heavy waggon. They had to be amputated at once. He remained totally unconscious all the time, and it was not until he awoke sober in the morning that he discovered that his legs were gone. He recovered completely. The question that then presented itself to me was, "Why could not people be made dead drunk before operations? Could it not be effected without upsetting their digestion and doing harm in other ways?" The subsequent discovery of *inhaling*, instead of drinking the intoxicating spirit, whether it be chloroform or ether, solved that question most happily.

The cries of the poor fellows who were operated on were characteristic; in fact, each class of operation seemed to evoke some peculiar form of them. All this was terrible, but only at first. It seemed after a while as though the cries were somehow disconnected with the operation, upon which the whole attention became fixed.

It was obvious that different persons felt pain with very different degrees of acuteness. I may here go quite out of chronological sequence, and refer to an experience in 1851, when I was on the point of starting from a mission station on my exploration of Damara Land, then wholly unknown but now a German possession. It will be again alluded to in a later chapter. A branch missionary outpost, twenty miles off, had lately been raided, and most of the people, other than the missionaries themselves, murdered. Of those who escaped, two women, each with both of their feet hacked off, made their way to the station, at which I saw them. The Damara women wear heavy copper rings on their ankles, put on when they are growing girls that the rings may not slip over their feet when they are adult. These coveted treasures can therefore be obtained only by the summary process of cutting off the feet. In this horribly mutilated state the two women crawled the whole of the twenty miles. The stumps had healed when I saw them. I asked how they staunched the blood. They explained by gesture that it was by stumping the bleeding ends into the sand, and they grinned with satisfaction while they explained.

I may yet travel onwards many more years to another illustrative anecdote. I happened to be President of the Anthropological Institute, when a very interesting memoir was read on the subject now in question. Numerous instances were given of a very startling character, but the one that seemed the most so was a story told there by the late Sir James Paget, as communicated to him by a trustworthy friend; he added that he felt compelled to believe it. It referred to a native New Zealander. It appeared that at the time in question it was the height of fashion for the Maoris to wear boots on great occasions, and not to appear barefooted. A youth had saved money and went to a store a long way off, where he purchased a pair of these precious articles. On returning home he tried to put them on, but one of his feet had a long projecting toe which prevented it from being thrust home. He went quite as a matter of course to fetch a bill-hook which was at hand, and, putting his foot on a log of wood, chopped off the end of his long toe and drew on the boot.

There was another occurrence in those pre-Pasteur days on which my mind dwelt often. It was a story corroborated by many analogous but much less striking instances that came under my own observation, of a man who had stumbled into a cauldron of scalding pitch. He was quickly pulled out, but the pitch had so enclosed and adhered to one of his

legs that nothing could be done with safety to remove
it. The other leg was cleaned as well as might be
and carefully dressed, and in that state, with one
leg cased in pitch, the other bandaged, he was
sent to bed. After many days, the leg that was
enclosed in pitch ceased to hurt, and the covering
became so loose that it was desirable and easy to
remove it, when lo and behold! instead of a vast
suppurating surface, the leg was found to be entirely
healed. The other leg, which had been less hurt and
carefully dressed, remained much longer unhealed.
It seemed clear that the art of dressing was far
behind what was possible, and that an application
of the dressing before "the air got into the wound"
was the thing to be aimed at. The subsequent
discovery by Pasteur of the germ theory, and the
practical application of it by Sir Joseph, now Lord
Lister, has overcome the difficulty.

I was so keen at my medical work, that, being
desirous of appreciating the effects of different
medicines, I began by taking small doses of all that
were included in the pharmacopœia, commencing with
the letter A. It was an interesting experience, but
had obvious drawbacks. However, I got nearly to
the end of the letter C, when I was stopped by the
effects of Croton oil. I had foolishly believed that
two drops of it could have no notable effects as a
purgative and emetic; but indeed they had, and I
can recall them now.

There were histories of occasional outbursts of
hysteria in the female wards; one took place whilst
I was there. It was a most curious and afflicting
spectacle of pure panic. One woman had begun to

scream and rave, then another followed suit, then another, and pandemonium seemed at hand. It was stopped by rather rough measures, gentle ones making matters worse. There was a current story of one of the surgeons having effectually stopped a most threatening outbreak, which the nurses began to join, in which an abundance of cold water was only part of the remedy employed.

Many protean forms of that strange disorder, hysteria, were frequently pointed out to me. The demoralisation that accompanied it was shown by the gross and palpable lies told by the patients in their desire at any cost to attract attention. A paroxysm of it may resemble a severe epileptic fit. I was informed in all seriousness by a friend, of a valuable way of distinguishing them, important for nurses to bear in mind, that in epilepsy the patient might and often did bite himself, his tongue for example, but in hysteria the patients never bit themselves but always other people.

Delirium tremens was a strange malady. The struggles were sometimes terrible, yet the pulse was feeble and the reserve of strength almost nil. The visions of the patients seemed indistinguishable by them from realities; in the few cases I saw, they were wholly of fish or of creeping things. One of the men implored me to take away the creature that was crawling over his counterpane, following its imagined movements with his finger and staring as at a ghost. Poor humanity! I often feel that the tableland of sanity upon which most of us dwell, is small in area, with unfenced precipices on every side, over any one of which we may fall.

The hysterical scream which so strongly affects other women is a forcible instance of the power of sound, whose limits are, as yet, imperfectly explored. The tones of a great actor or orator may thrill the whole being. An unemotional elderly gentleman told me years ago, that he was haunted by the recollection of the resonance of Pitt's voice when speaking of some event (I forget what it was) that gave him a "pang." There are many kinds of shrieks of a blood-curdling nature, of which that of a wounded horse on a battlefield is said to be one.

King's College.—After a brief vacation I was sent, again through Mr. Hodgson's ever active interest, for a year to King's College and to live as an inmate of the house of Professor Richard Partridge (1805–1873), together with four or five other pupils. His house was in New Street, Spring Gardens, now demolished through the extension of the Admiralty Buildings and the newly constructed entrance from Charing Cross into St. James's Park. My social surroundings were of a far higher order than those at Birmingham, and I rejoiced in them. Professor Partridge was, at that time, a brilliant man of about thirty-four years of age, yellow-haired, full of humour and of quips, as well as of shrewdness and kindliness; his intimate friends were all growing into distinction. He had known Charles Lamb well, and the genius of Elia seemed to haunt the house, though Charles Lamb had died four or five years before. I listened with admiration to the brilliant talk and repartees when Partridge had his bachelor dinners with fellow-cronies as guests. They included G. Dasent, later Sir George, the author and

Civil Service Commissioner; Professor Wheatstone, later Sir Charles, who conjointly with Cooke was the introducer of the electric telegraph; A. Smee the electrician, subsequently an authority on gardening, and others.

Professor Richard Partridge, F.R.S., familiarly called "Dickey," was brother to John Partridge, R.A., and Professor of Anatomy. It was commonly said that the brothers had each followed the occupation best fitted to the other. Certainly Richard Partridge was an admirable draughtsman, but was not, so far as I was then capable of judging, a man who really loved and revelled in science. He delighted in minute points of human anatomy and did not generalise, consequently the information given in his lectures seemed to me as dry as the geography of Pinnock's Catechism. For all that, they were enlivened by his never-failing humour. His instruction seemed to me deficient in the why and the wherefore. A human hand was just a human hand to him; its analogies with paws, hoofs, wings, claws, and fins were never alluded to.

I spent a happy time under his roof. We pupils had the drawing-room to read and write in, with a wardrobe and a hanging closet tenanted by a jointed skeleton which we could study at will. The days were spent in the Medical Department of King's College, which was quite disconnected with the classical side. All the pupils entered at the same door, but there we separated. The medicals turned sharply to the right, and many of them went downstairs to the dissection room, where much of my own time was spent.

The immediate chiefs of the dissection room were nominally my old travelling companion and tutor, William Bowman and John Simon, but Bowman had other College work to perform, and was rarely present. Mr. Simon, afterwards Sir John Simon (*b.* 1816), of the Board of Health, was practically the only Director. His quaint phrases, full of scientific insight and poetical in essence, were most attractive. His collected essays and reports are models of literary style applied to scientific subjects. He died three or four years ago, quite blind, at a very advanced age.

All the Professors whose lectures I had to attend, were notable men. Dr. Todd (1809–1860), the Professor of Physiology, gave a powerful impulse to his branch of science. He was then engaged in collaboration with Bowman in bringing out their Encyclopedia of Physiology, which was a remarkable work for those days. The signs of advance were all about and in the air. The microscope had rather suddenly attained a position of much enhanced importance; it was now mounted solidly, with really good working stages and with good glasses. Powell was the principal maker of it, and a Powell's microscope was an object almost of worship to advanced students. The manufacture of microscopes has rapidly and steadily advanced since those times, both in cheapness and in goodness : what was then a rarity is now in the possession of every student.

I enjoyed the lectures of Daniell (1790–1845) on Chemistry ; he was so simple and thorough. In those times the galvanic cell was becoming perfected, and the three forms then invented, the Smee, the Daniell, and the Grove (the latter being by my valued friend in later years, Justice Sir William Grove), still retain their names. Electrotyping was invented by Smee, and I recall well the humorously pathetic manner in which Daniell explained to his class how the neglect of drawing an obvious inference had prevented him from figuring as its discoverer. He had noticed the marvellous fidelity with which the marks of a file had appeared on a copper sheath electrically thrown down upon it, as the result of some chance experiment, but he had failed to infer that medals and the like might be copied by the same process.

It is needless to go into particulars of my course at King's College. They had much the same result on me in opening the mind that a similar experience must have on every keen medical student, but I do not remember any special characteristic worthy of record. I did pretty well at my studies. My chief competitor was George Johnson, afterwards Sir George (1818-1896), whose thoroughness of work and character I admired. He beat me in physiology, in which I came out second. I think the only prize I ever got all to myself was in the minor subject of Forensic Medicine, in which I delighted. It had a sort of Sherlock Holmes fascination for me, while the instances given as cautions, showing where the value of too confident medical assertions had been rudely upset by the shrewd cross-questioning of lawyers, confirmed what I was beginning vaguely to perceive, that doctors had the fault, equally with parsons, of being much too positive.

My friend Sir G. Johnson subsequently became the leader of one of the two opposed methods of dealing with cholera. His was the "eliminative" view, namely, that there was mischief in the system that Nature strove to eliminate, so he prescribed castor oil to expedite matters; others took the exactly opposite view, consequently there was open war between the two methods. I read somewhere that one of Johnson's most fiery opponents considered the number of deaths occasioned by his method to amount to eleven thousand. Leaving aside all question of the accuracy of the estimate of this particular treatment, it is easy to see that when a pestilence lies heavily on a nation, the numbers affected are so large that a proper or improper treatment may be capable of saving or of destroying many thousands of lives. By all means, then, let competitive methods be tested at hospitals on a sufficiently large scale to settle their relative merits. Of this I will speak further almost immediately.

One part of my duties was to attend King's College Hospital, but the position of a student there was far less instructive than that of an indoor pupil at the Birmingham Hospital, where responsibility was great and there was no crowding. The teaching was, however, greatly superior to the generality of that at Birmingham. The position of house pupil and resident medical officer has long since become highly and justly prized, and is now obtainable only after competition and by the best men.

Medical knowledge has advanced so far that more scientific treatment can be had in many small country towns than was formerly procurable even in London. Still, the experience haunts my memory of Dr. M. at the Birmingham Hospital, of his habitual drench of which I wrote, and of his remarkable success in turning out his patients nominally cured. There is still much lack of exact knowledge of what Nature can do without assistance from medicine, if aided only by cheering influences, rest, suggestion, and good nursing.

I wish that hospitals could be turned into places for experiment more than they are, in the following perfectly humane direction. Suppose two different and competing treatments of a particular malady ; I have just mentioned a case in point. Let the patients suffering under it be given the option of being placed under Dr. A. or Dr. B., the respective representatives of the two methods, and the results be statistically compared. A co-operation without partisanship between many large hospitals ought to speedily settle doubts that now hang unnecessarily long under dispute.

Medical statistics are, however, the least suitable of any I know for refined comparisons, because the conditions that cannot be, or at all events are not taken into account, are local, very influential, and apt to differ greatly. It is, however, humiliating to find how much has failed to attract attention for want of even the rudest statistics. I doubt whether the unaided apprehension of man suffices to distinguish between the frequency of what occurs on an average four times in ten events and one that occurs five times. Much grosser proportions have been wholly overlooked by doctors. I referred once to many dictionaries and works of medicine published before the time of Broca, some ninety years ago, and did not find a single reference to the almost invariable loss of speech associated with paralysis of the right side. Still more recently, the idea of consumption being communicated by any form of infection was stoutly denied by English medical men. As to rules of diet, the changes are ludicrous. Robert Frere, one of my fellow-pupils when with Professor Partridge, became through marriage in later years a managing partner in a very old and eminent firm of wine merchants. They had supplied George IV. with his brandy and the like. He told me that the books of the firm showed that every class of wine had in its turn been favoured by the doctors.

There were many incidents that I could tell about this time of my life that might be interesting in some sense, but which are foreign to the main purpose of such an autobiography as mine, which is to indicate how the growth of a mind has been affected by circumstances. I will, however, make one exception, which refers to a very narrow escape from drowning. I had been in a steamboat, crammed with people, to see the Oxford and Cambridge boat-race, and was returning with stream and tide. The arches of Old Battersea Bridge were narrow, and it required careful steering on such occasions to get safely through them. The steamboat on which I was yawed greatly. I was standing behind the right-hand paddle-box, when it crashed against one of the piers and split open just in front of me, giving a momentary view of the still revolving paddles. The shock sent me down among them. I was conscious of two taps on the back of my head, and then the water swirled over me. In a few seconds my wits had gathered themselves together, and I found myself submerged under a mass of wood, which afterwards proved to be the outer sheathing of the paddle-box. I dived to get clear of it, but found myself held back by projecting nails which had hooked into my clothes. My breath was becoming exhausted, so I passed my hand quickly but steadily all over myself, disentangling nails in two or three places, and then made my last dive for life. I fortunately rose clear, and utilised my former enemy the mass of wood as a raft. I was sufficiently unhurt to help another man who was also in the water and in distress, by pushing a piece of wood to him.

There was, of course, much commotion all about the scene. The steamboat drifted helplessly; boats put off from the shore; the men in the first boat that reached me tried to drive a hard bargain, asking a sovereign to take me in, but being in safety I was able to resist extortion. I then rowed to the ship, and my face was, I understood, a spectacle, being painted with blood that had flowed freely from a few scratches and was spread all over it by the wetting. There was much sympathy shown on the steamboat, and an especial interest in me on the part of the captain, who from the character of his questions obviously feared having to pay damages. So I at last landed, and, feeling little the worse after a short rest, cabbed home to Mr. Partridge's house. The only object that really suffered was my rather valuable watch. There is a short account of this accident in the Life of Leonard Horner, F.R.S., by his daughter K. M. Lyell, ii. 19. I did not hear that any notice of it got into the newspapers.

I will finish now what little I have to add about my medical experiences, skipping over four or five years in a few lines. While at Cambridge, of which I shall speak in a separate chapter, I attended a few lectures, chiefly by Dr. Haviland, in order to obtain some more of the necessary certificates to qualify me for undergoing an examination and obtaining a doctor's degree. After I left Cambridge, some more lectures had still to be attended, so I was sent for a short time as a pupil at St. George's Hospital. My dear father's death then occurred, as will be mentioned farther on, and the direction of my life became changed.

CHAPTER IV

SHORT TOUR TO THE EAST

Giessen—Linz—Rowboat to Vienna—Steam down Danube and overland to Black Sea—Constantinople—Smyrna—Quarantines at Syra
and Trieste—Adelsberg—Diligence from Milan to Boulogne—
Home

IN the spring of 1840 a passion for travel seized
me as if I had been a migratory bird. While
attending the lectures at King's College I could see
the sails of the lighters moving in sunshine on the
Thames, and it required all my efforts to disregard
the associations of travel which they aroused. On
fine mornings I could not keep still in the house in
Spring Gardens where I lived, but wandered in St.
James's Park. On these occasions I noticed that the
weathercock on the Horse Guards seemed to point
nearly always to the south-west. The explanation
proved to be that the fit seized me with violence
when a south-west wind was blowing. It was
arranged by my father that I should accompany Dr.
Allen Miller (1817–1870), subsequently a great chemist
and for many years Treasurer of the Royal Society,
to Giessen, where the more promising young chemists
of those days gathered to avail themselves of the
teaching of Liebig, then the foremost of the chemical
Professors in Germany. My father gave me a liberal
letter of credit, for, having been a banker himself, he

was unwilling that my balance should ever run low;
besides, he was always cautious in making ample
provision for unexpected contingencies. So to Giessen
I went, but soon finding that my chemical knowledge,
and indeed my knowledge of German, was by no
means sufficiently advanced for me to profit from
Liebig's teaching, I determined to throw that plan
over, to make a dash and go as far as my money
allowed, consistent with returning to England early in
October in time for my first term at Cambridge. I
had saturated myself since the age of nine with Byron's
poetry, which gave me a longing to see the East;
besides, a new route Eastwards had been opened,
between Czernavoda and Kustendji, the former lying
on that long reach of the Lower Danube where it most
nearly approaches the Black Sea, and Kustendji
situated on the Black Sea itself. A calculation of the
cost showed that my finances would suffice for this
and more, so away I went. A steamer ran twice or
thrice a week from Linz to Vienna, and once (I think)
in a fortnight from Vienna down the Danube, and the
times fitted nicely. But on arrival at Linz it proved
that the steamer bound for Vienna was disabled and
would not run for some days. This serious contretemps
threatened to ruin my whole scheme, which required
that I should reach Vienna in time for a particular
steamer.

I had made friends with an elderly British officer
at the hotel, who was in much the same plight as
myself, for it was as important to him as to me, though
for other reasons, to reach Vienna without delay. He
told me that he had found a boatman who would take
us all the way, some seventy miles down stream, for a

4

moderate sum, and that he was willing to go if I would join him. I accepted his proposal, he having assured me that the boat would be adequately manned, and that the journey would be both easy and interesting. His power of German conversation was even less than mine, and either he had not understood aright or he had been cheated, for when we had entered the boat in the dark by help of the faint and flickering light of a lantern, and had been pushed off into the current of the swiftly flowing Danube, I perceived that the boatmen consisted only of one old man and a boy. It was impossible to return, so we made the best of it. One of us two, and it was more frequently myself, for my companion wanted both youth and muscle, had to work an oar almost continuously in order to give steerage-way to the boat.

We toiled through the night and the following morning, hardly resting at all till we reached Mölk, where provisions and fruit were bought and another boatman engaged, and we went onwards after brief delay. We arrived as near to Vienna as the police regulations allowed, very late at night; but by unexpected good fortune the officials allowed us to land and to sleep hard by, so I was in good time for the steamer, and after a short stay was off in her. I had some agreeable fellow-passengers, and it was a momentous voyage to me.

The first stoppage was at Pesth, where I was quite unprepared for the grandeur of its quays and buildings. Thenceforward we entered comparative barbarism. There was a considerable delay at the famous rapids of the " Iron Gates," long since removed by blasting the rocks that gave them their name, and where the river ran strongly. I witnessed boats of no large size being towed up stream by the longest teams of men and horses that I have ever seen. If my memory does not play tricks, I counted no less than ninety-six horses hauling a single boat. I drove as far as time allowed among the Carpathians towards Mehadia, a then secluded watering-place, in the company of two Hungarians, with one of whom—a Kaunitz—I had struck up a travelling friendship, and who told me much about Hungary.

The position of Belgrade was imposing. It was then in Turkish occupation, and the Turks still wore turbans. The town being in quarantine, we were not allowed to land. The flat shores of Wallachia were most uninteresting and looked fever-haunted. The only human life visible for miles together was that of an occasional coast-guardsman perched in a crow's nest on the top of a pole, to prevent smugglers from crossing the Danube unseen. At one place we cut through a shoal of water snakes crossing the river, with their heads out of water and their bodies wriggling horizontally. It was a sight upon which a horrible nightmare might have been founded.

At length we arrived at our journey's end, where light waggons awaited us, which were drawn across the open country. I walked the greater part of the distance, and so reached the Black Sea at Kustendji. The steamer started in threatening weather, and particularly rough seas ensued. We rolled so badly and so briskly that a square chest containing seamen's things, which stood on the deck, was toppled over. In the morning, the historical Symplegades were in sight, and certainly the superstitious Greeks might well have accredited them, as they did, with the power of shutting like jaws and crushing vessels that attempted to pass between them, for the apparent width of the intervening space changes rapidly with changing perspective. Then we steamed through the glorious Bosphorus, whose sides were far less built upon than now, past Therapia to Constantinople, or Stamboul, as it was commonly called.

I revelled in the glory of the place and in the picturesque and turbaned groups. The hotel kept by Miseri was then a small establishment, more like a pension. He had been courier to a connection of mine, and I was taken in and made very comfortable. The numerous acquaintances I picked up there and the stories I heard of the current rascalities gave an insight into a phase of humanity which I did not esteem but was glad to know about.

Though I am now inclined to twaddle about what was then so new, so strange and exhilarating to me, it would not interest readers who are probably familiar with far more graphic accounts of this capital of the East than I have skill to write. The sherbet, iced with snow from the neighbouring Mount Olympus, shares, I suppose, with similar sherbet at Granada, iced with snow from the Sierrra Nevada, the honour of parentage to our very modern ice-creams. In my youth the only good ice-cream maker in London was Gunter in Berkeley Square, and the very existence of such a luxury as ice-cream had then, as I know, been recently scoffed at by the educated daughters of a clergyman in South Wales. After about six days' stay in Constantinople, I had to move onwards, taking a steamer to Smyrna. Olympus stood grandly above

the shores of the Sea of Marmora ; then came the
Hellespont, then the Troad, then Smyrna.

My allowance of time was drawing to a close, for
I had to make ample allowance for long detention in
quarantines, which were in those times an especial
nuisance. They were put on or taken off with
apparent caprice, sometimes it was said for purely
commercial reasons. So I was able to allow only two
or three days for seeing the environs of Smyrna, and
then started in a steamer to the island of Syra,
where I was placed for ten days in quarantine. My
rooms were like those of a khan, wholly unfurnished,
the guardian supplying bedding and food at moderate
cost. He followed me as a prisoner under his charge,
with a long stick wherewith to ward me from touching
or being touched by any body or thing that was not in
the same quarantine as myself. The quarantine
buildings enclosed a large square. My rooms opened
at the back into a cheerful covered balcony which
looked on the sea. My neighbouring occupant was
a lady, a near relative to Arthur Cayley, the great
mathematician, whom I even then had learnt to
revere, and whose pupil I became during one of my
happy long vacations at Cambridge.

The laws of quarantine were curiously minute.
Metal, such as a coin, was not supposed to be so
deeply infected but that a simple washing would
purify it ; paper must be pricked and fumigated ;
but clothing had to undergo as much quarantine as
the wearer, and even more, as will be seen later on.
It was ruled that if any part of a cloth or fabric of
fibres was touched by a person in quarantine, the
whole of it became equally tainted. So I put to my

guardian the case of touching one end of a very long rope, but could get no reasonable answer, any more than a child can when he puts searching questions. Violation of quarantine is a very serious offence. A soldier would shoot a person without mercy, and with the approbation of his superiors, if that appeared to be the only way of preventing it.

The nine or ten days' rest in quarantine at Syra was by no means ungrateful. I made myself occupation, and they passed pleasantly. The process of giving "*pratique*" was amusing. We were drawn up in a row, and the medical officer walked up and down sternly scrutinising us. Then he gave the order of "Put out your tongues," which we all did simultaneously, and he passed along the line at two paces distance from it, looking at our tongues. Then he added, "Do exactly as I do," whereupon he clapped himself sharply under the left armpit with his right hand, and under the right armpit with the left hand. Similarly on the left and right groins. This was to prove that none of the glandular swellings that give the name of "bubonic" plague were there, otherwise the pain of the performance would have been intolerable. Then, with a sudden change from a stern aspect, he put on a most friendly and courteous smile, and stepping forwards he shook each of us cordially by the hand, and we were freed. A couple of days had to pass before the next steamer started for Trieste, which I occupied in rambling about the island, living for one day almost wholly on figs—which was unwise, because too much of them affects the kidneys.

I started with the steamer, had a few, but memorable, hours at Athens, lay for two days in

quarantine off Ancona, and was landed in the quarantine at Trieste. What Turkey was to Greece in
respect of quarantine, that Greece was to Turkey.

There was a curious custom at Trieste of " making
Spoglio," as they phrased it. When three or four days
of the normal length of quarantine had still to run, it
was permissible to strip and leave all clothes behind,
to bathe, to put on new clothes, and to be free. The
process is based on the assumption that the well-
washed human body, if in apparent health after say
a week's seclusion, may justly be considered free from
infection, whereas the clothes worn by it must remain
still longer in quarantine. What happened was this.
We were inspected by the doctor, and then directed
to the edge of a covered quay, opposite to which was
another quay where old-clothes men displayed their
wares; a strip of sea water, perhaps 4 or 5 feet deep
and 20 wide, separated the two quays. A bargain
had to be made with one of the old-clothes men by
shouting across the water. I was to leave everything
I had on me, excepting coin or other metal, and papers
which were about to be fumigated, in exchange for
the offered clothes. When the bargain was concluded,
I stripped, plunged in, and emerged on the opposite
quay stark naked, to be newly clothed and to receive
freedom. The clothes-man got my old things in due
time—that was his affair. The new clothes were thin,
and the trousers were made of a sort of calico and
deficient in the fashionable cut of my old ones; but
as it was not then late in the year the thinness
mattered little in those latitudes, and I did not care
about the rest.

I occupied two of the days I had saved by making

Spoglio, in visiting the wonderful caves of Adelsberg. A view over the Adriatic when driving up the mountain-side on the way to that place, remains still in my mind as one of the three or four most glorious views that I have had the privilege to see. The long walk underground at Adelsberg, the black and vicious stream that ran through it, looking like a river of death, and the fantastic stalactites and stalagmites were indeed astonishing. I bought two of the curious creatures called Proteus, that live in these underground waters. They have no real eyes, but sightless dots in the place of them; their colour is that of the buried portion of stems of celery (etiolated, as it is commonly called), and they have both gills and lungs. They were the first living creatures of their kind brought to England. I gave them to King's College; one soon died, the other lived and was yearly lectured on, as I heard, until fate in the form of a cat ended him.

I went from Trieste by steamer to Venice, and thence by diligence to Milan, whence I travelled by diligence to Geneva, with the bottle containing the two Proteus under my thin coat, for fear of the water freezing while crossing the Alps. At Geneva I had a few evening hours to spare, which I spent at the theatre, and thence on by diligence to Boulogne. It took me either seven days and eight nights, or conversely, to reach Boulogne from Milan, and it was of course tiring to sit up and be shaken in a diligence during that long time. My legs began to swell before I reached Boulogne, but the two or three hours of lying down in the Channel steamer quite restored them.

So I reached my home in Leamington safely and in good time, and my dear kind father took my escapade humorously. He was pleased with it rather than otherwise, for I had much to tell and had obviously gained a great deal of experience. This little expedition proved to be an important factor in moulding my after-life. It vastly widened my views of humanity and civilisation, and it confirmed aspirations for travel which were afterwards indulged.

CHAPTER V

CAMBRIDGE

Trinity College—First vacation at the Lakes—Second vacation at Aberfeldy—College friends—Entire breakdown in health—Third vacation in Germany—My father's death

IT was a notable day in my life when, in the year 1840, escorted by my father on the top of a stage coach, I caught my first view of the principal buildings of Cambridge. There was no railway to Cambridge then. I had been entered at Trinity College, where rooms were assigned to me on the first floor of B. New Court. My tutor was J. W. Blakesley (1808–1885), an accomplished classical scholar, contemporary with Tennyson and his set, and subsequently Dean of Lincoln. The then Master of the College, who, however, resigned his post after the close of my first term, was Christopher Wordsworth (1774–1846), brother of the poet and father of three distinguished classical scholars, — John; Charles, Bishop of St. Andrew's; and Christopher, the headmaster of Harrow. The biographies of them all appear in the *Dict. Nat. Biog.* I found but few old friends among the undergraduates besides Matthew Boulton, but gradually fell into my place. I soon became conscious of the power and thoroughness of the work about me, as of a far superior order to anything I had previously witnessed. At the same time I wondered at its narrowness, for not a soul seemed to have the slightest knowledge of, or interest in, what I had acquired in my medical education and what we have since learnt to call Biology. The religious dogmas were of a more archaic type than I had latterly learnt to hold. I thought that just as the medicals wanted the thoroughness of the classicals and of the mathematicians, so these wanted at least an elementary knowledge of what was familiar to the medicals. Great and salutary changes have long since been introduced, and the above criticism, which was perfectly just at the time, is now, I believe and trust, almost wholly out of date.

I stood far behind the majority of my fellow-freshmen in classics, but less so in elementary mathematics, which were then much neglected in schools; for I had an innate love of them, and had indulged in some little private study. I pass lightly over my first year, which was a period of general progress, without much of note, until the first vacation arrived.

I then formed one of a reading party who went to Keswick in Cumberland, and had rooms in the same house with the two tutors, Matheson and Eddis. It was called "Browtop," and was then a detached villa with a wide prospect, situated in the district that now bears that name. One other pupil lived there also; the rest had lodgings in the town. Being in those years careless of rain and little sensitive to the enervating air of the Lake District, I found myself perfectly happy. The hills being moderate in height and the distances small, an afternoon sufficed easily for most of the excursions, so the whole morning was left free for reading. Matheson, the mathematical tutor, was a well-known Fellow of Trinity College, a considerable pianist and a good walker. He also knew the country and many of its residents. Among these was the Rev. Frederic Myers (1811–1851), Vicar of Keswick, who had married into the Marshall family, and who showed me much kindness. He was father to the as yet unborn poet and spiritualist, Frederic W. H. Myers (1843–1901), and his house was a social centre.

I saw a most amusing scene in its drawing-room, which those who recollect the formidable presence of Dr. Whewell will appreciate. All male animals, including men, when they are in love, are apt to behave in ways that seem ludicrous to bystanders. Whewell was not exempt from the common lot, though he had to sustain his new dignity of " Master of Trinity." He was then paying court to the lady who became his first wife, and his behaviour reminded me irresistibly of a turkey-cock similarly engaged. I fancied that I could almost hear the rustling of his stiffened feathers, and did overhear these sonorous lines of Milton rolled out to the lady *à propos* of I know not what, "cycle and epicycle, orb and orb," with hollow o's and prolonged trills on the r's.

The following skit indicates the feeling in regard to Whewell's manner that was current in Cambridge after he had assumed his office. I was reminded of it not so very many months ago, by the late Lord Kelvin :—

"You may roam where you will through the realms of infinity
And find nothing so great as the Master of Trinity."

Those who have read Whewell's Life, which was written by a loving hand and dwells mainly on his kindly, domestic character, will gather little idea of the rough power of the man and his too frequent overbearing attitude. In after-days he invited me to the Lodge, where I found him most unexpectedly gracious.

It may be worth mentioning that at the time of which I am writing, brakes to carriages were unknown in England except in the Lake Country, where the many hills made it difficult to travel without restraint, unless by frequently stopping to put on or take off the drag. Their use gradually spread, as the first sentimental opposition to them subsided. A near relative of my own, who was a devoted whip and drove his own four-horse drag for many years, was at first contemptuous towards brakes, but soon changed his mind, and ever afterwards used one.

One of the longer excursions was to Scawfell, where I found a small encampment of ordnance surveyors with theodolite and heliostat. Their immediate object was to obtain by direct observation the bearing of Snowdon, ninety-six miles off (as I think they said), to form the side of one of their principal triangles. A corresponding station was set up on the top of Snowdon, whence after many days' waiting in vain the long-wished-for star of light reflected from the sun by the mirror on Snowdon, became faintly but clearly visible through the telescope at Scawfell. It had been seen on three days altogether, two of which were successive. The obstruction to light by a few miles of mist, etc., in the lower layers of the atmosphere, contrasts forcibly with the ease with which every detail of the far more distant moon becomes visible when risen but a few degrees above the horizon.

Talking of such things reminds me of an elementary but very neat little problem that was set about this time in one of the College examination papers. It has often served me as a rough reminder of the constants involved, so I give it :—

"The tops of two masts, each ten feet above calm water, are just visible to one another at a distance of eight miles; what is the diameter of the earth? Aerial refraction is not to be taken into account." I leave its solution to the reader.

One of the features of my stay at the Lakes was the wrestling and other field sports, then much more homely in their accessories than they are now. I took lessons from one of the family of Ivens, among whom were many noted wrestlers. My teacher was the light-weight champion of the year. It was interesting to observe the wary approach and half-catchings of the opponents before one of them succeeded in grappling ; then the tug-of-war began.

An event occurred at this time closely similar in many respects, but not in its most painful details, to one previously related by De Quincey in his reminiscences of S. T. Coleridge, as having occurred in the Lake District in the early years of last century. I was quite ignorant of it till very lately, when I happened to be reading his book. My story is that of a Polish Count, O., who appeared at Keswick with scant introductions, took a house, and made himself most agreeable. I fell at once under his influence, for he seemed to me extraordinarily accomplished. He had all sorts of books and instruments, and even a tame monkey! So the Count throve and prospered for a while. But a lady resident in the neighbourhood who had been connected in her youth with one of the German Courts, and who studied the Almanach de Gotha and the like, insisted that the Count's claims to the title were totally unfounded. So a small warfare raged. In the meantime the Count won the affections of a simple girl, the orphan child of a somewhat wealthy "statesman," that is what we should call a yeoman farmer. He married her, and afterwards ran away with as much of her money as he could get hold of, leaving her with the questionable title of Countess as her only consolation. This finale occurred after I had left.

I grieve deeply that I knew little at that time of the Lake Poets, except Byron's lines on the correct poetical creed—

"Thou shalt believe in Milton, Dryden, Pope ;
  Thou shalt not trust in Wordsworth, Coleridge, Southey. . . ."

In consequence, I made no effort to obtain the honour of seeing and possibly receiving some slight introduction to any one of its then living members. Neither did I ever see Dr. Arnold, though I walked with Strickland, one of our reading party and a former pupil of his, as far as his door, which he entered to spend half an hour with him, while I waited and envied.

Strickland was the son of a well-known Yorkshire baronet. He joined me in many pleasant walks from London after my college days, of which I especially recollect one in the then rural Isle of Wight, when there was little more than a single house at Shanklin, and that was its pretty, rustic hotel. The times of travel from London so fitted in, that the walk from Ryde about Easter-time began well before twilight, and we reached Shanklin not too late to be taken in and to thoroughly enjoy the moonlit evening. Strickland was a strong swimmer, but he got into some difficulty next morning owing to the surf and undercurrents at the place where he entered the sea. He returned safely to shore, to my great relief, but much tired from long battling with the water.

His end was tragic. It occurred in North America, when winter had just set in, near some well-known watering-place whose name I forget, separated by a low range of hills from another watering place about sixteen miles off. The road between the two was perfectly simple and easy in summer, but not so in the snowdrifts and darkness of winter. Strickland would attempt it, though much was said to dissuade him : he never reached his destination. A relief party tracked his wanderings. He seemed to have acted as one demented by the hardship, for he had stripped off his clothes and thrown them away, one after the other, even his boots, so that his dead body was almost wholly undressed. That was the story I heard from two persons.

On returning to Cambridge after the first long vacation, I was put steadily to mathematical work, coming at length under that most distinguished Cambridge tutor, William Hopkins (1793–1866), mathematician and geologist. He kindly took a good deal of interest in me and gave me much encouragement, but the hopes he fostered were shattered by serious illness, which precluded severe study during my third year, as will be mentioned farther on. At a later date I found myself his colleague as Joint Secretary to the British Association, but his health had by then declined and his fine intellect begun to fail. I never had a tutor whom I reverenced and loved so entirely as Hopkins.

It was early in my second year that I entered into a close friendship with two Etonians. The one was Henry Fitzmaurice Hallam (1824–1850), the younger son of the historian Henry Hallam (1777–1859) and brother to Arthur Hallam (1811–1833), the subject of Tennyson's *In Memoriam*. The other friend was F. Campbell, the eldest son of Lord Campbell (1779–1861), then Lord Chief-Justice, and afterwards Lord Chancellor. F. Campbell became in later years, through succession, Lord Stratheden and Campbell. I owe much to each of these fast friends, but in different ways.

Harry Hallam had a singular sweetness and attractiveness of manner, with a love of harmless banter and paradox, and was keenly sympathetic with all his many friends. He won the Second Chancellor's Medal. Through him I became introduced to his father's house, still shadowed by the sudden death of his son Arthur and of a daughter. Mr. Hallam was very kind to me, and the friendship of him and of his family was one of the corner-stones of my life-history. I met many eminent persons at his house. Harry Hallam, like his brother and sister, died suddenly and young, to my poignant grief. His death occurred while I was away in South Africa. I have visited the quiet church at Clevedon where

5

all the Hallams lie, each memorial stone bearing a briefly pathetic inscription, and kneeling alone in a pew by their side, spent the greater part of a solitary hour in unrestrained tears.

F. Campbell had set for himself an ideal of public life that was too high for his powers, and many would say that he greatly failed in it. It may be so, but he had what I prized beyond anything else, a capacity for steady friendship, and a disposition unalloyed by pettiness. I always found help when consulting him about any of my own difficulties, because he put things in fresh lights and always with noble intent. He died in 1893. Through being his friend, I was entertained with much kindness by his father at Stratheden House, and received important help on more than one occasion.

It was mainly through these two men, Hallam and Campbell, that I first became acquainted with most of the ablest undergraduates of that day. Of these Maine (Sir Henry S. Maine, 1822–1888) ranked the highest. He had a great charm of manner with much beauty of feature, and was one of the few non-Trinity men who became thoroughly at home in Trinity itself. In later years, when he had become an eminent jurist and had filled with distinction the highest legal post in India, I used to enjoy long talks with him at the Athenæum Club, mostly on topics connected with Primitive Culture.

The subject of prehistoric civilisation was novel even so late as the early fifties, and was discussed independently from two different sides. The line of approach that Maine followed was to investigate the customs of the so-called Aryan races. The other line was by the study of living savage races, and of such inferences regarding the past as might be drawn from implements and bones preserved in prehistoric graves and caverns. The horizon of the Antiquarians was so narrow at about the date of my Cambridge days, that the whole history of the early world was literally believed, by many of the best informed men, to be contained in the Pentateuch. It was also practically supposed that nothing more of importance could be learnt of the origins of civilisation during classical times than was to be found definitely stated in classical authors.

Sir H. Maine considerably extended this narrow horizon through his close analysis of classical writings in the light of his Indian experiences, but he was always tempted to look on what was really a very advanced form of civilisation as if it had been primitive, and thereby laid himself open to violent attack. Among his opponents, J. F. MacLennan (1827-1881), the author of *Marriage by Capture*, etc., was eminently impetuous, and Maine, knowing that I was well acquainted with him, begged me to do what I could to moderate his controversial tone; I tried in vain. This, however, is travelling many years ahead. I had often occasion to consult Sir H. Maine on subjects that I had then in hand, and always found him a most helpful adviser.

It is difficult to select illustrative episodes of my Cambridge days. William Johnson Cory, then known as Johnson of King's (1823-1892), "Poet, and Master at Eton," was a remarkable character. He was easily the first classic of his year, as tested by the brilliancy of his performance in gaining the Craven

Scholarship soon after joining the University. At that time he was eccentric, very short-sighted, and Johnsonian in appearance, but these peculiarities wore off so much that, on his calling on me some years afterwards, fashionably dressed and polished in manner, I did not at first recognise him. He took an active part in a small Epigram Club which flourished for a while and then ceased, but which gave rise to some good verses. I recollect the roll of the first line of one by Maine—" King Daniel of Derrinane . . ."— that referred to a recent action of Daniel O'Connell.

Tom Taylor (1817-1880), "Dramatist and Editor of *Punch*," was full of vigour and versatility, but a few years older than those of whom I have been speaking. He had recently been elected Fellow of the College. In those days *Punch* was newly started, and Tom Taylor thought he could do better, so he founded a weekly comic paper called *Puck*, for which he endeavoured to obtain contributors. It was fairly good, but did not live long. Many years later he became editor of the very periodical he then wished to crush.

I saw much of Joseph and E. Kay, half-brothers of Sir James Kay-Shuttleworth (1804-1877), who was the "Founder of English Popular Education." Joseph Kay (1821-1878), "Economist," was appointed "Travelling Bachelor," a University post that at that time attracted little competition, because the conditions attached to its tenure were inconvenient to most rising men. Its possession, therefore, carried little weight. But Joseph Kay utilised to the full his position of "Travelling Bachelor of the University of Cambridge" in obtaining help abroad, and he wrote and published

a valuable Report with that title, which attracted
much attention. He took in it an opposite position
to one previously occupied by Whewell. I beg to be
pardoned if my memory plays tricks, but my impression is that Whewell's efforts to subdue his own
indignation at being bearded in this way by a mere
"Travelling Bachelor" were all the more amusing
because he was impotent to retort. Joseph Kay was
perfectly in order in asserting his rank; he was
judged by competent outsiders to have written very
ably, and he was no longer a resident in Trinity
College within immediate reach of Whewell's wrath.

E. Kay (1822–1897), afterwards Lord Justice of
Appeal, had rooms on the same staircase as myself,
and we wasted a great deal of time together, both in
term and in my second summer vacation. But
however idle he may have been at College, he richly
made up for it afterwards by hard and steady legal
work, out of which he finally emerged as a Judge
with a large fortune made at the Bar.

Charles Buxton (1823–1871), son of the philanthropist Sir T. Fowell Buxton (1786–1845) and
father of the present Postmaster-General, was another
intimate friend. He was a far-off relative of my own,
and one of the most favourable examples of a Rugby
product under Dr. Arnold. Other similar examples
of highly favourable products occur at once to the
memory, such as Dean Stanley, Dean Lake, and
Walrond, but unquestionably the common opinion of
Cambridge undergraduates then assigned the epithet
of "prig" to most Rugby boys. I can exactly recall
the combination of qualities that occasioned the
offence; they were partly an unconscious Phariseeism

combined with want of "go," and partly a Rugby voice and manner. Eton boys were rated far higher than they. I do not recollect whether any generalisation was formed at that time in respect to Harrow boys, who were then few in number. To return to Charles Buxton, he gave me the idea of perfection in respect to a highly honourable class of mind. This did not include exceptional brilliance, such as characterised some of the men mentioned above, but it did include most of the manly virtues and as much common sense as was consistent with a charming dash of originality. His elder brother Fowell, who has lately died, had rooms on the same staircase as myself.

W. G. Clark (1821–1878) was another contemporary of whom I saw much then and in after years. His strong bent had been towards diplomacy, but he wanted the fortune and connections necessary for success in such a career, so his desire remained unfulfilled. He loved to bring back impressions of travel, whether made in the Peloponnesus or in the rear of Garibaldi. He was Public Orator of the University for many years, and Vice-Master of Trinity College. Consequently, as a matter of course in those days, he was an ordained clergyman. But he chafed under the fetters of orthodoxy, and became a prominent member of the small group of men who procured the Act that allowed clergymen to retire from their office without retaining clerical disabilities. His career was clouded towards its end by insidious mental disease. He lived long retired in almost complete solitude in a Yorkshire inn, but sometimes sent bits of elegant Greek poetry to old classical friends, as to Justice Denman. A small volume of poems published under his initials contains some gems. He had lost a favourite male cousin in youth whose death affected him deeply and gave the chief motive to the book of poems in question.[1]

My second long vacation was spent with a reading party in Aberfeldy, in Perthshire, under the guidance of two tutors as usual, of whom one was Arthur Cayley (1821–1895), whose mathematical work soon gained a world-wide reputation. He and Sylvester (1814–1897) became the two leading mathematicians of England. Cayley was reputed to be the more solid, Sylvester the more daring and brilliant. I saw much of Sylvester a dozen or more years after the date of which I now speak, and for a brief time also at the English Lakes. He was a great friend of Cayley, and corresponded with him very often about his own numerous new ideas, becoming subsequently depressed or elated according to the tenor of the answer. Over and over again I have heard him say, "I must send this to Cayley," or again, "Cayley has pointed out a difficulty." He was charmingly naïve, and both were men of prodigious mental power. When the time came for adjudging the Copley Medal to one or other of them, the highest honour of the Royal Society, which it annually bestows on the foremost man in science of whatever branch, in all Europe, there was much discussion as to which of the two should first have it. I was a member of its Council

[1] One of the verses still haunts my memory and deserves reproduction :—

"The brook sings not so cheerily as of yore,
The young spring leaf is withered and upcurled,
The rose is scentless, and the sunbeam cold,
Truly there's something wanting in the world."

at the time; the opinions of most of us, including myself, were of course largely guided by those of the eminent mathematicians who were also members of it, and by the result of private inquiries. The opinions in favour of Sylvester prevailed; Cayley received the Medal a few years subsequently.

Never was a man whose outer physique so belied his powers as that of Cayley. There was something eerie and uncanny in his ways, that inclined strangers to pronounce him neither to be wholly sane nor gifted with much intelligence, which was the very reverse of the truth. Again, he appeared so frail as to be incapable of ordinary physical work; not a bit of it. One morning he coached us as usual and dined early with us at our usual hour. The next morning he did the same, all just as before, but it afterwards transpired that he had not been to bed at all in the meantime, but had tramped all night through over the moors to and about Loch Rannoch. As to memory, I found by pure accident that he could repeat poetry by the yard so to speak, and that of many kinds. His shy, retiring ways did no justice whatever to his gigantic mental capacity.

I was, in a very humble way, able to compare the work of various mathematical teachers with that of Cayley. The latter moved his symbols in battalions, along broad roads, careless of short cuts, and he managed them with the easy command of a great general. The very look of his papers, written in firm handwriting and well proportioned lengths of line, bore thoroughness and accuracy on their face. This is not over fanciful. William Spottiswoode (1825–1883), himself a mathematician and President of the

Royal Society, of whom I shall have to speak later, laid much stress on the general aspect of mathematical papers as indicating in many ways the value of their contents, and I could quote other authorities to a similar effect.

We had a pleasant and a social time at Aberfeldy, for the residents in the neighbourhood were very kind to us. Sir Neil and Lady Menzies of Menzies Castle, to whom I had an introduction, lived amid Highland surroundings. One of these consisted of a full-dressed piper who strutted up and down the long hall during dinner with the self-sufficiency of the drum-major of a regimental band, squirling on his abominable instrument. But there was also an abundance of Southern culture.

The visit of the Queen to Lord Breadalbane at the neighbouring Castle of Taymouth gave rise to the following permanent impression on me. On returning to my rooms after a walk, I found all my books and things taken away and replaced by the gear of a cavalry officer, who was sitting uninvited at my own table as lord and master of it. I could hardly contain my wrath, but he was courteous and amused, though firm. He was billeted there, consequently I must give way and yield my occupancy to him. He had been told there was another room available for me to which my things had been taken, but go I must and at once. This little incident made me realise the odiousness and too probable insolence of military rule, and the lesson sank deep. I gained on the spot a Quaker-like repugnance to the sight of the accoutrements of a soldier, that exists to this day under certain conditions, and its source is still recognisable.

On returning to Cambridge the old life re-
commenced, but on an enlarged scale, and more
friends were made, among whom were George
Denman (1819–1896), afterwards a Judge, and the
son of Lord Chief-Justice Denman (1779–1854). He
combined classical capacity with power of muscle and
endurance, both in a very high degree, for he was
Senior Classic of his year and Stroke Oar of the
University crew. He lived a double life, warily looking after his own boat crew, the First Trinity, and
joining their rollickings in order to keep them within
bounds, but doing hard mental work at other hours.
I think he was perhaps the most respected of all the
undergraduates. In after years he told me the
following extraordinary anecdote of Macaulay's
memory. He, Denman, had obtained the prize for
Greek verse and had to recite his composition.
Macaulay was a guest at Trinity Lodge and heard
the recitation. Some years after, when Denman had
half forgotten the occurrence and imperfectly recollected what he had then written, he was introduced
to Macaulay, who exclaimed at once, "Why, it was
you who recited those verses," which he straightway
repeated.

Memories so crowd on me that I find it difficult
to stop. Something ought to have been said of a
singularly attractive man with quaint turns of thought,
H. Vaughan Johnson, who lived on the same staircase
as myself, and who collaborated in legal work with
E. Kay, of whom I have already spoken. He married
a sister of my friend, then F. Campbell, afterwards
Lord Stratheden and Campbell.

Also I should mention W. F. Gibbs, who became

tutor to the then Prince of Wales, now King
Edward VII. Gibbs obtained his Trinity Scholarship
at the same time as F. Gell, who was afterwards
Bishop of Madras. Gibbs was gifted with agility;
Gell was very short-sighted, and the reverse of agile,
but he possessed a grand nose, the finest I have ever
seen, and a glory to the College. These two, as
Gibbs told me, exuberant with joy from gaining their
scholarships, rushed down the avenue of limes at the
back of the College and through the gate at the end,
where a row of low bars confronted them; Gibbs,
who led, jumped lightly over them, but Gell, who
followed, blundered, tripped, fell heavily on his
face, and ruined his grand nose for ever. The bars
are still there; whenever I pass that way I recall the
tragedy.

Two events may be mentioned to show how long
the duelling spirit lingered. One was a row at the
Union which nearly dismembered it. I partly forget
how it originated, and it would hardly be worth while
to record it if I did. It culminated in the formation
of two fiercely opposed parties, P. and C., and by a
leading member of the C. party being bludgeoned in
the dark by two members of the P. party. They
had awaited his exit from the dark staircase leading
from his rooms into Neville Court. The tumult that
this caused among the already excited undergraduates
is barely conceivable. The C. party, to which I
belonged, formed itself into a Committee and sent to
an Indian officer, then living with his family in
Cambridge, entreating him to come and advise us
how to act. The officer himself happened to be
delayed for half an hour, but he sent in advance,

quite as a matter of course, a neat box containing a pair of duelling pistols ready for use.

I may add that a special meeting of the Union was forthwith called, for which it was obviously necessary to provide an exceptionally strong but neutral President. A man known as "First Trinity" Young (I forget his Christian name), who died in early life or he might have highly distinguished himself, was selected for the purpose, and he executed admirably his most difficult task. It gave me a lesson in administration. He began with a brief but emphatic request for cordial support from both sides, adding that every question had more than one aspect. Humorous but apt remarks were thrown out by him now and then. An equally patient hearing was given to all parties, and a few occasional interruptions were firmly repressed. The meeting parted with its members much more disposed towards working relations than before; so the extremity of the crisis was passed.

Its consequence was, however, the constitution of an opposition society, called the "Historical," in which more attention should be paid to decorum and to the amenities of debate than had latterly been customary in the Union. About sixty members joined it, and, partly because I was then living out of College in a house where there was a possible meeting room, I was asked to preside, which I did. My old friend Dr. H. Holden (1823–1896), with whom I was speaking some few years ago of this very incident, assured me that among the active members of the "Historical" was Stanley, afterwards the 15th Earl of Derby (1826–1893). He entered the University not long before I quitted it, during, I suppose, my absence of one term from Cambridge through illness. Anyhow, I do not in the least recollect his presence.

Speaking of the still lingering practice of duelling, C. Bristed, an American who came to Cambridge for a couple of years or so, and whose racy ways made him everywhere an acceptable guest, had a strange experience. Some few years after we had left the University, F. Campbell asked us both to dine with him at Stratheden House, where he was at the moment the only member of his family in residence. Bristed gave us there the full account of a duel in which he had unexpectedly become engaged. It occurred near a German watering - place that lay within a short distance of French territory. He had been criticising his future opponent pretty freely in a local paper, with the result that on leaving church with his young wife, where they had just joined in taking the Sacrament, a note was handed to him containing a challenge, and suggesting a place in French territory for the encounter. There seemed no other feasible course than to accept that most untimely challenge, which he did. On arriving at the ground, the combatants were placed 40 paces apart, with instructions to walk towards one another, each to fire his one shot whenever he thought proper. Bristed, who was rather short-sighted, said that his opponent looked absurdly far away, and that he considered the safest plan for himself was to "draw" his adversary's shot before they came nearer together, which he did. He fired harmlessly, and a harmless shot came in reply. All the time he was recounting this very irregular proceeding, I kept the corner of my eye fixed on a portrait of the Lord Chief-Justice, that hung opposite, and thought how incongruous the conversation was with its presence.

I received a kindly welcome from time to time after leaving Cambridge, in the homes of not a few of my fellow-undergraduates. One was that of Robert, afterwards Sir Robert Dalyell. His father, Captain Sir William Dalyell, was a naval veteran with a scar across his face left by a severe gash, who had quarters in Greenwich Hospital as one of the Captains in command, the constitution of Greenwich Hospital being then totally different from what it is now. The family consisted of himself, Lady Dalyell, and their two daughters. Numerous friends appeared every Sunday. We visitors walked and had tea, spending healthful and delightful summer afternoons, usually returning to London by river. The life of a young bachelor in not over elegant lodgings is vastly cheered by such occasional outings. They give great pleasure all round with very little expenditure either of exertion or of cost.

The family of Crompton Hutton, who lived at Putney Park, were most kind in a similar way, to myself, to E. Kay, and many others. That family was soon sadly broken up by deaths. One of the merriest of the sisters in those days was the wife, and latterly the widow, of Lord Lingen, who herself has died since I first wrote these lines. Lord Lingen was, I need hardly add, for a long time one of the most valuable civil servants of his country, first at the Education Office and afterwards at the Treasury.

It was during my third year at Cambridge that I

broke down entirely in health and had to lose a term and go home. I suffered from intermittent pulse and a variety of brain symptoms of an alarming kind. A mill seemed to be working inside my head; I could not banish obsessing ideas; at times I could hardly read a book, and found it painful even to look at a printed page. Fortunately, I did not suffer from sleeplessness, and my digestion failed but little. Even a brief interval of complete mental rest did me good, and it seemed as if a long dose of it might wholly restore me. It would have been madness to continue the kind of studious life that I had been leading. I had been much too zealous, had worked too irregularly and in too many directions, and had done myself serious harm. It was as though I had tried to make a steam-engine perform more work than it was constructed for, by tampering with its safety valve and thereby straining its mechanism. Happily, the human body may sometimes repair itself, which the steam-engine cannot.

As it had become impossible for me to continue reading for mathematical honours, I abandoned all further intention of trying for them, and occupied part of my remaining time at Cambridge in attending medical lectures to fill up the necessary quota of attendances that should qualify for a medical degree. I spent my third long vacation in travelling with my sister Emma in Germany. We stayed some weeks in Dresden, where we joined the Hallams and accompanied them during a little further travel, and then I took my sister round by Vienna and back home. Those were days of travelling by voiturier and diligence.

There was a good deal of talk at that time about animal magnetism. Its practice in Saxony was forbidden by law, but an Austrian acquaintance in Dresden invited me to his house across the frontier, where I saw the elementary part of its practice, namely, its inducing catalepsy and insensibility to pain. I afterwards practised it at home, and magnetised some eighty persons in this way; but it is an unwholesome procedure, and I have never attempted it since. One experience was, however, of interest. I had been assured that success was the effect of strength of will on the part of the magnetiser, so at first I exerted all the will-power I possessed, which was fatiguing. I then, by way of experiment, intermitted a little, looking all the time in the same way as before, and found myself equally successful. So I intermitted more and more, and at last succeeded in letting my mind ramble freely while I maintained the same owl-like demeanour. This acted just as well. The safe conclusion was that the effect is purely subjective on the part of the patient, and that will-power on the part of the operator has nothing to do with it.

A main object of giving the foregoing brief notices of notable persons with whom I had the privilege of being acquainted at Cambridge, is to show the enormous advantages offered by a University to those who care to profit by them. The body of undergraduates contains a very large majority of men of mediocre gifts and tastes, but it has also a strong infusion of the highest intellects of their age and country, picked out of all the schools of England. Among any body of young educated Englishmen collected at random, some few will probably be found who are destined to rise to distinction, but among a group of those who are ranked as the foremost in a University, more than one half of them will do so.

For my own part, I had hoped to take respectable mathematical honours, though perhaps it was never in my power to do so, notwithstanding the assurances of my eminent tutor, Mr. Hopkins. But the utter breakdown of my health in my third year, as already explained, made further study of a severe kind impossible. I therefore followed my bent in reading what I could, and my time was by no means wasted. I contented myself with a Poll Degree. Judge therefore of my surprise a few years ago, while passing a winter on the Riviera, when a telegram reached me saying I had been elected to the rare honour of an Honorary Fellowship in Trinity College. I thought at first it must be a mistake, but it was not. Nay more, hearing that a copy of a portrait recently made of me by the late Charles Furse (see frontispiece) would be acceptable, I had one made and offered it to the authorities of the College. It now hangs in its Hall among those of men with whom I feel it the highest possible honour to be associated in any way.

I must recur briefly to the close of my medical education. As already mentioned, I attended some lectures during one term at Cambridge, but had not even admittance to the then small Addenbrook Hospital. I have little to tell about this period that would interest others than myself. It was thought well that I should complete my course in London at St. George's, for the purpose of seeing new conditions of medical treatment. I attended these necessarily in a desultory way, on account of an impending domestic sorrow. My dear father's originally fine constitution, long tried by severe asthma and gout, had at length seriously given way. He required continual medical and surgical treatment and trusted in me, so to him I went. The end came in October 1844 at Hastings. His remains had to be taken to Leamington. It was a wretched journey, for the railway was not even then completed the whole way.

The effect of his death was to remove the main bond that kept our family together, and we soon became more or less separated. Two of my sisters married within the year, and I found myself with a sufficient fortune to make me independent of the medical profession. So my status of pupilhood was closed, and I had henceforth to be my own director. Being much upset and craving for a healthier life, I abandoned all thought of becoming a physician, but felt most grateful for the enlarged insight into Nature that I had acquired through medical experiences.

CHAPTER VI

EGYPT AND THE SOUDAN

Family matters—Malta and Alexandria—Nile—Korosko—Berber by
desert — Boat to Khartum and White Nile — Bayouda Desert to
Dongola—Wady Halfa and Cairo—Recent visit to Professor Petrie's
camp at Abydos

THE home side of my surroundings has been
only slightly alluded to, not that it was of
small importance to myself, but because it belonged
to a different phase of my life from that with which
I am here chiefly concerned. When I had outgrown
the tuition of my sister Adele, I led in one sense
a solitary life. For though I joined my other two
unmarried sisters in their social amusements, I was
always treated by them and their companions as a
boy, and I felt during this time like an only child
with aunts. Their affection to me was deep, so was
mine to them, but it was not and could not be
reciprocated on equal terms. But I received in full
measure the priceless treasure of a home, in which
each member knew the essential characteristics, good
and bad, of all the others, and who loved each other
all the same, and would support him or her through
thick and thin. The younger of my brothers, Erasmus,
was mostly away; in the first instance in the navy,
afterwards in farming his property in Somersetshire,

or again in service as an officer in the Militia. My elder brother Darwin was a great favourite among his friends from his early life onwards. He used me as his fag when I was a boy, and taught me to be fairly smart. I imbibed many common-sense maxims from him, but our ideals of life differed to an almost absurd degree: he had not the slightest care for literature or science, and I had no taste for country pursuits. Our differences of temperament became more marked the older we grew. These few remarks, in connection with what has previously been said, will give a supplementary idea of what my surroundings had been during much of my boyhood. It was now the year 1845, when I was twenty-three years old, and the acuteness of my late bereavement had passed away.

After the necessary legal business was finished, the members of the family gradually adapted themselves to their new conditions. My sister Emma lived thenceforth with my mother, whose house, whether at Claverdon or Leamington, I always thought of as "home." Emma soon became my loving and beloved correspondent, continuing so during the remaining seventy years of her long life, ever devoted to my interests and keenly sympathetic. I was indeed fortunate in possessing such an unselfish and affectionate sister. My sister Lucy was in suffering health, from the results of acute rheumatic fever when a child, and lived only three years longer. My sisters Bessy and Adele were then either married or about to be married; my eldest brother Darwin was married and living with his young wife and her mother, Mrs. Philips, at her country house, called

"Edstone," between Stratford-on-Avon and Henley-on-Arden; and my second brother Erasmus was, as already said, at his estate at Loxton in Somersetshire.

I was therefore free, and I eagerly desired a complete change; besides, I had many "wild oats" yet to sow. So I started on travel, this time to Egypt. At Malta I found my old friend Robert Frere, of whom I have already spoken. He was acting medically towards his uncle, Hookham Frere, much as I had been acting towards my own father. Hookham Frere was too unwell to be seen, or I should greatly have valued the privilege of a few words with so accomplished a man, whatever his diplomatic shortcomings may have been. Not the less so because of the amusing parody written jointly by himself and Canning of my grandfather Darwin's *Loves of the Plants* under the title of *Loves of the Triangles*, which gave a *coup de grâce* to the turgid poetry that had become a temporary craze in my grandfather's time.

At Malta I took steamer to Alexandria, and found two Cambridge friends on board, who had been travelling in Greece. They were Montagu Boulton, the third and youngest brother of Matthew Boulton, and Hedworth Barclay, a very distant kinsman of my own and the son of David Barclay of Eastwick Park. We ultimately agreed to join. Boulton had a first-rate courier named Evard, who had also been groom of the chamber to one of the most fashionable of English families. Barclay had a good Greek cook, Christopher, and I was to contribute a dragoman, which I did. His name was Ali.

Mehemet Ali was at that time the ruler of Egypt. Barclay had an audience of him, and received the usual firman entitling us to impress men to pull up our boat at certain well-known places where the stream is exceptionally strong. I myself saw the old greybeard driving, but that was all. Shepherd's Hotel then looked out upon rice-fields, and modern Cairo did not exist, but Waghorn's overland wagons to Suez had been established. After some stay at Cairo, we hired a dahabeyah; Barclay put on board a keg of his own porter, and so we started, intending to live luxuriously and in grand style. We also engaged an Arab lad as coffee-bearer and to make himself generally useful, who went by the name of Bob. He turned out to be a lad of parts.

The mornings were delightful. We rolled out of our beds half awake and tumbled ourselves into the river, climbing back very wide awake indeed into the boat by help of the big rudder, to the exquisite enjoyment of the first cup of coffee and a pipe. We chattered with Bob, the captain, sailors, and others, and soon smattered in Arabic. Boulton studied it classically as well, working very hard. So the voyage proceeded in the usual way. We were pulled safely up the First Cataract, and onward we went.

When near Korosko, men had to be impressed, but a person in a rather shabby Egyptian dress, but of Egyptian rank as a Bey, claimed and insisted on precedence. We were cross, and relieved our minds by the use of uncomplimentary English words. But by the time we had walked together to Korosko we had become fairly friendly, for he was a far more interesting man than we had supposed, and had much to tell us in French. He invited us to see his hut, where everything was perfectly clean and well ordered. Small as it was, a scientific and literary air pervaded it. There were maps, good books and scientific instruments of various kinds, so my heart warmed towards him. Then he began to address us in fairly good English, and made us understand that he was quite aware of our phrases when we were cross, and that he forgave us, but did so in a dignified way. There was one thing we could do well which he could not, and that was to provide a really good dinner. Evard and the cook rose at once to the occasion, and nothing could have been managed in better style under the circumstances.

The stranger proved to be Arnaud Bey, one of the distinguished St. Simonians who, having been banished from France, helped greatly to civilise Egypt in the days of Mehemet Ali. He had just returned from a long exploratory journey after gold and other valuable products in the districts about the Blue Nile. It will be hard now for a reader to put himself in the attitude of geographical ignorance that was then almost universal in respect to those places. Arnaud said at last, "Why do you content yourself like other tourists to go no farther than Wady Halfa? Why not travel overland by camel from this very place, Korosko, to Khartum? The Sheikh of the intervening Bishari Desert is in the village at this very moment. I know him well, and can easily arrange that he shall take you to Berber at moderate cost. You will then find your way by boat to Khartum." We were amazed at the proposition, for the very names of those places were unknown to us.   He drew a map on a small piece of paper for us to keep, on which he marked bits of useful information.   At length, after hours of eating and drinking and talking, we fell wholly

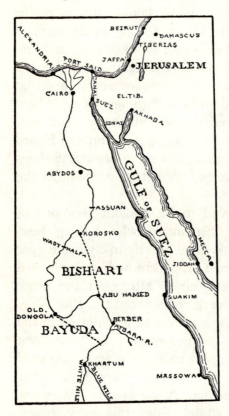

into his plan.   The Sheikh was sent for, and I shall never forget his entrance. The cabin reeked with the smells of a recent carouse, when the door opened and there stood the tall Sheikh, marked with sand on his forehead that indicated recent prostration in prayer. The pure moonlight flooded the Bacchanalian cabin, and the clear cool desert air poured in.   I felt swinish in the presence of his Moslem purity and imposing mien. For all that, we soon came to terms,

and were to start the day after the morrow.   The boat was to be sent to Wady Halfa under Bob in chief command to await our return there, and we three and our three servants were to travel into the unknown on the backs of beasts strange to our experience. So it all befell.

A more complete change can hardly be imagined than that from a luxurious cabin to nightly open-air bivouacs on the cold sand. Our first day was the customary march of little more than an hour, to be assured that nothing needful had been omitted. The next day the real journey began. The track we followed was presumably the same that has been followed since the most ancient days; it bore marks of its continued use during recent times in the whitened bones with which it was strewed. Sometimes we came across a camel whose skin had not yet disappeared, but formed a hollow shell including marrowless and porous bones. These desiccated remains were of most unexpected lightness. My arm is far from strong, but I easily lifted with one hand and held aloft the quarter of a camel in this dried-up state.

The ribbed rocks looked like the bones of the earth from which all the flesh, in the shape of soil and vegetation, had been blown away as sand and dust. Travellers by the railway that now runs along that very track can ill appreciate the effect the desert had on such as myself at that time. Ali proved an excellent and devoted servant. I long bore in mind his kindness to me on one bitterly cold night, for the nights were sometimes extremely chill, in quietly taking off his own jacket and wrapping it round my shivering body.

Many strangers joined our slowly moving caravan. One group was such as is frequently seen on similar occasions; it consisted of a husband on foot, with his wife and child mounted on a donkey, like the often-painted subject of the Flight of the Holy

Family into Egypt. Another personage was a middle-aged and rather mild-looking individual, who possessed little more than a sword, and was on his way to Abyssinia, where some fighting was expected with neighbouring savage tribes. He proposed to take part in it, and to make his profit from the slaves he captured. He was an old hand at this, and his businesslike account of the process was explicit. It was a moot question with him on each occasion when a man had been captured, whether to mutilate him at once or not. If so, the man was apt to die, and would certainly require costly attention for a long time ; on the other hand, if he recovered, his market value was greatly increased. I shall have a little to say later on of some results of the particular slave-hunting expedition which this worthy person went to join.

A caravan yields so many strange experiences and affords so many occasions of mutual helpfulness and of friendships, that it is easy to understand the importance of the Hadj pilgrimage in uniting Moslems. I have often wished that something of the sort could be revived among ourselves, such as the famous Canterbury Pilgrimage of Chaucer, but the religious motive for real pilgrimages is generally wanting in Protestant countries. The Congresses of large itinerant societies like the British Association, in some few respects may be considered as taking the place of pilgrimages, but they want the long hours and days of open-air life, hard exercise, and leisure.

After four days' travel from morning to evening, we came to a half-way place where a brack but drinkable water was to be had, which replaced the redolent stuff that our water-skins afforded, and so on for four more days, when we reached the Nile at Abu Hamed, having cut across its huge bend. Oh! the delights to such tourists as we were, of a temporary exemption from the discomforts of the desert, and of unlimited rations of water. We travelled farther by the side of the Nile for another three days or so, till Berber was reached, when we paid our dues and said good-bye to the camels. The Governor of Berber was very civil; the sherbet he gave us, though made from limes and not from lemons, tasted heavenly. He gave me a monkey, and I bought another, and these two were my constant companions on camel-back and everywhere else for many months, until I reached England.

A boat had here to be hired to take us up to Khartum. We got one in which the part below decks was much too low to stand in, and it swarmed with cockroaches, but it sufficed. The people at Berber were unruly, and so obstructive that the boatmen feared to enter with us into their own boat. However, we showed determination, and pushed off into the stream, with the result that first one and then another of the men ran alongside and plunged into the water and swam to the boat and turned its head up stream. We then set sail to Khartum.

In due time we passed Shendy, the scene of the recent massacre of Abbas Pasha, a younger son of Mehemet Ali. He was sent to collect imposts and to overawe the people. At Shendy he and his soldiers committed all sorts of outrages, and finally he demanded the daughter of the Deftader (or Tax-gatherer) in a form of marriage that was equivalent to temporary concubinage, which was a grave insult to her father, the most important man in the place. The Deftader was unable to resist; so he resigned himself, but gave orders secretly. While Abbas Pasha with his suite were at dinner and stupid with what they had drunk, the Pasha noticed that great bundles of stalks of the native corn were being brought in and stacked about the tent. He asked and was told that it was forage and litter for his Highness's horses. When enough of this straw had been brought in, a signal was given to fire it, and every man who attempted to break through was massacred, including of course Abbas himself. The Deftader escaped to Abyssinia; something more of him will be said shortly.

Finally we reached Khartum, then a group of huts with a wagon-roofed hall for the audiences of the Pasha. We heard of an extraordinary Frank, believed to be English, who had arrived some weeks previously. We went to call on him, knocked at the door, were told to enter, which we did, and came into the presence of a white man nearly naked, as agile as a panther, with head shorn except for the Moslem tuft, reeking with butter, and with a leopard skin thrown over his shoulder. He was recognised at once by my companions as an undergraduate friend, Mansfield Parkyns. He had got into a College scrape, and, leaving Cambridge prematurely, found his way to Abyssinia, where during years of adventure he had made friends with the just-mentioned Deftader of Shendy, and was then acting as an intermediary and the bringer of a substantial present whereby to obtain, if possible, his forgiveness and restoration.

Of the many travellers whom I have known I should place Mansfield Parkyns (1823–1894) as perhaps the most gifted with natural advantages for that career. He easily held his own under difficulties, won hearts by his sympathy, and could touch any amount of pitch without being himself defiled. He was consequently an admirable guide in that then sink of iniquity, Khartum. The saying was that when a man was such a reprobate that he could not live in Europe, he went to Constantinople; if too bad to be tolerated in Constantinople, he went to Cairo, and thenceforward under similar compulsion to Khartum. Half a dozen or so of these trebly refined villains resided there as slave-dealers; they were pallid, haggard, fever-stricken, profane, and obscene. Mansfield Parkyns complacently tolerated and mastered them all. The abominations of their habitual conversation exceeded in a far-away degree any other I have ever listened to, but it was clever. When one of them was out of the room, the others freely related his adventures to us, in which some anecdote like this was frequent. "So he said, 'Let us be friends; come drink a cup of coffee and smoke a pipe,' then he put poison into the coffee." There is a gourd whose dried seeds are said to be poisonous and not very unlike coffee in taste, which is particularly convenient in such cases. With all their villainy there was something of interest in their talk, but I had soon quite enough of it. Still, the experience was acceptable, for one wants to know the very worst of everything as well as the very best.

Some few years later, when trade had thriven and Khartum had become less barbarous, it was

deemed expedient to appoint an English Consul,
partly to watch and report on matters connected with
the slave trade. Mr. Petherick, who had been an
ivory dealer in the Soudan, was the first to hold that
post. I often saw him after his return ; he was
extremely cheery, and apparently frank in conversation, but very reticent on much that I wanted to
hear. I could not discover what had been the end
of my villainous acquaintances, nor how far the society
of Khartum had become purified by the time he
arrived there.

We had a few days still to spare, and Parkyns
was glad to join us in a short cruise up the White
Nile. His birthday and mine proved to be the
same, and we had an appropriate jollification. Our
house or hut looked over the swift and broad Blue
Nile on to the waste beyond, where pillars of whirling
sand were constantly forming at that time of year,
February. Many of them careered simultaneously,
but soon dissipated. I have never been caught in
one ; it would no doubt be disagreeable, but I never
saw one that behaved as if it were dangerous.

It was a strange sight on turning the corner
where the two Niles meet, to change from the Blue
Nile, which sparkled and rushed like a clear Highland
river, into the stagnant and foul, but deep White
Nile. We sailed through mournful scenery up a
width of water visited by great flocks of pelicans.
The river had few marked banks, but lapped upon
grassy shores like a flooded mere. The water was
so stagnant, that when we anchored for the night the
offal thrown overboard by the cook hung about the
boat, and a man had to be sent each morning with

a pitcher to get less undrinkable water from a distance. Heads of hippopotami bobbed up at times all about us in the mid river, but were very shy of approach. At that date, I should have said there were crocodiles on nearly every sandbank on the Nile below the Cataracts, for considerably more than half of the way thence to Cairo.

Beyond the despondency caused by the air and the mournful character of the scenery, I have little to say, except that our journey upwards was concluded somewhat earlier than intended, through an adventure. One of my two companions, attended by Parkyns, lay out at night to shoot a hippopotamus, whose recent tracks were only too apparent. They returned in the dark and very early morning in much excitement, and tried to make us understand that we ought to wake up and return at once, for some unintelligible reason. However, to please them, we yielded to their insistence, roused up the crew and sailed homewards. It turned out, some hours later, that the real reason was that my sportsman-companion had shot, not a hippopotamus, but a cow that was coming down to the river to drink. There really seemed no feasible way of making amends for the mistake, and a certainty of clamour and excessive claims if we confessed it. So we disappeared from that district, much as a pestilence would have done.

Our return journey past Khartum was by our boat to Matemma, opposite to Shendy, where we discharged it, and hired camels to take us a six days' journey, I think, across the Bayouda Desert to Dongola. We had become by that time used to camel-riding, we were well mounted, and travelled even as much as eighteen hours out of the twenty-four, on more than one day. The Polar Star and the pointers of the Great Bear served as the hand of a huge sidereal clock to tell the weary time.

At length we reached our destination. It is the habit of dragomans to tell fibs about their masters, to enhance their own importance; anyhow, we were treated to a review as distinguished strangers. I then had little experience with horses; Boulton was not a much better horseman than myself. Barclay was, but even he found himself in difficulty when sitting in a Turkish saddle with short stirrups and holding a rein armed with so powerful a curb that it required the lightest of hands to use it properly. However, we all passed the ordeal, without ludicrous mishap.

From Dongola we rode three days across the desert on the opposite side of the Nile, to cut off a small bend, and thenceforward by the west side of the Nile itself, so far as the very broken ground permitted. Semney was a surprise; a compact little temple, high above a spot where the whole Nile at that time of the year flowed through a channel so narrow that a cricketer ought to be able to throw a stone across. I tried, but, being bad at throwing, failed by a little. On the other hand, at the Sixth Cataract, between Berber and Shendy, where the river is broad, I had waded right across it to shoot ducks.

We had felt no small anxiety about the fate of our dahabeyah, but there she was at Wady Halfa in spick and span order; Bob, that bit of a boy, having risen to the level of his responsibilities and maintained perfect discipline. It appeared that the rais, or captain, was once refractory, but Bob boldly gave the order to the sailors to flog him, and flogged he was by his own crew, and ate the bread of humility.

My excuses for speaking at such length about countries since so familiarly known are that it will help to give some idea of how they struck a tourist-traveller in the time of Mehemet Ali, upwards of sixty years ago, and because this little excursion formed one of the principal landmarks of my life. That chance meeting with Arnaud Bey had important after-results to me by suggesting scientific objects to my future wanderings. I often thought of writing to him in order to bring myself to his remembrance, and to sincerely thank him, but no sufficiently appropriate occasion arose, and it is now too late.

In the winter 1900–1901 I visited Egypt again, and, calling at the Geographical Society there, learnt how important and honoured a place Arnaud Bey had occupied in its history. He had died not many months previously, and I looked at his portrait with regret and kindly remembrance. Being asked to communicate a brief memoir to the Society at its approaching meeting, I selected for my subject a comparison between Egypt then and fifty years previously. I took that opportunity to express my heartfelt gratitude to Arnaud, which posthumous tribute was all I had the power to pay.

During this same visit to Egypt I spent one of the most interesting weeks of my life at Professor Petrie's camp. It was by pure chance that when booking my place to Egypt, in the London office, I found Professor Petrie on some similar errand. He then and there invited me and my niece to join him

7

and Mrs. Petrie at Abydos, where he and his very capable party were about to excavate. Abydos lies on the western side of the Nile, roughly one-third of the way between Thebes and Cairo. We were met at the railway station by that most capable lady, then Miss, now Dr. Alice Johnson, mounted on the one horse that the camp possessed, and who with kurbash in hand and voluble Arabic extricated us quickly from a crowd of troublesome natives, and rode with us a distance of eight miles or so to the camp. This consisted of a row of mud huts with a space in front, the whole enclosed with a low mud wall and a wicket gate. The pottery, etc., that had recently been dug up was arranged in front of the huts. They had only mats for doors. One of the huts was the dining-room, and the others were for members of the party, the farthest from the entrance being that of Mr. and Mrs. Petrie. I was prepared for cold nights, but found them more severe than I expected. Being little short of eighty years old, I had lost much of the resisting power of youth, and heaped every scrap of clothing I could find over my body, with only partial success. I amused myself on one occasion by counting the number of layers of these that lay on my chest, and found it to be seventeen. A single skin rug capable of excluding the nimble dry air would have been worth more than half of these flimsy coverings. Our host and hostess were peculiarly independent of ordinary comfort, but the consumption of marmalade at their table was enormous.

I had no idea before of the strenuous life led by a great excavator. The mere digging can be delegated, but the rest seemed to occupy every faculty of our hosts at full stretch from early morning to late evening every day. There was drawing, copying, photographing, recording, comparison of specimens, piecing of them together, discussing them and planning new work, besides attending to the discipline of many men not concentrated at one spot, but dispersed among different diggings.

An amusing scene occurred at a stated hour every morning, when the fellahs who had found any curios and wanted to sell them were seated in a long row at a fixed distance from the camp. They brought in rotation what they had to sell. Professor Petrie knew by long experience exactly how much the various articles would fetch if taken to the dealers in the large towns, and offered that amount for what he cared to buy. The Arabs quite understood the system, namely, that by accepting what was offered they would get just as much as if they took a long journey in hopes of a better bargain, so the traffic was quick. The objects were bought out of funds variously provided, but the Egyptian Government reserved some rights of purchase in the end.

The conversation at meal-time was usually most interesting. Much was going on, and the originality and fertility of the ideas of Professor Petrie and the ingenuity of his explanations were marvellous. The actual digging was of course monotonous and laborious, but the faculties of those of the party who superintended each locality were kept on the alert. They had to record and to make maps as well as to keep the labourers to their work, and to supervise them narrowly. At nightfall the men, who had mostly worked for Professor Petrie during previous years, returned to their own huts, a little way behind one corner of the camp, and there they indulged about once a week in strange performances, not unlike those of dancing and howling dervishes. Their nature seemed to require occasional doses of these ebullitions.

We were fortunate at being present at the impressive feast of the full moon, which included solemn chants. It was dignified in every respect, and appeared to have a deeper religious significance than might have been expected possible with these men.

CHAPTER VII

SYRIA

Beyrout—Fever—Death of dragoman at Damascus—Jaffa—Descent of Jordan—Home

OUR company parted at Alexandria. Barclay returned home, I went to Syria, and Boulton desired to go farther East, to study Arabic and Oriental modes of thought and expression. Our paths crossed only once in Syria. Owing to misadventures, and to my great regret, I never saw him after. He made his way to the British forces, then engaged in the siege of Mooltan, and was the guest of their commander, General Whish. He stationed himself, against advice, in a loopholed tower to witness the progress of the fight, a matchlock ball penetrated his eye and killed him on the spot. I heard the story many years afterwards from General Whish himself.

I sailed from Alexandria to Beyrout with my dragoman Ali and my two pet monkeys. We were then put into quarantine, where Ali found a party of negress girls who had been captured on the borders of Abyssinia during the very fighting for which my acquaintance in the caravan was bound. They had been taken to Beyrout *via* the Red Sea. The girls were delighted to talk to us of places known to them as well as to ourselves. They seemed as merry as possible at the prospect of being sold and of soon finding, each of them, a master and a home.

A journey so far as Khartum was then thought something of a feat, even in Syria, and Ali, as I am convinced, greatly fibbed about my social importance. It must have been on that account that the Governor of the Quarantine, or whatever his title may have been, relaxed his restrictions on my behalf so greatly as to call down severe newspaper criticism on his acts of favouritism. In fact, we made a champagne picnic together in two boats, under the sole condition of the party in the one not touching any one in the other. For a similar reason, as I suppose, I was invited and entertained in a most stately way at the palace of a Druse chief, situated among the hills.

I bought travelling gear at Beyrout, and went inland to buy a pair of horses for myself and Ali, because it was not easy to hire good riding-horses, though baggage-horses could always be had. I set myself up in style, with tent and extra walls, a canteen, and handsome coffee and pipe apparatus. On arrival at the place where the horses were to be bought, I camped on ground intersected with ditches of stagnant water—a most insanitary-looking place. I caught there a sharp intermittent fever which plagued me for years, and, though often kept in abeyance for a long time together, has occasionally recurred most unexpectedly. It is only a few weeks now since I had an attack of it. I returned with my horses to Beyrout, but was too unwell to make much use of them.

After some wanderings, I settled in Damascus,

at first in the house of a medical man who enabled
me to witness some gorgeous Jewish domestic cere-
monies. I also took elementary lessons in Hebrew
at his house, for which the little I knew of Arabic
made an excellent preparation. A sad grief befell me
there in the death of my faithful dragoman, Ali,
through violent dysentery. All the last duties to the
Moslem dead, the washings, the shrouding, and the
wailings, took place in the courtyard. My own
presence, as a Christian, at the funeral would have
been seriously resented by the Moslems, though I
was able to arrange about his tombstone. The
sculptors here adopt a very simple process for their
illiterate workmen. A flat face is given to the stone,
on which the inscription is painted in black. Then
all that is not painted is chipped away. The populace
at Damascus was then in a fanatical humour and
Christians had to be careful. There had been a
frightful persecution of Jews a little previously, and
there were others of Christians subsequently.

Ali had some trifling personal property, and
wages were due to him. I sent these to his wife in
Cairo, who was the only relative I ever heard him
mention, together with a little present for herself,
and thought my duty fulfilled and that all was
finished. On the contrary, I had inadvertently
roused a hornet's nest of greedy claimants. An
official Arabic letter was sent to me demanding
various payments to numerous relatives, together
with a threat of legal proceedings if not attended to.
My banker, to whom I referred it, advised me to
get out of the reach of the law as soon as I conveniently could, or I might find myself fleeced, and

perhaps entangled interminably. Fortunately, this circumstance occurred about the time when I should have been returning to England on my own account, so I "re-levanted," if it may be so expressed. Defaulters ordinarily "levant," or run from Europe to the Levant; I ran in the opposite direction.

At Damascus in the hot time of the year there was more than one delicious retreat in public coffee-places with gardens, through which one of the innumerable runnels of clear river water was conducted. I also took an interesting ride through the outskirts of the town, where a vast amount of dried apricot is prepared. It looks like greasy brown paper, is wrapped in rolls, and is largely consumed. Each orchard has a smoothed place like a small threshing-floor, as well as a big cauldron over an oven into which the apricots are put. The resulting slush is ladled out and spread over the floor; when it is sufficiently hardened, it is rolled off it as if it were a sheet of oilcloth. The cost of preparation is so small and the results so good that this manufacture might be found remunerative in other countries where apricots grow in abundance.

I spent some happy days at Aden on the Lebanon, a little below the famous cedars. The Sheikh was only too glad to entertain me, because one of the miserable tribal fights was expected, and he was glad of the presence of armed persons in his house, to protect it. Nothing, however, happened, beyond a few harmless shots. I afterwards revelled in the glorious beauty of the gorges leading down to the Mediterranean, and rank the view down one of them as the very finest my eyes have ever rested on. Mr. J. G. Frazer, in his *Adonis, Isis, and Osiris*, has collected similar expressions from many other travellers.

I returned to Beyrout, where, finding one of my horses killed by a fall over a cliff, and being unfit to enjoy or even to endure more riding, I sold the other, and found my way to Jaffa on board an empty collier. The part of its deck that I wanted was cleaned, and the voyage was brief and not unpleasant.

The soil about Jaffa is perfectly dry and wonderfully fertile, but only on the strict condition of its being amply supplied with water. Its environs were traversed by dusty roads between dull mud walls, on whose other side the richly watered gardens lay; so pedestrians, as might be expected, were thirsty and covetous. I saw a sort of pump handle with a spout on the side of the road, and an inscription above bearing some such encouraging text as "Drink! Here is water." Accordingly we pumped, and a little water did certainly come; but however hard we pumped there issued no more than a scanty streamlet out of the spout. We heard, all the same, a sound of abundance of water that never reached us, the cause of which was soon discovered to be an ingeniously arranged division, by means of which the pumper got only a small fraction of the water he raised, and the garden got all the rest. It was an excellent example of the higher forms of commercial enterprise. They enrich all round, but the merchant to whose initiative they are due gets by far the biggest share.

I was too unwell for a long day's ride on horseback, and hired a camel, which was not a usual conveyance, to take me from Jaffa to Jerusalem. The exaltation I felt at the first sight of the walls was far too high to last long. It was broken in the night by the miaulings of cats, the flat roofs of the houses forming an almost unlimited playground for those unscriptural and half-diabolical creatures.

In those days the course of the Jordan had been untravelled, as I was assured, since the memory of man, and the Dead Sea had never been navigated, with one solitary and most painful exception a year or two previously. Captain Costigan, whose accomplished married sister, Mrs. Bradshaw, I counted among my Leamington friends, had transported a boat to the Dead Sea. His man, or men, played him false, emptying the water keg in order that they might sooner get at the wine. He started with, I think, only a single man, the wind was unfavourable to return, he had to toil at the oar under the blazing sun, caught sunstroke and died.

The peace among the tribes who occupied the valley of the Jordan, which had been favourable to him, still continued, and I determined on an expedition down it, having then temporarily thrown off the ague. It seemed possible that the Jordan might be descended on a small raft of inflated water skins, or "kelligs," so I procured half a dozen of them, with the necessary lashings and other gear, and started with a few horsemen for Tiberias. I put the raft together just below the small bridge through which the Jordan runs out of the lake, and my escort travelled by the side of the river to render assistance when needed, and to form camp from time to time. It was rather a hare-brained attempt, though amusing to plan. The river was very small and shallow, but carried the light raft well; however, it was soon whirled under overhanging trees, and I was nearly combed off it. Then matters grew worse, and decidedly dangerous. The horsemen rode by the side, and were highly amused at my difficulties. At length I became convinced that it would be madness to persevere, so I left the raft, dressed myself, mounted my led horse, and we rode on down the valley. It is all so perfectly known and mapped now that it would be absurd to recount the little that I could tell, but I became more and more impressed with the weirdness of the great fissure in the earth's crust through which the Jordan flows. Even the Lake of Tiberias is 300 feet below the level of the sea, and the Dead Sea is about 1000 feet deeper still, and its climate very sultry in consequence.

My first camping-place was among the tents of the Emir Rourbah. It was an important encampment of Bedouins, whose dress I had been instructed to wear, and on no account to appear in the hated Turkish fez. When I arrived, there were watchers on every point of vantage. I was kindly received and shown much of their everyday life. The Emir had a quantity of chain armour, such as was in common use among the chiefs in the Soudan. I was surprised to find how effectual it was in spreading over a large surface the sensation of what otherwise would have been a painfully sharp blow. Matters progressed very pleasantly until the thoughtless omission of a Moslem ceremony soured my welcome. It may sound trifling, but it was effective all the same. I had shot a desert partridge, but not killed it, so, taking it up, I knocked its head, English fashion, against the stock of my gun. I ought to have cut its throat with my knife, while repeating the Moslem formula. I caught sight of a look of abhorrence on the face of my companions, and thereupon evidently ceased to be considered as one of themselves, but as a hateful and hypocritical Christian; so I was glad to be allowed soon to depart.

After a brief stay about Jericho, where I tasted and foolishly bathed in the nasty, sticky, dense water of the bituminous Dead Sea, which stuck in my hair for the day, I returned to Jerusalem with the view of transporting a boat. But finding that I was wanted at home on some legal business, that it was desirable to be out of the way of the claimants to the little property of poor Ali, my late dragoman, and feeling ill and used-up, I set sail with my two monkeys homewards.

I was put in quarantine in the Lazarette of Marseilles for, I think, ten days. Its superior officer was a military martinet. One of my monkeys got loose and ran all about the Lazarette, where, according to rule, he ought to have put every article that he touched into at least the same quarantine as himself, and there were bales of goods in store. The officer was transported with rage, and actually ran after the nimble monkey with drawn sword, to the intense amusement of the onlookers and of the monkey. I quietly captured him at last. The officer vented his feelings in appropriate language, but as he could do no more, the breach of quarantine regulations was overlooked, and so the matter ended.

When I reached London, on a chilly November

day, I failed to find a comfortable night's lodging for my pets, but an old friend who was living in apartments kindly undertook their charge. He handed them with many instructions to his landlady, who thought and perhaps said, " Drat the beasts ! " and shut them up in the cold scullery, where they were found the next morning dead in one another's arms.

CHAPTER VIII

HUNTING AND SHOOTING

Leamington—Moors—Orkney and Shetland—Balloon—*Telotype*

I RETURNED to my mother and sister, who then occupied Claverdon, much in need of a little rest. I was also conscious that with all my varied experiences I was ignorant of the very A B C of the life of an English country gentleman, such as most of the friends of my family had been familiar with from childhood. I was totally unused to hunting, and I had no proper experience of shooting. This deficiency was remedied during the next three or four years. Under the advice of my eldest brother, I bought a hunter and a hack, and began to hunt at the rate of about three days per fortnight in Warwickshire, at neighbouring meets.

The next year I established myself at Leamington, jobbed horses, and hunted methodically. There was a small "Hunt Club," supposed to be somewhat select, to which I belonged, and where I dined when not otherwise engaged. The hunting men most to the fore in Leamington in those days included some who had considerable gifts, each in their respective ways. Foremost among them was Jack Mytton, son of the more famous Jack Mytton (1796-1834) who was notorious for his daring feats and other ex-

travagances, who wasted a large fortune and died
unhappily. His life has been published; a brief
account of it may be read in the *Dictionary of
National Biography*. The son's career seemed
moulded on that of his father, and he too wasted
a fortune that had somehow accrued to him, and died
prematurely. There was no question as to his ability
and power over others.

A more or less unfortunate fate befell most of
my other companions at the Hunt Club. Many of
the small party who habitually dined there were social
favourites, and two at least of them were of more than
average social rank. Five of these men contrived to
ruin themselves by betting and gambling, and to end
unhappily. For all that, they were bright companions
in the heyday of their fortunes. They lived in good
style and as a rule not very prodigally, though all
had fits of recklessness. One of the most valuable
qualities in a man of moderately independent means
who has to live in a society of this kind is a careless-
ness to the attraction of gambling.

A Leamington friend, Fazakerley, asked me to
the Highlands to shoot. His moor was called Culrain ;
it was about fifteen miles long by three broad, and
the small house on it was three miles from Bonar
Bridge. I bought a beautiful Irish setter which a
friend chose for me, and we shot in the leisurely
fashion of those days, when driving game was never
practised. I slept in a neighbouring bothy, for the
house was small, and I quickly obtained some knowledge of English sport on the moors. At the end of
the season, the weather being still fine, I made my
way to John O'Groat's House, opposite the Orkneys,

whence, after being wind-bound for a while, I sailed in the post boat, which was then the only means of conveying letters from island to island, and so reached the so-called " Mainland," and settled at Kirkwall.

The next year I started before the grouse season began, and spent a most interesting summer among the Shetlands, using rowboats as the usual means of conveyance, and occupying myself with seal-shooting and bird-nesting. I could write much about all this, and on the weird experiences of a fisher society living in a treeless land, with whale-jaws for posts, and with no knife in their pockets larger than a penknife, having only tobacco and string to cut with it. Their social hierarchy was such, that a man who had been to Hudson's Bay had taken, to speak in the language of a University, a " Poll Degree." Those who had visited Baffin Bay were considered to have gained " Honours."

A shoal of whales (the cawing whale, averaging perhaps 20 feet in length) came ashore whilst I was in Shetland, and I hurriedly rode several miles to be in time to see them. Nearly one hundred were lying dead on the beach, but they looked small as they were scattered over the shore of the bay. The excitement of driving in the shoals is said to be an event not easily forgotten. It was all over by the time I arrived.

I would not shoot a seal now, but youths are murderous by instinct, and so was I. There was much of interest in the conditions under which they were shot. The early rise in the long summer day, the row to the leeward side of a likely holm, or small island; creeping up to a good vantage point and waiting there until the head of a seal is seen to bob up ; then stalking the animal by running from cover to cover whenever he sinks out of sight. Then, on reaching the beach, going cautiously between the big boulders to a good shooting-place and poking the rifle over one of the stones, shielding it and self from sight as carefully as possible. There one has to wait, perhaps with the tide coming in over one's legs, until in the course of his antics the seal's head rises within sure shooting distance ; then a careful aim, and a bang. The boatmen hearing the sound, come rowing as hard as they can round the corner, lest the seal should sink and be lost. He ought to be shot dead, or not touched at all. The oozing blubber of the animal makes a circular calm round the spot where he is shot, with the bloodstain in the middle. A boat-hook secures the seal even if he should have sunk four or five feet. His market value is a few shillings ; the boatmen get him as their perquisite.

I heard a story about the domesticity of the seal, as having recurred, with variations in detail, at more than one place. A young seal was caught and became quite at home with the fisherman, coming to his house for company, for warmth in the winter-time, and for food. It was petted until its size made it too big for a pet and troublesome to the children. Then the fisherman, sad at heart, took it with him in his boat, far away to the fishing-ground, and threw it overboard. Some days later, when the family were at supper, rather dismal at the loss of their old friend, they heard the familiar sound of scuffling and scratching, and on opening the door, in flopped the seal.

I used to watch the breeding-places of the sea birds, of which there were multitudes, of perhaps twenty

8

different kinds. The stormy petrels make their nests deep in beaches of shingle. An intelligent man initiated me into the way of taking them. We crept as silently as might be to where the twitterings could be heard, and, having carefully located the spot, tossed away the shingle as fast as we could, and usually found the bird on its nest. Its oily smell is very strong and rank. The popular belief is that if you cram a wick between the beak and down the gullet of a dried-up petrel and light it, the bird will burn like a lamp.

The hardships of what was called deep-sea fishing were great. It was conducted in open whale-boats with six rowers, who were generally thirty-six hours absent, and sometimes longer. In bad weather they had to keep to their oars, and could get little or no sleep all the time. I was told that on returning they went half stupid to bed, and, partly awakening to feed from time to time, slept for full twenty-four hours on end.

I could tell many tales of what I heard and saw, such as that at one lighthouse (I think in North Ronaldshay) the keeper, wishing to alleviate the solitude of his life, cast about for a suitable pet. That which he selected did credit to his genius. It was a toad in a bottle, requiring no care, little if any food, easily placed on any shelf, and always showing its bright eye.

When I finally left Shetland, which was after the grouse season, I took as a present to my brother for the large pool at Edstone, a crate full of many different kinds of sea birds, which I was assured would live in fresh water and pick up snails in the garden, as tamed gulls do. The railway people put

the crate in a very exposed truck on a chill autumn
night, which killed three-quarters of them at least.
The remainder throve at Edstone for a while, the
latest survivor being an oyster-catcher, who came to
his end thus. It had been freezing hard in the night,
followed by soft snow, and then re-freezing. Next
morning they found the tracks of a fox on the snow-
covered ice, going to a place where the yellow legs
and nothing else of the bird remained frozen in.
The oyster-catcher's legs had been entrapped by the
frost, and his body had been snapped up by the fox.

During the many weeks and months that I spent
in London between 1846 and 1850, which is the time
to which this chapter refers, I took walks with
friends, and sometimes rides with Harry Hallam, once
on a most pleasant riding tour with him in South
Wales, and I went to meets of the Queen's Stag
Hounds.

Among many other things, I was eager to know
the sensations of ballooning; I venture to give my
own impression of it. There were occasional nightly
ascents from the then existing Cremorne Gardens,
and foolishly thinking that I could sneak in under
cover of darkness, I engaged a seat. The evening
arrived, and I found it was advertised as a Gala
Festival, and I was anything but secluded from
observation. A number of fireworks were attached
to the car, and after an oration from the aeronaut, up
we went. It was very curious to observe the up-
turned faces of the crowd below, which seemed to
recede, for I had no sensation of being myself in movement. The fireworks went off, and doubtless made
an effective display, and then all seemed singularly

still. I was surprised at feeling no giddiness, but the car is so deep and the swelling of the balloon so voluminous that there is always much to steady the eye. The chief cause of giddiness when standing on a small isolated platform seems to lie in the absence of anything for the eye to "hold on by," meaning by this, anything that shows a sensible change of perspective, however slightly the body may move. Consciousness of altering one's position is due to two things, the change in perspective, and the sensations arising in the well-known "semicircular canals" of the ear. When the latter sensation is present unaccompanied by the former, mental distress results.

The balloon was open below, and owing perhaps to some optical illusion, it seemed to be filled with a singularly pure and beautiful medium. The quietness and sense of repose were the chief feelings that I experienced; next the clearness with which some noises, such as the barkings of dogs, reached us when we were still at a considerable height. Besides myself, there were only the aeronaut and his boy; the former alternately boisterous and maudlin. He told me that his wife frequently dreamed that he would come to an ill end, and so he did, breaking his thigh not long after in a balloon descent and dying from it. The "bump-bag" and the grapnel were new to me. The bump-bag is useful in permitting a quick descent to be made in order to catch a particular field in the line of drift. More gas is let out than is necessary for a normal descent, then when the car is still some feet above the ground the bump-bag rests on it, its weight is removed, and the lightened balloon descends slowly through those remaining few feet.

We drifted for an hour or more in the quiet dim night, learning our course by watching what could be seen of the country below, for of course there is nothing in the balloon itself to tell whether it is moving backwards, forwards, or sideways. It drifts with the air, so relatively to the air it is perfectly still. When it was time to descend, the valve was opened and bits of torn-up paper thrown out, which dashed upwards, as it were. In other words, we dashed downwards through them. At length we approached what the aeronaut thought would be a suitable field to descend upon, and let go the grapnel, which is a light but strong steel anchor with four pointed arms. It failed to catch hold, and we went drifting on towards a large decorous family mansion, with hothouses by the side and a lawn in front; sheep were placidly lying in the field. The horrid grapnel bobbed and scratched the ground among the sheep, fortunately without hooking one, and caught in the fence round the lawn. Then the valve was opened wide, letting out volumes of stinking gas; the rooks in a neighbouring rookery which we had brushed on our way, were vociferous, the dogs everywhere about barked furiously, and the natives in the neighbouring village were awakened and ran to the scene.

In the midst of the hubbub the hall door opened wide and let out a glare of light, in which a portly butler with two man-servants in livery appeared to be framed, looking horrified, as well they might be, by the sudden disorderly invasion of visitants from the sky. After some delay, we were invited to enter, and found the unhappy owner of the mansion in his dining-room by his uncleared late dessert, with decanters of wine, utterly perplexed as to the character of the welcome he ought to offer. The aeronaut gulped the wine offered to him, declaring with much rigmarole that it was a scientific (!) ascent. I cowered, and was utterly ashamed. After a miserable hour's delay, and thanks chiefly to the exertions of the boy, a postchaise was procured, the balloon was packed into its own car together with all its gear, and the car was hoisted on the roof of the chaise. The boy insinuated himself somewhere, and the aeronaut and I reached London in the small hours of the morning. I was so afraid of meeting in society the ill-used master of the mansion that I determinedly abstained from finding out who he was. The moral that I drew from the trip is, that the ascent and travel in calm weather in a balloon is most delightful; the return to earth most disagreeable, and dangerous in even a slight wind.

Among the many trifling events that occurred about that time, I may mention a yachting fiasco. I had a fancy to see Iceland, and, having had a little yachting experience on a brief third visit to Shetland, whither I and a companion sailed in an old Revenue cutter, hired I forget at what port, and being assured that with a similar vessel the trip might safely be made, I went to Ryde to hire one. The owner of a cutter that seemed suitable made no difficulty, so I hired it for a month. On arriving on board, in order to test the capabilities of the vessel and its crew, I told the captain to set sail to Hastings. He was suave, but pointed out the impossibility with the then wind and tide of getting there. I did not clearly understand his arguments, but answered, "Never mind; it will suit me equally well to go in the opposite direction to Penzance." The captain was still suave, but even more obstructive than before ; at length it turned out that he had no idea of sailing beyond the Solent and its neighbourhood. Being resourceful, I accordingly went to Lymington, and used the yacht as an hotel, getting a couple of days' hunting in the New Forest, and compromising about the hire of the yacht.

It will be thought from what appears in this chapter that I was leading a very idle life, but it was not so. I read a good deal all the time, and digested what I read by much thinking about it. It has always been my unwholesome way of work to brood much at irregular times.

The one definite scientific piece of work in these years that is worth mentioning refers to the then newly introduced electric telegraph. I had always a liking for electricity, and had some cells in a drawer of my study table with wires leading from them through the woodwork, to which apparatus could be attached. All this would be thought very elementary now, but some new things have to be done by such means when a science is in its infancy. I wished to print telegraphic messages and to govern heavy machinery by an extremely feeble force.

The method adopted may be explained thus. Suppose a telegraphic needle of the most delicate construction conceivable, having the three possible movements of right, neutral, left, to be momentarily lifted off its support by an arm that squeezes it against a little cushion above. However delicate the needle may be, its projecting ends will be stiff enough to push another freely suspended (but non-magnetic) needle of a much stronger and heavier build, in the

same direction as itself. This process may be repeated on a third needle of considerably larger size
and greater strength; and if desired, on a fourth.
The force required to keep all this going is independent of that which moves the first needle, and is
applied by a reciprocating beam worked by ordinary
power. The synchronising of the two stations is a
simple matter, no great precision being wanted in
order that the electric impulses should be delivered
to the first needle at the right times. Without going
further into this long bygone matter, I may say that
I printed what I had to tell in a pamphlet entitled
the *Telotype* (No. 1 in the text of my Memoirs in
the Appendix). The pamphlet was post-dated, after
the manner of some publishers, as being in June 1850.
It was really printed in 1849; I had left England for
my travels on April 5, 1850. The pamphlet had
long since gone into the limbo of the forgotten, so
it was a surprise to me, not many years ago, to meet
one of the most prominent electricians of the day, who
told me that he had seen and procured it for the
library of the Electrical Society. Moreover, he spoke
appreciatively of my youthful attempt. *Requiescat in
pace.* There was more in the pamphlet than is
described above.

CHAPTER IX

SOUTH-WEST AFRICA

Royal Geographical Society—Ch. J. Andersson—Cape Town—Walfish
Bay—Reach Damara Land—Hans—Negotiations with Namaqua
chiefs—Revs. Rath and Hahn—Wagons brought up

TRAVELLERS of the present generation need
some effort of imagination to put themselves
into the mental positions of those who were living in
1849. Blank spaces in the map of the world were
then both large and numerous, and the positions of
many towns, rivers, and notable districts were untrustworthy. The whole interior of South Africa and
much of that of North Africa were quite unknown to
civilised man. Similarly as regards that of the great
continent of Australia. The unknown geography of
the North Polar regions preserved some of the earlier
glamour attached to the possibility of finding a navi-
gable North-West passage from England to China,
which inspection of the globe shows to be far shorter
than that round the Cape. The South Polar regions
had only been touched here and there. The geography
of Central Asia was in great confusion, the true
position of many places familiar in ancient history
being most uncertain, while vast areas remained
wholly unexplored, in the common sense of that
word. It was a time when the ideas of persons

interested in geography were in a justifiable state of ferment.

My own inclinations were to travel in South Africa, which had a potent attraction for those who wished to combine the joy of exploration with that of encountering big game. The book of Harris, describing the enormous herds of diverse animals that he found on the grassy plains of South Africa, had directed many sportsmen thither who abundantly confirmed his account. Gordon Cumming had just returned to England. Oswell, then in company with Livingstone, and with another companion, Murray, had recently made a joint expedition, in which the desert country which hitherto limited the range of travel to the northward had been traversed, and Lake Ngami discovered. Consequently the well-watered districts beyond this desert could now be reached by wagon from the Cape. I felt keenly desirous of taking advantage of this new opening, and inquired much of those who had recently returned from South Africa concerning the conditions and requirements of travel there. But I wanted to have some worthy object as a goal and to do more than amuse myself.

It happened at this critical moment of my life that I was walking with my cousin, Captain Douglas Galton, R.E., then one of the most rising officers of the Engineers, and subsequently Sir Douglas Galton, K.C.B., of whom I have already spoken. He suggested my putting myself in communication with the Royal Geographical Society, where I could learn precisely whereabouts exploration was especially desirable, and where I should be sure to receive influential support. He offered introductions to some of its leading members, which I gladly accepted, and this determined my line of life for many years to come.

The immediate helpfulness to a traveller of such a Society is very great. It has the further advantage of pledging him to undertake work that is authoritatively judged to be valuable. My vague plans were now carefully discussed, made more definite, and approved, and I obtained introductions to many persons useful to me in their respective ways. I was introduced to the then Colonial Secretary, Lord Grey, who gave instructions in my favour to the Governor of the Cape.

My outfit was procured, and other preparations were far advanced, when my kind friend, Sir Hyde Parker, whose acquaintance I first made when shooting at Culrain, strongly urged me to engage a companion. He told me that a young Swede whose history he knew intimately was then in England, and that I could not do better than come to terms with him. This was Charles J. Andersson, who became my travelling-friend and second in command. He spoke English fluently, through having been brought up by Charles Lloyd, a well-known Scandinavian sportsman and writer, but an Englishman of Quaker extraction. I may mention here that I made Mr. Lloyd's acquaintance some years later, when his face had been frightfully scarred with wounds made by a bear. He told me that an old wounded she-bear had turned upon him, and actually got his head between her jaws to crack it, but her rounded teeth failed to find at once a sufficiently sharp hold and only tore the flesh. His companion shot the animal in time.

Andersson was accustomed to the rough life of a

sportsman, and had been sent to England to push his way to fortune as he best could. His capital wherewith to begin consisted of a crate of live capercailzie, two bear cubs, and the skin of one of their parents. He was then so naïve that, seeing an auctioneer's placard about a forthcoming sale of farm stock, in which was included " 20,000 Swedes," he, not knowing that in the language of farmers "Swedes" meant "turnips," confessed afterwards to a thrill of terror lest they should be his compatriots, and lest he himself might be pounced upon and sold as a slave together with them.

I was most fortunate in securing Andersson, because a second in command proved at times to be a necessity, and he always did his part admirably. He was remarkably strong and agile. When on board our full-rigged sailing-ship he began for amusement to climb the rigging. A sailor followed him, as is the wont of sailors, with a piece of twine to lash his feet as soon as he had gone as high as he dared, and to keep him bound there until he had consented to "pay his footing." Andersson perceived the game, and completely vanquished the sailor by descending from the maintop to the deck, hand over hand down the mainstay, which was too daring a feat for the sailor to emulate. Consequently Andersson became highly respected by all the crew.

One of the effects of association with the leading members of the Royal Geographical Society was to show me that the world of English interests was very much wider and more earnest than that of the coteries among which I had chiefly lived, and that many men were thoroughly able to understand and criticise my proposed course justly, whose good opinion if I succeeded would be of far more value to me than the approbation of a multitude of less well-informed persons, however numerous or laudatory they might be.

I left England on April 5, 1850. My voyage deserves a few words of description, because it was made under conditions that are now obsolete, which had some advantages to counterbalance their many disadvantages. The ship was called the *Dalhousie*, an old teak-built East Indiaman, quite incapable of beating against a head wind, and occupying nearly eighty days in reaching Cape Town. It was chiefly used on this journey to carry emigrants at cheap rates with rough accommodation, but a few cabin passengers were taken besides, who had the use of the high poop to themselves. In a long voyage like that of ours, the elements count for much, and the manipulation of the ship is of continual interest. The charm of the Northern Trades, of the calms and sudden squalls of the Equatorial Belt, and of the crisp, strong Southern Trades cannot possibly be experienced in an equal degree by those on board a fast steamer, that rushes through all of them at an equal speed and holds its course almost regardless of wind and weather. I was glad, too, of the abundant opportunities of familiarising myself with the sextant, by which I mean a much closer acquaintance with its manipulation and adjustments than nautical persons are usually contented with or require. I had left England without any practical instruction either in obtaining latitudes and longitudes, or in surveying, for I failed to find anybody who would give it, consistently with the limited time then at my disposal. The excellent facilities now afforded by the Royal Geographical Society for the instruction of intending travellers did not then exist; indeed, I had a large part in their introduction many years later. I was, however, familiar with the requisite book-work, and relied on what I could pick up on board ship and elsewhere to supplement it. Let me anticipate that I took very kindly indeed to instrumental work, and learnt in time to get more out of my sextants, etc., than most persons. Land work admits of far greater exactitude with that instrument than sea work, where the true position of the horizon is never known, owing to uncertainties of refraction, and is not seen at all at night. The sun, which is the principal object of observation at sea, is little used on land, where the altitudes of stars are obtainable with great accuracy from their reflections in a small trough of mercury. Also the hand can be so rested that the images of the star and of its reflection shall be quite steady when seen through the telescope. Moreover, the two images, whether of the star and its reflection, or of the star and the moon, can be toned to an exactly equal degree of brightness. The sextant is a very powerful instrument for its size, in the hands of those who have patience and skill to get the most out of it.

I was received very kindly at the Cape by the Governor, Sir Harry Smith, and by his lady, whose name is perpetuated in that of the well-known town "Ladysmith," called after her. But the news from the frontier recently received at Cape Town scattered my plans like a bombshell. The Boers, who had been very unruly, had affirmed their intention of keeping the newly discovered lands about Lake Ngami to themselves and of refusing passage through their territory to every Englishman. Sir Harry Smith said it would be useless for me to attempt to go as I had proposed. After a tedious journey of more than two months by ox wagon, I should meet with Boers who would politely but firmly tell me that I must go no farther. If I attempted to force a way, they would shoot me, and he would be powerless to prevent them.

I had made many friends in Cape Town, and numerous suggestions were offered as to other ways of reaching the district of Lake Ngami. The one I adopted had many arguments in its favour. A cattle-dealer then in Cape Town had made occasional ventures to Walfish Bay. The coast around it was desert, but the Namaqua Hottentots drove cattle there for sale, which would otherwise have been sent overland to the Cape by what is practically a four months' journey. The country between Walfish Bay and the Namaquas could be traversed by wagons. There were mission stations in Namaqualand, whose headquarters were in Cape Town. Nay more, a new missionary was waiting for an opportunity to go there, and if I took him with the other things now waiting to be sent, I should be helpful to the missionaries, and they would doubtless be all the more inclined to help me. Again, to the north of the yellow Namaquas were the black Damaras, the interior of whose land was as yet quite unknown, though two or three mission stations had been established along its southern border.

Here, then, was a land ready to be explored, by

which a new way through grassy country might be found leading through Walfish Bay to the interior, and at the same time south of the territory claimed and practically barred by the Portuguese. Sir Harry Smith desired to use every opportunity of disavowing the complicity of the Cape Government with the attacks of the Boers on the natives, and he requested me to use such occasions as I might have, of doing so. He caused a document to be drawn up to express this and to serve as my credentials. It was written in English, Dutch, and Portuguese, with a huge seal appended to it, protected by a tin case.

The story of my journey has been so fully told [1] in print that I shall go but little into the details of it here. Moreover, the country has of late been so traded through and fought over, and in large part occupied by the Germans, that it has, I presume, become mapped with considerable exactness.

It will be seen by my sketch map that the country I travelled over proved to be inhabited by three principal and widely different races, occupying three roughly parallel belts of country running from west to east. The southernmost were the Namaquas. They were yellow Hottentots, with hair growing in tufts on their heads, and speaking a language full of clicks. They had a strain of Dutch blood, and most of them spoke a little of the Dutch language. Their race reaches down through more and more civilised tribes to the Cape Colony. Captain, afterwards Sir James Alexander (1803–1885), had travelled right

---

[1] *Narrative of an Explorer in Tropical South-West Africa.* By F. Galton (Murray), 2nd edition, Ward, Locke, & Co., Minerva Press, 1889. *Lake N'gami; Explorations in South-West Africa.* By Ch. Andersson (Longman), 1856. Also papers by both in the Journal of the Royal Geographical Society.

through their territory from the Cape to Walfish Bay,
and back.   Mission stations were planted among
them, of which the two northernmost, numbered
1 and 5 on the map, were called Schepmansdorf and
Rehoboth respectively.   The Kuisip river-bed, down
which water runs only once in every few years, and
ends in Walfish Bay, makes a northern limit to the
Namaquas, which they were apt to transgress.

The Swakop river-bed, in which water runs every

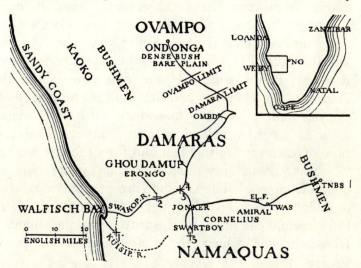

year after the rains, and which enters the sea some
forty miles north of Walfish Bay, is the southern
limit of the Damaras.   Two mission stations (2 and
3), called Otchimbingue and Barmen respectively, were
established on the Swakop.   A third, marked 4 on
the map, had been established, but destroyed shortly
before my arrival by a murderous raid of Namaquas,
under Jonker, whose name will be found on the map,
and the position of whose home is shown by a

9

dot. The land between the Swakop and the Kuisip is a high desert plateau and uninhabited. The Damaras extend northward up to about the line where "Damara Limit" is written on the map, and they extend far to the east. The Kaoko plain, of which I learnt little that was definite, lies to the west, between them and the sea.

"Damara" is a corruption of the Hottentot word "Damup," used indiscriminately for numerous Bantu tribes that have no general name in their language, but severally call themselves Ovaherero, Ovapantieru, etc. In a similar way the Arabic word "Caffre" (Kaffir, or infidel) comprehends many different Bantu tribes on the east side of South Africa. The Damaras and the Caffres are clearly of the same race. To the immediate north of Damara Land is a narrow belt of country ill fitted for habitation. Northward of this belt and from the line where "Ovampo Limit" is written on the map, is the country of the Ovampo. The Ovampo are pure negroes, but of a high type. Their country extends northwards a little beyond the limits of the map, up to the Cunene River, beyond which the Portuguese claim possession.

In addition to the Damaras, small tribes are scattered over their territory of two totally distinct races of Hottentot and Negro. Both of these tribes now speak the Hottentot language. The first of them are the Bushmen, so called by the Namaquas, and who are pure Hottentots. They are usually small men, but not so very small as the Bushmen proper of Cape Colony are, or rather were, for those exist no longer. On the other hand, the Ghou

Damup are as purely negro as the Ovampo. The Bushmen and the Ghou Damup are equally hunted and equally ill-treated by the Damaras, and they live wherever they can find safety. The Ghou Damup are apparently the inferior of the two.

I suppose that the country was inhabited long ago by the progenitors of the Ghou Damup, probably a branch of the Ovampo; that the Hottentots invaded it, and lorded over the Ghou Damup for so many years that the latter wholly forgot their native tongue, and spoke the Hottentot language instead; lastly, that the Hottentots, and of course the Ghou Damup also, were in their turn overrun by the progenitors of the Damaras, and became dispersed among them as they are at the present time.

The Bushmen are nomadic and good hunters. The Ghou Damup are sedentary, living on roots and the like, but they have a stronghold in Erongo, to the north-west of the Mission Station No. 2 on the map. They live there in marvellously rocky and easily defensible quarters, totally unsuitable to the pastoral Damaras, who have no object to gain by attacking and ousting them if they could. I visited also a large encampment of Bushmen in quite another part of the country, and stayed by them for four days, at the place marked Tbs (= Tounobis), on the extreme right hand of the map.

It was reckoned to be a six or seven days' sail from Cape Town to Walfish Bay, so I hired a small schooner, and with the help of many kind friends got all my equipment on board. It consisted of a light cart, two Cape wagons, nine mules from which a

team could be selected to draw the cart, when it was
laden with articles of barter to buy oxen, and two if
not three skilled drivers and other necessary men ; also
two horses which were not expected to live long, and
did not, and a few dogs. The gear of the missionary and the young missionary himself were also
taken on board. We started from Cape Town in the
second week of August 1850.

On arriving at Walfish Bay, we found ourselves
faced by as desolate and sandy a shore as even
Africa can show, which is saying a great deal.
There was a small empty wooden hut on the beach,
very useful as a storehouse ; a few natives appeared,
and one consented to act as a messenger to the
mission station twenty miles off, in return for a stick
of tobacco and a biscuit. This is No. 1 on the map
(Schepmansdorf). We landed the things as best we
could from the schooner, which was anchored one-
third of a mile from the shore. The animals had to
swim, the rest of the cargo was taken in many
instalments by the dinghey. The missionary, Mr.
Bam, and his then guest and helper Mr. Stewardson,
a former cattle-trader, made their appearance the
next night, riding on oxen, which is a usual mode
of travel in these parts.

In the meantime we had visited the watering-
place "Sand Fontein," three miles off, of which we
had heard, and which is marked by a dot on the map.
It was at that time a puddle of nasty water, but gave
a sufficient quantity of it for the mules and horses.
A cask of good drinking water was brought ashore
for ourselves and placed in the storehouse.

It was agreed that all my possessions should be

carried to Mr. Bam's station, No. 1 on the map, and it was finally arranged that Mr. Stewardson should guide us up country to Mission Station No. 2.

My disasters began soon. The journey across the arid plain that separated the Kuisip from the Swakop taxed the strength of the mules, who were wholly unused to such a strain. It was necessary to give them immediate rest and food as soon as the pasturage of the Swakop was reached. Tracks of wild animals were looked for on the sand of the river-bed, but none were found, so Stewardson urged that our mules and horses should be left free during the night to rest and feed themselves. The result was that a troop of lions dashed down upon them in the dark, killing one mule and one of my two horses. The remainder galloped off unscathed, and were recovered in the afternoon. The tracks of the lions by the side of those of the animals up to the two fatal springs told the story clearly. I had no reserve of food, so it was necessary to utilise the horse flesh, which I cut off and stored in an apparently safe hole in the side of a cliff. When I returned towards nightfall to remove it, one of my enemies had out-generalled me. He had clambered from behind and unseen to a ledge five or six yards above the hiding-place, and could be seen there by the party below, crouched like a cat above a mouse-hole. I got down safely, meat and all, and saw the head and the pricked ears of the brute as he kept his position. A shot struck the rock under his chin, and he decamped.

I had little further trouble with lions during my journey, though they were often heard roaring at night. I think I only lost one cow, and apparently a

few of my remaining mules after I had no further use
for them. All eight of the mules decamped later on,
when I had provided myself with oxen; three of
them reached Schepmansdorf; those that disappeared
on the way had probably been killed by lions. The
very first animal I shot in Africa was a lion, just after
my first arrival at Schepmansdorf. It had crossed
from the Swakop to the Kuisip and had seized a
small dog in the yard of the mission station, while
I was asleep in an almost doorless hut that opened
on the same yard. So much for lions.

I pass over all the other difficulties, troubles, and
events that intervened, which have been related in
the books above mentioned. Suffice it to say that
by the end of September I was installed at Station
No. 2 under the kind care of Mr. Rath, the resident
missionary. Here I had the good fortune to meet
Hans Larsen, a Dane, who spoke English perfectly.
He had been a sailor, but obtained permission to quit
his ship at Walfish Bay and to enter the service of
a cattle-dealer. When that particular venture was
concluded, he joined a second cattle-dealer, and finally
found himself at large with a small herd of oxen,
which he intended to drive overland and to sell at
Cape Town. I had been most strongly urged to
acquire his services if I could, and I did so to my
very great advantage, partly, I may add, through my
medical experience. He was willing from the first
to go, were it not for a most painful whitlow which
disabled his arm, and gave him so much pain that
he could hardly sleep or eat; and he was totally unfit
for the expected severe manual work. He therefore
had to make his acceptance dependent on getting

well. Now the sore was of a chronic kind, very familiar to me when at the Birmingham Hospital. There was an outgrowth of what patients like to call "proud flesh," upon which a slight cautery often acts like a charm. It stimulates the vitality of the part and causes it to act normally. It did so in this case. I rubbed the sore lightly over with nitrate of silver, which hurt at the time, but eventually gave him the first good night's rest he had enjoyed for months. Thenceforward his finger rapidly improved and healed, and he felt and looked himself again.

I bought all his live stock of fifty oxen and one hundred sheep and goats at a single swoop, by a cheque on Cape Town for £71. Hans himself became a most valuable and efficient servant and friend. In brief, he and Andersson went down to the coast with the new oxen, to break them in and to bring up the wagons, while I remained partly at the Mission Station No. 2, and afterwards at No. 3, where Mr. Hugo Hahn, a very accomplished man, who had married an English wife, was the resident missionary.

Mr. Hahn possessed all the extant knowledge about the Damaras, and was greatly interested in my proposed expedition. Information about the wretched state of the country was gradually obtained. It came to this, that the four tribes of Namaquas under Jonker, Cornelius, Amiral, and Swartboy respectively, well provided with horses and guns, had made many successive raids upon the Damaras, lifting cattle and selling them. They usually sent the stolen animals overland to the Cape. Sometimes when opportunity occurred they sold them to traders at Walfish Bay. The Damaras were not only perpetually fighting among themselves, but also provoking retaliation from the Namaquas, which the latter only too gladly indulged in. Lastly, the Namaquas, who in the first instance welcomed missionaries, were now opposed to them and to every outside influence or criticism, and determined to do just what they liked both to one another and to the Damaras. More especially they had recently determined that no white man should pass through their country to the interior. They were, in short, behaving in a similar, but still more marked spirit of exclusion to that of the Boers.

The attack under Jonker on the Mission Station No. 3 on the map was their latest iniquity. They behaved like demons. Among other things they cut off the feet of the women to get their ankle rings, as related in Chapter III. Unless these misdoings could be stopped, my journey would soon come to an end. The Damaras believed that I and my party were merely Hottentots in disguise, and acting as spies. To make a long story short, I took Hans and two intelligent men and rode on ox-back to Jonker himself, and rated him soundly, in English first, to relieve my mind, and then in Dutch through my interpreters, brandishing my paper with the big seal, and thoroughly frightened him. Arrangements, which I cannot go into now, were made for a meeting between myself and the other Namaqua chiefs, and ultimately a *modus vivendi* was secured, which lasted all the time I was in the country and for a while afterwards.

These negotiations occupied fully three months, during which every nerve was strained to get the expedition into readiness to start. Andersson, Hans, and nearly all the men had gone down with the cart and newly-bought oxen to Station No. 1, whence they brought back the two wagons most successfully, though having first to break in the oxen. Then, whilst Andersson was encamped at Station No. 2, I rode with Hans to the mountain stronghold of the Ghou Damup, Erongo. Finally, in March, I made my start northwards from the place where Station No. 3 formerly stood, every step being henceforth through new country.

CHAPTER X

LANDS OF THE DAMARAS, OVAMPO, AND NAMAQUAS

M Y first objective was Ovambondé, a place which proved to be of exaggerated interest. It is marked B on the map. It was the only definite spot, generally known to the Damaras, that I could hear of in a northerly direction. Without some definite goal it would have been necessary to travel unguided through a country so choked with bushes bearing cruel thorns that we might have found ourselves in impassable blind issues time after time.

The plateau on which we were to travel was some 6000 feet above the level of the sea, as calculated by the usual method from the temperature of boiling water. It had a crisp sandy surface good for travel, but the thorn-bushes were a serious obstacle. Water was a daily cause for anxiety, and was usually to be procured only at places where the natives had recently dug for it with success. The country is deluged at the time of the rainy season, and pools remain for a while at many places, but they soon disappear, partly through evaporation, but principally from percolation through the sandy soil. Here and there a thin layer of less porous earth holds the water longer. The pool may then become sanded over, but water can be reached without trouble by digging and scraping. During a large part of the journey this looking out for signs of water and digging wells, after the first four hours' journey had been accomplished, was the almost daily occupation. The giving of drink to the oxen, three at a time, out of an improvised trench covered with canvas, into which the water was ladled, was a common feature at each encampment.

The digging for water was laborious. Sometimes the well was already dug by natives, but dry, and had to be so much deepened as to require a chain of three men to utilise it. One raised the water-vessel to another who stood a stage higher, and he to a third who stood breast high above the surface of the ground and poured its contents into the trough. On one of these occasions we had fallen fast asleep, dogs and all, utterly wearied, and found in the morning, to our astonishment, the tracks of elephants all about us. They had drunk at the well, disturbed nobody, and disappeared into the not distant bush, whither I followed them in vain.

The caravan at starting consisted of ten Europeans and about eighteen natives, or twenty-eight in all. The two wagons were both laden. The large one had a solid deck over its cargo, and the space above deck was curtained into two compartments, in which Andersson and I slept when the ground was wet; as a rule we bivouacked in the open. The available space above the deck of the wagon was too low to read or write in with comfort. The small wagon held the clothes of the men in addition to its regular freight, and nobody slept in it except during the heavy rains. At first the natives of my party were constantly changing, and in addition to my own party there were occasional hangers-on.

As regards commissariat, my biscuit and every kind of vegetable food had been eaten up. I had plenty of tea, coffee, and some sugar, and a few trifles besides, but no wine or spirits except for medicine. Our sustenance was henceforth to be the flesh of the oxen and sheep driven with us, eked out by occasional game. The charge of the cattle was our constant anxiety and care; if lost or stolen, we should be starved. The estimate was that one sheep—they were very lean—afforded twenty meals, and I found that men on full work required two meals daily. An ox was reckoned equal to seven sheep, and would therefore feed twenty-four people for three days. The gross total of oxen, cows, and calves in the caravan was ninety-four; that of sheep was twenty-four. Seventy-five of the oxen were broken in; nine of these as ride-oxen and a few others as pack-oxen, the remainder only for draught. I considered myself to be provided for ten weeks, exclusive of game, while still preserving a sufficiency of trained oxen.

I had many things for barter, but could not foresee whether, or how far, they would be accepted in exchange for cattle. It afterwards appeared that two sticks of cavendish tobacco was a usual equivalent for one sheep, and a rod of iron or a gun for perhaps eight oxen.

I soon saw some of the horrors of savagedom.
My dogs found a wretched native whose muscles
along the back of his neck had been severed to the
bone, but whose throat was uninjured. He had
crawled under thorn-bushes to die, whence we extricated him. His head rolled horribly, but he could
speak a little. I did what I could in the way of
splints and bandages, but he soon died. Then, while
staying with a most gentlemanly chief, Kahichené, who
was himself killed soon afterwards, and his followers
dispersed, two of my fore-oxen were stolen. They
are by far the most important animals in a team.
The chief sent trackers after them. They and the
thief were brought back; I begged for the man's life,
for ox-stealing is a capital offence. He was spared
while I was there, but clubbed, as I understood, after
I had left. But enough of these gruesome stories.
I had to hold a little court of justice on most days,
usually followed by corporal punishment, deftly administered. At a signal from me the culprit's legs
were seized from behind, he was thrown face forward
on the ground and held, while Hans applied the
awarded number of whip strokes. This rough-and-
ready justice became popular. Women, as usual,
were the most common causes of quarrel.

The Damaras were for the most part thieving
and murderous, dirty, and of a low type; but their
chiefs were more or less highly bred. These people
seldom die natural deaths; many are killed when
fighting, many are murdered, and sick persons are
as a rule smothered by their relatives. It was
fortunate for me that there was at that time no
paramount chief in Damara land, unless it were a man

like Kahichené.   The smaller ones feared our weapons
and the mystery attached to white men coming from
afar, who might be in friendly relations with their
dreaded enemies, so I was able to slip through their
lawless country with comparative ease.

Ovambondé proved to be of no importance.   It
was nothing more than a long reach in a then dry
river-bed, which would, however, assume a very
different aspect after heavy rains.   By the time we
had arrived there, the tales concerning a different
race called the Ovampo, who lived to the northwards
beyond the Damaras, had become more and more
consistent and exciting, and gave a fresh impetus
to proceed.   The Damara limit is marked on the
map; the axle of one of my wagons broke just
before reaching it.   Consequently I made a camp
near a friendly Damara chief, and left the wagons,
with Hans and the drivers, to be repaired in the way
familiar to Boers, and started for Ovampo land with
Andersson and three men on ride-oxen.   I also took
three laden pack-oxen and a few loose ones in reserve,
to furnish food if needed.

A caravan travels every six months from Ovampo
land to buy Damara cattle, stopping at the very place
where we had been.   Another caravan similarly travels
along the Kaoko (see map) between Damara land
and the sea.   We met one of the former of these
caravans a little after we had started, so we returned
for a while to our old camp, and finally went back to
Ovampo land with it.   These Ovampo were under
strict discipline, secret and very resolute.   I could
not do what I liked in their company, but had to
depend on their plans.   The will of their king

Nangoro was supreme. I could not enter the country, trade in it, or leave it, except with his permission.

The border-land between the Damaras and the Ovampo seemed to be a natural frontier unsuitable for occupation. We passed bleak plains and then a wide belt of thorn-bushes, which after a day's journey ceased suddenly and disclosed a broad stretch of fields of maize, a strange and welcome sight. After a day's march through these, we reached the place where Nangoro lived.

I did much to make myself agreeable, investing Nangoro with a big theatrical crown that I had bought in Drury Lane for some such purpose. But I have reason to believe that I deeply wounded his pride by the non-acceptance of his niece as, I presume, a temporary wife. I found her installed in my tent in negress finery, raddled with red ochre and butter, and as capable of leaving a mark on anything she touched as a well-inked printer's roller. I was dressed in my one well-preserved suit of white linen, so I had her ejected with scant ceremony. The Damaras are very hospitable in this way, and consider the missionaries to be actuated by pride in not reciprocating.

We were treated with strict courtesy, but, except at the very first, without friendliness; a sense of growing constraint was everywhere, and there were ugly signs of an intention to allow our oxen to die of hunger, and then to make an easy end of us afterwards. The Ovampo carry on a trade with the Portuguese half-castes to the north, and knew and despised the guns used by them; but ours were shown, by their bullet marks after firing at a distant tree, to be of a much higher order and to be feared. Probably that new view of their value helped us considerably. We were quite at the mercy of Nangoro; our cattle grew thinner daily on the very scant pasturage to which they were restricted, and Nangoro would not give me permission to go farther. It was as much as our oxen could do to take us back at all, and having at length received permission, or orders (I know not which), to return, I did so with mixed feelings—regret at having to turn back, relief at getting away safely. The Ovampo were suspicious of us, but seemed particularly happy and social among themselves, and to be a people well worthy of friendly study. But the spirit of what is elsewhere known as "taboo" reigned everywhere, and simple inquiries were too frequently met with the rejoinder of "You must not ask." I had very good interpreters between the Damara and Ovampo languages.

My fears of ill-usage were shown not to be fanciful, by the fact that a party who followed me some years later were attacked as they departed, and had to fire in self-defence. According to one of many rumours, a stray bullet killed Nangoro himself, at a considerable distance, while he was sitting within his own stockade. The party got safely away, but were in great danger.

The return journey to the wagons was indeed difficult. One bitterly cold encampment in a hollow on the bleak plain, where we were comparatively safe from a night attack, seriously tried the constitution of some of my best ride-oxen, who never afterwards became as serviceable as they were before. The wagon was however mended, all had gone well

with the men left behind, and we started homewards.

Ultimately the whole party was brought safely
back to Station No. 3 on August 3, 1851, where
we were most heartily welcomed and congratulated
by Mr. Hahn after our long absence of five months,
during which no news whatever of us had reached
him. In the meantime I had spent ninety days in
actual travel, independently of such excursions as
were needed from time to time to look out for
practicable routes. Of these ninety days, fifty were
occupied in travel to Nangoro and forty in returning.
The return distance in time was 168 hours, equal
to 462 miles. Our road had passed through a
dangerous and difficult country; it traversed the
whole breadth of Damara land, and had reached
the capital of the country beyond it to the north.

Some little news had reached Mr. Hahn from
Europe through the hands of a cattle-trader. It
included an English newspaper, but no letters for
myself; it was now one year and four months since I
had heard a single word from my home. Peace had
been kept during my absence between the Hottentots
and Damaras.

A ship was expected for the missionaries not
earlier than December, so I should have a clear four
months for further travel and yet be able to catch that
ship. I determined on a quick journey to the eastwards of the Namaqua country, and dispatched
messengers at once with letters to the Cape, in doing
which the Namaqua chief Swartboy assisted me. I
thereby made arrangements to confirm those partly
made by the missionaries about the time of departure

10

of their ship, that it might not arrive too soon.   I then
divided my party and settled matters relating to the
future of the wagons and their contents, also in regard
to my three remaining mules, the rest of which had
died or been killed by lions long since.   Then I started
afresh on August 13, taking one wagon with me,
Andersson, three of my best servants, and five or six
of my most active Damaras, and went in the first
instance to Jonker.

He received me kindly, and I had the good fortune
to find in this place a fairly educated man, Erhardt,
imported by the missionaries as a schoolmaster, who
spoke Dutch and English perfectly, and Hottentot
fairly well.   I engaged his services, especially as he
undertook to guide me as far as Elephant Fountain
(E.F. on the map), which had been the *ultima Thule*
of the missionaries.   I was also asked to settle some
disputes between the other Namaqua chiefs, who
were all very friendly to me now.   I proposed to
push farther forward from Elephant Fountain as far
as time, the exceptional drought of the year, and the
weakened stamina of my oxen permitted.

We left Jonker August 30, and arrived at
Elephant Fountain September 11, where I found
myself at last in a country of big game.   There was a
copious spring, and herds of all kinds of animals came
to drink.   It received its name from the large number
of tusks found in the water at this place when the
Namaquas first reached it, as though it had been a
spot to which elephants travelled to die, according to
a well-known legend.   It was then overgrown with
reeds, and formed a notable covert for wild beasts.   It
lies in a corner of the district then claimed by the

chief Amiral. Farther to the south of it the country becomes desert. Amiral joined me, by arrangement, at Elephant Fountain for a shooting expedition. He and his people seemed much more civilised than the other Namaquas, and nearer in character to the Dutch Boers.

I left my wagon with two men, together with those of Amiral and some of his own men whom he left behind to guard them, and starting on ride-oxen with Andersson we reached Twas, the farthest point yet visited by Amiral, on about the 28th. In front of us lay an arid plain, especially arid in this very dry year, which had to be crossed in order to reach the next watering place, well known to the Bushmen, but not to Amiral, and called Tounobis.

My oxen were tired and footsore, but we went. It proved to be a journey of 20½ hours actual desert travel, and led us suddenly into an ideal country of big game. The ground, adjacent to a broad river-bed, was trodden with the tracks of all sorts of animals, elephants, rhinoceros, lions, and a vast variety of smaller game. Crowds of Bushmen were encamped near to the water, busy with their pitfalls and with securing an elephant that had fallen into one of them during the previous night. We became great friends with the Bushmen, and sat late into the night hearing their stories about themselves and the recent doings of a body of strange Namaquas coming from the south, who in the preceding year had swept past them and onwards to Lake Ngami, leaving unmistakable signs of their expedition, and marauding as usual as they went. This much, therefore, was established, that a feasible road existed from Walfish

Bay to the interior, of which I had myself travelled
as far as Tounobis, and the remaining few days'
journey had been travelled during the preceding year
by marauding Namaquas.

After staying a week at Tounobis, Amiral wished
to return home, and I was not in a position to travel
farther afield, because the next stage towards Lake
Ngami was described by all as being more severe
than the last one, and with my tired oxen it was
as much as we could do to get back at all. So I
returned, and, ultimately, found myself back on the
shores of Walfish Bay on December 5. The wished-
for schooner arrived on January 16, 1852. I finally
parted with Andersson, Hans, and most of the men,
and retaining only three with me for the possibility of
a short travel in Portuguese territory, which came to
nothing, I sailed to St. Helena, whence I returned
straight to England.

This, in a few words, is an outline of my journey.
The distances were (as carefully calculated), Walfish
Bay to Station No. 3 (Barmen) 207 miles, Barmen to
Nangoro 512 miles, Barmen to Tounobis 311 miles,
—total 1030 miles, and nearly as many back ; besides
other side expeditions, especially that to Erongo, and
another of little interest that has not been alluded to
above.

This bald outline of a very eventful journey has
taken little notice of the risks and adventures which
characterised it and are recorded in my book. They
must be imagined by the reader, otherwise the following paragraph will seem overcharged, which it is not.

I had little conception of the severity of the
anxiety under which I had been living until I found

myself on board the little vessel that took me away, and I felt at last able to sleep in complete security. I had indeed to be thankful that all ended so well. I did not lose one of my many men either through violence or sickness during the long and harassing journey. It was undertaken with servants who at starting were found to be anything but qualified for their work, who grumbled, held back, and even mutinied, and over whom I had none other than a moral control. The very cattle that were to carry me had to be broken in, and I had to call into service an indolent and cruel set of natives speaking an unknown tongue. The country was suffering the atrocities of savage warfare when I arrived—tribe against tribe and race against race—which had to be stopped before I could proceed. I had no food to depend on except the cattle I drove with me, which might any night decamp or be swept off by a raid. That all this was gone through successfully I am indebted in the highest degree both to Andersson and Hans, to whom I have had to make too scant reference here for want of space.

Andersson remained behind to investigate the natural history of the countries we had opened out, and wrote histories of his journeys and observations. He ultimately died in Damara land. Hans found his way to the gold diggings of Australia, but with the exception of one letter that he sent me before starting I lost all communication with him, to my very great regret. He must have met with mischance. I reached England exactly two years after leaving it, that is on April 5, 1852, more than fifty-six years ago.

I began this chapter by showing how largely the Geographical Society aided me in preparing for the journey. I conclude it by showing how still more deeply I became indebted to it for its approbation. The Society awarded to me one of their two annual gold medals in 1854, "for having at his [my] own cost and in furtherance of the expressed desire of the Society, fitted out an expedition to explore the centre of South Africa, and for having so successfully conducted it through the countries of the Namaquas, the Damaras, and the Ovampo (a journey of about 1700 miles), as to enable this Society to publish a valuable memoir and map in the last volume of the Journal, relating to a country hitherto unknown; the astronomical observations determining the latitude and longitude of places having been most accurately made by himself."

The President, Sir Roderick Murchison, in presenting the medal to me at the Anniversary Meeting (I quote from the *Times*), having read the above paragraph in the Report, said that Mr. Galton had a distinct claim on the Society before all other African travellers, because he had fitted out the expedition at his own expense in furtherance of their expressed wishes, and had zealously accomplished that which he had so disinterestedly undertaken. Then, turning to Mr. Galton, he added: "It is now my pleasing duty to place in your hands this testimony of the approbation of the Royal Geographical Society. I am sure you will receive it, as we intend it, as the highest honour which we can possibly confer. You left a happy home to visit a country never before penetrated by a civilised being. You have accomplished that which every geographer in this room must feel is of eminent advantage to the science in which we take so deep an interest. Accept, with these expressions, my belief that, so long as England possesses travellers with the resolution you have displayed, and so long as private gentlemen will devote themselves to accomplish what you have achieved, we shall always be able to boast that this country produces the best geographers of the day."

The Geographical Medal gave me an established position in the scientific world. In connection with subsequent work, it caused me to be elected a Fellow of the Royal Society in 1856, and to receive in the same year the very high honour of election to the Athenæum Club under Rule II., which provides that the Council may elect not more than nine persons in each year on the ground of distinction in Science, Literature, Art, or Public Service, being at the average rate of a little more than two elections annually, under each of these four broad heads. The recipient is thereby saved many, sometimes sixteen or more, years of waiting, before his turn would arrive to be balloted for in the ordinary course of election. So I have much to be grateful for to the Royal Geographical Society, and I loyally did my best to promote its interests during the many years that I served on its Council in various capacities.

CHAPTER XI

AFTER RETURN HOME—MARRIAGE

Yacht to Norway—Dover—Marriage—Relations of my own ; those
of my wife

ON returning to England, my gratification was
great in finding all my immediate relatives well
and eager to welcome me. But I was rather used up
in health, and desired to get out of the way of being
lionised, which is exceedingly wearisome to the lion
after the first excitement and novelty of the process
have worn away. So I gladly accepted an invitation
from Sir Hyde Parker to yacht and fish with him in
Norway. He was a famed fisherman, and had landed
in Norway the largest salmon on record with a fly,
66 lb. in weight, authoritatively confirmed. Several
of his yachting friends were to have sailed at the
same time ; but their plans were affected by the
electioneering then going on ; consequently, after the
loss of some precious days, we were accompanied
only by the yachts of Mr. Bentinck and Mr. Milner
Gibson.

The former told us interesting anecdotes of Lord
Brougham's early rise at the Bar, how eagerly his
help was sought by the smart men of those days
when they got into scrapes, as being more likely
to get them out of their difficulties than any one

else. The extraordinary versatility and energy of
Lord Brougham had made a great impression on me
at that time and long previously, and I listened
eagerly to anecdotes of him. A timid and rather
elderly lady had told me that Lord Brougham was
once a guest at her brother's house, where his
appearance was awaited with awe. The great man
arrived, talked incessantly and wonderfully well during
dinner, but retired early on account of business letters.
Later on, while she was preparing for bed, an awful
yell or scream, which she could only describe in the
negative terms of unearthly and totally unlike anything
she had ever heard before, rang through the corridor.
She tremblingly snatched up whatever dress was
at hand, and issued in terror to learn what had
happened. She met Lord Brougham's valet with a
candle in his hand, walking leisurely, and cried to
him, "What is it? What is it?" He answered
unconcernedly, "It is only his Lordship calling for
me ; that is his usual way."

There is a remarkably good wax effigy of Lord
Brougham as a young man in Madame Tussaud's
collection, perhaps the most real-looking of any there.
Later on I was taken to see him in his house at
Cannes, a few years before his death. Doubts had
recently been expressed in the newspapers about his
version of the circumstances attending the dissolution
of Parliament by William IV., which made Lord
Brougham exceedingly wroth. It was fine but sad
to witness the unmeasured indignation of the old hero,
punctuating his remarks as he sat, by heavy digs
into the sand with the point of his umbrella, held in
both hands like a dagger.

Notwithstanding the Norway cruise, my health remained out of sorts, and a little later in the year, while some of my old fever was on me, I could not resist a dangerous exposure in order to witness the funeral of the Duke of Wellington. This made me seriously ill; I could hardly stand, but somehow made my way to my mother's house at Claverdon, where she and my sister Emma nursed me tenderly, and then, as I got better, it was agreed that we should all go together to Dover for a complete change.

There I recovered completely, and became engaged to my future wife, the daughter of the Very Rev. George Butler, Dean of Peterborough, who had been Headmaster of Harrow during many years. My wife had three sisters and four brothers, the latter all highly distinguished for scholastic and administrative ability.

I shrink, yet cannot wholly refrain from speaking of the affection I freely received from them, their relatives and their friends, all owing to that happy marriage, which lasted forty-four years, and ended at Royat in 1897, followed by a grave in the cemetery at Clermont Ferrand.

I shall say little about my purely domestic life, which, however full of interest to myself, would be uninteresting to strangers, so I attempt no more than to give brief accounts of the friendships and events that followed my marriage in 1853 up to about 1866. This interval of thirteen years occupies a fairly well defined part of my life owing to two reasons, namely, that my scientific interests during its latter half became concentrated on heredity, and because it was in 1866 that my health suffered a more serious breakdown than had happened to it before. During the whole of this interval I find from old diaries that I frequently suffered from giddiness and other maladies prejudicial to mental effort, but that I invariably became well again on completely changing my habits, as by touring abroad and taking plenty of out-of-door exercise. The warning I received in 1866 was more emphatic and alarming than previously, and made a revision of my mode of life a matter of primary importance. Those who have not suffered from mental breakdown can hardly realise the incapacity it causes, or, when the worst is past, the closeness of analogy between a sprained brain and a sprained joint. In both cases, after recovery seems to others to be complete, there remains for a long time an impossibility of performing certain minor actions without pain and serious mischief, mental in the one and bodily in the other. This was a frequent experience with me respecting small problems, which successively obsessed me day and night, as I tried in vain to think them out. These affected mere twigs, so to speak, rather than large boughs of the mental processes, but for all that most painfully.

My own family became dispersed in four groups. My mother and my sister Emma lived together in Leamington, and their house became a second home to my wife and myself. My mother always showed the greatest affection to me throughout her long life, which closed in 1874. After her death, the house and garden devolved upon my sister Emma. She cared for the interests of the family as a whole, and for each of us severally. She was invaluable to my wife and myself, and became my regular correspondent, whose weekly letters were awaited and read by us both with eagerness.

My eldest sister lived during the time with which I am now concerned, with her husband and her two growing children, in the country, about seven miles from Leamington.

My sister Adele lost her husband not long after her marriage, and settled successively in various places at home and abroad, devoting herself, as already said, to the education of her little girl. She died in 1883.

My second brother, Erasmus, lived for a while on his property at Loxton, in Somersetshire, five miles from Weston-super-Mare, but joined the 2nd Warwickshire Militia during many years, of which he became Major. He is now the only survivor of my six brothers and sisters, and is ninety-three years of age.

I turn from my own family to that of my wife. Her father was Dean of Peterborough, previously Headmaster of Harrow during many years, and before his appointment the Senior Wrangler at Cambridge, in the year in which Copley, the future Lord Lyndhurst, was second. There was no Classical class list in existence in Cambridge in those days, but the fact of Dr. Butler's election to the Head-mastership of Harrow at a very early age testifies to his reputation as a classical scholar as well as a mathematician. He had been noted for athletic powers, and he much prized a medal awarded to him by the Humane Society for having saved the life of a drowning woman when long past his middle age.

He afterwards overtaxed his heart by exertion to catch a train, which, among other effects, brought on a considerable degree of blindness, and made him in many respects invalided before the age of eighty. But his mind was apparently in full vigour, and his interests were most keen. Few persons had a more courtly demeanour. I was fated never to know him as a father-in-law. When I reached the Deanery from London, in order to be formally accepted into the family, I found the blinds drawn, and learnt that the Dean had died suddenly at luncheon. There had been some discussion in the morning about Cathedral matters in the Chapter House, and the excitement told fatally upon him, as it was always feared that any exceptional emotion might do. I was taken upstairs to look upon his dead face.

The Dean was father of an exceptionally gifted family. All of his four sons distinguished themselves highly at the Universities. The youngest was the Senior Classic of his year, subsequently Headmaster of Harrow, as his father had been before him, then for a brief time Dean of Gloucester, now and for many past years Master of Trinity College, Cambridge.

The same gifts of nature have descended in large measure to the grandchildren. Out of the eighteen grandsons of Dr. George Butler, Dean of Peterborough, a full half have already shown exceptional ability. Five have won a University Scholarship or prize, two others have given promise of high administrative power in India, one of whom now occupies the important post of Foreign Secretary to the Indian Government. Out of the five granddaughters, one has obtained a First Class in History at Oxford. This by no means exhausts the achievements of the grandchildren. The Butler family well deserve study as an instance of hereditary gifts, but this is hardly the place for it.

Neither can I enlarge as I could have done on the far greater importance of being married into a family that is good in character, in health, and in ability, than into one that is either very wealthy or very noble, but lacks these primary qualifications. The enlargement afforded to the previous family interests through marriage is so great that much must be lost when first cousins marry one another.

I protest against the opinions of those sentimental people who think that marriage concerns only the two principals; it has in reality the wider effect of an alliance between each of them and a new family. Moreover, the interests of the unborn should be taken far more seriously into account than they now are. Enough is already known of the laws of heredity to make it certain that the marriage of one class of persons will lead on the whole to good results, and that of another class to evil ones, however doubtful the result may be in particular cases. Of this I shall speak more fully in the final chapter.

As regards the earlier domestic life of my wife and myself, we lived in a flat in Victoria Street for three years; then I bought the long lease of 42 Rutland Gate, which has been my home ever since. We followed the usual routine of social life of persons of our class, making tours every year, usually abroad. The doctors sometimes sent one or both of us to undergo a cure at some watering-place   In this way we visited and, some of them more than once, Spa, Vichy, Contréxéville, Wildbad, Baden, Royat, and Mont Dore les Bains. We also often went to the Riviera and elsewhere. My finances had at this time to be considered rather carefully, as an income which was sure to arrive eventually was long delayed, and the property that was to yield it entailed a cost that almost swallowed up its profits. But there was no real stint; we had quite sufficient fortune for an unpretending establishment, with abundant leisure besides.

Certainly we led a life that many in our social rank might envy. Among our friends were not a few notable persons, a full half of whom were first known to me through the connections of· my wife. Then I was blessed with an abundance of animal spirits and hopefulness, though they were dashed temporarily over and over again by the great readiness with which my brain became overtaxed; however, I always recuperated quickly. Once I had a bad reminder of my old Syrian ague, but, thanks to quinine (which the ancients would have deified had they known of its virtues), the malady passed away so far out of sight as to have since recurred only at long intervals.

One of the pleasantest description of events in those days were the long walks I took, especially at Easter-time, with one or other of my brothers-in-law, or with their or my own friends. Let me venture to describe my own views as to provisions suitable for a day's walk during a homely tramp. They are such as can be procured at any town however small, are tasty, easy to carry, exempt from butter, which is apt to leak out of paper parcels, and are highly nutritious. They

are two slices of bread half an inch thick, a slice of
cheese of nearly the same thickness, and a handful of
sultana raisins. The raisins supply what bread and
cheese lack; they play the same part that cranberries do
in pemmican, that nasty, and otherwise scarcely eatable
food of Arctic travellers. The luncheon rations that I
advocate are compact, and require nothing besides
water to afford a satisfactory and sustaining midday
meal. If sultanas cannot be got, common raisins will
do; lumps of sugar make a substitute, but a very
imperfect one.

We frequently enjoyed the hospitality of the Headmaster of Harrow and his wife. One delightful way of
spending Sunday in those days was to walk to Harrow
along what was then a comparatively countrified road, to
take afternoon tea at the house of my wife's mother,
Mrs. Butler, who resided on the outskirts of Harrow,
to go to the evening service at the School Chapel,
to have a good square tea-supper at the Headmaster's, presided over by his attractive wife (*née*
Elliot), where interesting people were nearly always
present; afterwards to walk or rail home in the
evening, usually with a companion.

CHAPTER XII

"ART OF TRAVEL"

Compilation of the *Art of Travel*—Lectures at Aldershot—
Heliostat—Rifle screen—*Reader* newspaper

I WAS rather unsettled during a few years, wishing to undertake a fresh bit of geographical exploration, or even to establish myself in some colony ; but I mistrusted my powers, for the health that had been much tried had not wholly recovered. On the other hand, there was abundance of useful work at home. Geographical exploration had become a topic of general interest. Burton had penetrated to Mecca. Japan was opened, and Laurence Oliphant had returned thence. Dr. Barth had come back at last from his long exploration of North Africa, including districts which are now under British and French rule and well mapped, but at that time were either partially or quite unknown. It is very different now ; a letter can be sent for a penny to Kano, and Timbuctoo has become a French military station. Arctic expeditions by land and sea were then much to the fore ; Dr. Rae (1813–1893) had performed his great journeys in Arctic North America, with a wonderfully small and inexpensive equipment. Lesseps was engaged in obtaining support for making the Suez Canal, and I must say that the British engineers who pooh-poohed its possibility at the meeting of the Royal Geographical Society, where it was the subject of a paper by Lesseps, have proved untrustworthy guides and prophets. I threw myself into the thick of the discussions and criticisms of whatever had just been done, and into the preparations for what was about to be undertaken, and was in short a very active member of the Council.

It was not long after my marriage that the character of a piece of work that lay before me was clearly perceived. It was ready to be taken in hand and most suitable to my powers. It was to aid others in the exploration of the then unknown parts of the world, especially of Africa, of whose total length as much had been seen by me in my two journeys as perhaps by any one else then living. Being placed on the Council of the Royal Geographical Society, I thoroughly utilised that position to fulfil my object. The ignorance of travellers in any one country of the arts of travel employed in others was great, and I tried to make a compendium of them all. Having easy access to every traveller of note in England, I read many books of travel, or rather skimmed them for the purpose. Amongst others, I turned over every page in Pinkerton's well-known series of large quarto volumes of the narratives of travellers.

The result was that sufficient material was gathered for the composition of a small book entitled the *Art of Travel* (Murray). It soon reached a second edition, and was afterwards rewritten and much enlarged to form a third edition, which was stereotyped, and even now continues to be sold. I also took considerable part in the first edition of the

Hints to Travellers issued by the Geographical Society, which has long since quite outgrown its original form, all its chapters having been rewritten, each of them by experts. In its present shape it is a most trustworthy guide to travellers for such instrumental and other scientific work as they need to be acquainted with. The Anthropological "Notes and Queries" are a similar and most useful compendium relating to that branch of science. I had some share in this, but by no means a large one.

I cannot resist quoting the following letter from my cousin Charles Darwin, the great naturalist, whose opinion as the author of the *Voyage of the Beagle* was naturally valued by me most highly. I had asked him for hints while engaged on the first edition of the *Art of Travel*, and sent him a copy of it, to which he now refers. This was four years before the publication of the *Origin of Species* :—

"DOWN, *Jan.* 10, ?1855

"MY DEAR GALTON,—I received your kind present yesterday. I always thought your idea of your Book a very good one, and that you would do it capitally, and from what I have seen my forethought is, I am sure, *quite* justified. I hope that your volume will have a large sale, but what I fully expect is that it will have a long sale, and if you save from some disasters half a dozen explorers, I feel sure that you will think yourself well rewarded for all the trouble your volume must have cost you.—Believe me, my dear Galton, yours very truly,   C. DARWIN "

The outbreak of the Crimean War showed the helplessness of our soldiers in the most elementary matters of camp-life. Believing that something could be done by myself towards removing this extraordinary and culpable ignorance, I offered to give lectures on the subject, gratuitously, at the then newly founded camp at Aldershot. As may be imagined from what is otherwise known of the confusion of the War Office at that time, no answer at all was sent to my letters, until I ventured to apply personally to the then Premier, Lord Palmerston, who at once caused me to be installed. It is evident from my old notebooks that I worked very hard to frame a suitable course of practical instruction and of lectures for those who cared to profit by them.

General Knowles (1797–1883) was then in command, and he gave me both moral and material help. He assigned me two huts, and made arrangements about hours. My second brother, Erasmus, was in camp as Captain in the 2nd Warwickshire Militia, and his presence was most grateful to me. I myself took a small house about two miles from my hut, and walked there and back each day. Several officers came, and not a few of them showed interest. A lecture was also given by me at the United Service Institution, and the newspapers warmly backed the attempt. The War Office requested that ten (I think) reproductions should be made of a cabinet with four drawers, containing models of what was exhibited in my lectures. One of the cabinets was sent to the South Kensington Museum, and may be there still. One was sent to Woolwich. The others were distributed elsewhere. I do not think that my lectures had much other result, because the rude teachings of the Crimean War soon superseded mine, and the army generally became expert in much of what I had wished should be known by them.

A small contrivance of my own, over which I spent a great deal of time, may be alluded to here; it is described at length in the *Art of Travel*, and in other publications, as a "Hand Heliostat" [10]. I contrived and practised with it long before the present system of sun-signalling had been invented. The use of a heliostat for creating a point of light, visible at great distances for purposes of Ordnance triangulation, had long been fully recognised; a description of its employment from Snowdon to Scawfell has already been given in Chapter V. The difficulty in using a portable instrument is to direct the flash with sufficient accuracy of aim. If the part of the landscape upon which the flash falls could actually be seen by the operator, it would always appear to be of exactly the same size as the disc of the sun itself, whatever the distance may be; in other words, it subtends an angle of about 30 minutes of a degree. My plan was to divert a small part of the flash so as to create a mock-sun in the field of view of the instrument, which the operator could throw, by judicious handling, upon any desired spot in the landscape, with the assurance that persons on the ground covered by the mock-sun could see the flash. The instrument is now used in nautical surveys, as I was told by the late Hydrographer, Sir William Wharton, to enable shore parties to make their exact whereabouts visible to those on the ship. The heliostat that I usually carried with me went easily into a large waistcoat pocket, and was very efficient at a distance of ten miles. I should have been glad to possess one on many occasions when travelling in Damara Land. However, without additional complications, it could not be made into a really serviceable instrument for transmitting verbal messages. It would then require nearly as much trouble to carry as the present sun-signalling apparatus, while it would be less rapid and sure.[1]

It is interesting to flash with a small mirror against a light-coloured surface that lies in shadow, as through an open window against the opposite wall of the room behind. The size and shape of the mirror is then seen to have very little influence on the size or shape of the mock-sun, even at moderate distances. In long-range signalling their influence is wholly inappreciable.

I may describe here another contrivance, partly belonging to Art-of-Travel matters, partly military, that I sent to the United Service Institution [12]. It was appropriate to the days of " Brown Bess," but useless as a protection against modern musket bullets with their flat trajectories. I showed it was easy to provide a screen under which A. could hit B. at any distance beyond, say, 200 yards, while on the other hand B. could not hit A., although he might see him clearly. The balls of B. would be intercepted by the target. The principle on which the target gave pro-

---

[1] Anyhow, the optical principle on which it worked was pretty. A part of the flash struck one end of a strip cut out of the middle of a glass lens, and was brought by it to a focus (a burning spot) on an otherwise shaded porcelain screen. The eye looking through the other end of the strip saw the burning spot as a mock-sun. Now, by a well-known optical law, the apparent position of the burning spot is the same whatever be the part of the lens that makes it, or through which it is viewed. So the mock-sun seen by the eye covers the same part of the landscape that is simultaneously covered by the flash. The eye sees, it is true, only one portion of the mock-sun, whence the position of the rest has to be inferred.

tection was that the flight of a bullet does not describe a symmetrical curve. Its course is nearly straight at first, then gradually curves downward until it may be said to plunge. If A. and B. are in full sight of one another but at some little distance apart, and fire at one another, the courses of the incoming and outgoing bullet are different. That of the incoming bullet is higher by several inches or feet than the outgoing. Consequently, if a shield be interposed, near to A., above his line of shooting and at such a height that it will not interfere with his outgoing shot, it will effectually prevent a shot of B. from touching him, and conversely. The numerical conditions are worked out on the paper. The idea took the fancy of some of the audience, as one that might possibly be of much service.

I was a humble sharer in an undertaking started by Herbert Spencer, of establishing a weekly newspaper of literature and science, that was to eclipse the existing ones. His contention was that, if a few selected men were to combine each to write one article weekly, on a subject within his own province, a periodical might be produced that would have great weight and authority. The late Sir Frederick Pollock undertook its general editorship, to be helped in all details by a paid sub-editor, Mr. B., while he would keep the more purely literary portion in his own hands. Tom Hughes (the auther of *Tom Brown*) lent us his rooms and his co-operation. Tyndall undertook Physical Science; Huxley took Physiology, with reservation, as he could not afford to give much gratuitous work; Spencer, of course, took Philosophy; my part was to look after Travels and Geography, and there were a few others. We subscribed £100 each; Spencer persuaded a City friend to do a little more in order to start the concern, so a Limited Liability Company was formed, and the newspaper was called *The Reader*. It was an amusing experience, owing to Mr. B.'s insistence, from a commercial point of view, about the necessity of obtaining advertisements by all sorts of ingenious means, but some of which, in our opinions, were not quite above-board. Then it was brought home to us that, as our venture was one of limited liability, whatever we bought must be paid for at once, while what we were to receive would not be paid for many months. We were like children in the hands of Mr. B., who knew all the ins and outs of the commercial conditions of success, concerning which we were almost childishly ignorant. The newspaper proved dull, notwithstanding some really good articles. The management was naturally too amateurish; promised articles were delayed, and the time of the committee was too much wasted in frequent discussions about first principles, upon which Spencer loved to dilate. So *The Reader* did not thrive. Its expenditure exceeded its incomings, our reserve fund melted away, and the newspaper came to an end after about a year's existence. We each lost our hundred pounds, but no more, and had gained an unexpected view of the seamy side of journalistic enterprise.

CHAPTER XIII

SOCIAL LIFE

Interesting visits—Explorers of those days—Other notabilities
and friends

ENTRIES in old diaries recall many pleasant
social meetings at home, whether dinners,
breakfasts, or simple gatherings of friends, where
there was generally some traveller or other lion of
the day whom people were glad to meet. I made
occasional excursions to visit Charles Darwin at
Down, usually at luncheon-time, always with a sense
of the utmost veneration as well as of the warmest
affection, which his invariably hearty greeting greatly
encouraged. I think his intellectual characteristic
that struck me most forcibly was the aptness of his
questionings; he got thereby very quickly to the
bottom of what was in the mind of the person he
conversed with, and to the value of it.

I enjoyed two interesting visits to Lord Ashburton
at the Grange, under the presidency of the first and
second Lady Ashburton respectively. Carlyle was a
guest on both occasions. On my first meeting him
he surprised me by his unexpectedly courteous and
even polished manner, but he became more like
his ordinary self later on. On the second occasion
he seemed to me the greatest bore that a house

could tolerate. He had a well-known story then to the fore, which W. H. Brookfield (1809–1874), who was a very constant guest, told me he had indulged in five times that day already, and undertook that he should repeat it for my benefit a sixth time, which he did. Then Carlyle raved about the degeneracy of the modern English without any facts in justification, and contributed nothing that I could find to the information or pleasure of the society. He, however, executed a performance with great seriousness which was decidedly funny, by hopping gravely on one leg up and down within the pillars of the portico, which he had discovered to be a prompt way of warming himself in the then chilly weather.

It is difficult to select events out of the very many that were then interesting to me. One was a visit to Mr. Webb at Newstead Abbey, the old home of the poet Lord Byron, which he had recently purchased. Mr. Webb had been a first-class African sportsman, of whom mention will be made in the next chapter in connection with the identification of Dr. Livingstone's remains. The mementoes of Lord Byron at Newstead Abbey were well cared for, and most touching to me, for I had in my youth an unlimited admiration of his works; so I drank greedily with my eyes all that I saw connected with him. I will here anticipate very many years, and mention a tragedy that occurred only two autumns ago to Lord Byron's grandson and representative, Lord Lovelace. My niece, who has managed my home since the death of my wife, spent a few summer weeks with me in the pretty village of Ockham. The night before leaving it to return home to London we were invited to Ockham Park after tea-time, for a quiet farewell call. Lord Lovelace was exceptionally agreeable, the conversation was general, and the evening passed by most pleasantly. It had been arranged that his carriage should take us back ; he accompanied us to it, and wished us good-bye in the most friendly and courteous manner. No one outside his household, and very few of these, saw him again alive. It appeared that he dressed himself for dinner, and after coming downstairs fell dead on the floor.

I saw much of Richard, afterwards Sir Richard, Burton and of Lawrence Oliphant in those days. There were exceedingly pleasant social gatherings held after each meeting of the Geographical Society of geographers and others, who were invited by Admiral Murray to his rooms in the Albany. He was an excellent host, and justly popular among a great variety of men whom he had the tact to bring harmoniously together in his chambers. Bishop Wilberforce, who prided himself on worldly *savoir faire*, was occasionally a guest ; Burton was habitually there, but his usual conversation in those days was not exactly of a stamp suitable to episcopal society. I was present at the first introduction of these two men, whose behaviour was most comic, each trying to act the part appropriate to the other, and, I must add, doing it most successfully, and to all appearance quite naturally. Burton was a great reader, generally to be seen at the Athenæum with a folio volume before him, and he was a prodigious note-taker during his travels. He lent me his notebook on Zanzibar, of which I shall shortly speak again, and I was astonished at the variety and amount of information he had written in it, in his small, clear handwriting.

Lawrence Oliphant had a most winning manner and a marvellous facility of expression. I have served on more Council meetings than could easily be reckoned, and am only too familiar with the often recurring difficulty of finding a phrase that shall cover just as much of the question under discussion as is generally accepted, without touching any part on which there is disagreement. Oliphant had the art of hitting upon the appropriate phrase on these occasions more deftly and aptly than any one else whom I can remember. We worked together most pleasantly as joint secretaries under the presidency of John Crawfurd, the Ethnologist, who nicknamed us his two sons.

I had the great pleasure of again falling in with Mansfield Parkyns of Abyssinian fame, at Admiral Murray's hospitable gatherings.

Among many other distinguished travellers who were in England during the fifties, I should mention Dr. Barth, who was a learned and simple-minded man. The five volumes of his travels in North Africa have the merits and demerits of many German books, being full of information but deterrent in form. I suspect that few Englishmen have read them through as conscientiously as I did. He was a great believer in the importance of the Hausa language to traders and settlers. It was then practically unknown even to professed linguists, so he brought over with him a bright Hausa boy to help him and others in learning it. I never knew exactly what happened, but it seems there was evidence that the boy had expressed a wish to go back to Africa, as he well may have done in moments of temporary depression, whereupon the zealous secretary of a philanthropic Society threatened poor Barth with an action for kidnapping if he did not send the boy back at once. Barth was amazed, and sought advice, which was that considering the sectarian bitterness with which the action would probably be carried on, the ease with which thoughtless expressions might be twisted into deliberate words, and the certain cost and tediousness of legal proceedings, it would be wiser for him to submit and to send back the boy. This he did with no little grief, and so all attempt to lexiconise and grammarise the Hausa language was thrown back for many years, during which a knowledge of it would have been of material use in various British operations on the West Coast of Africa.

A long subsequent attempt was, however, made with success by a small committee, of whom I was one and Major Leonard Darwin another, under the Presidency of Sir George Goldie, through whose efforts sufficient funds were collected to enable Mr. Robinson to study the Hausa language seriously and on the spot. Opportunities for learning it have now been afforded, and are used at Cambridge by prospective military and civil servants in West Africa.

Mr. Crawfurd (1783–1868) was then a vigorous old man of considerable moral weight and of great experience, with not a few amusing peculiarities (Sir Roderick Murchison called him laughingly, in public, the Objector General). He had been secretary to Sir Stamford Raffles, and, according to what he told to me, and I presume also to others, he was the sole

originator of the idea of making Singapore a free
port, and had trouble in convincing Sir Stamford
that it would be wise to do this.   He became its first
Governor, and the descriptions he gave of his multifarious occupations in that new post, with a very
small staff, were amusing.   He established a newspaper and wrote much of it himself.   The settlement
quickly grew in size and wealth, and had attained much
importance by the time he retired.   He compiled
the first Malay Dictionary and Grammar.   Having
failed in England to secure a seat in Parliament, he
engaged heart and soul in Ethnology and Geography,
spoke very frequently at meetings, always with reason,
and he wrote many ethnological papers, all good, but
perhaps few of first rank.   He was a very kind and
helpful friend to me.   He caught his death illness
through handing ladies to their carriage on the
occasion of one of his Soirées, on a bitter night.   He
died believing in his delirium that he was speaking
at the Ethnological Society (since merged into the
Anthropological), to which he was devoted.

Mr. George Bentham (1800–1884), the botanist,
was a great friend of Mr. Crawfurd, and he became a
kind friend to myself and to my wife.   He was son of
General Bentham, who obtained one of the highest
positions as constructor of ships in the Russian Navy,
and he was nephew to Jeremy Bentham.   Mr. George
Bentham was the companion in youth of John Stuart
Mill, of whom he had much to tell.   In his early
manhood he took to logic, and wrote an important
paper, in which he pointed out that the distinctiveness
of a certain logical operation in common use had been
overlooked and never received a name.   I myself am

ignorant of logical subtleties, and repeat the following
much as a parrot might. He called the operation in
question the "Quantification of the Predicate." Years
passed by, during which he abandoned logic and gave
all his time to systematic botany, for which his logical
training was helpful. He had been President of the
Linnæan Society for many years, and his name had
become familiar to every botanist and dabbler in
botany. At this time a letter in some newspaper (I
think the *Athenæum*) was brought to his notice, in
which the writer dwelt on the importance of this
"Quantification of the Predicate." He mentioned
the name of its young author, adding that he had
taken much pains, in vain, to learn what had become
of him,—could any reader supply information?

Mr. Bentham called one morning in 1880, together
with Sir Joseph (then Mr.) Hooker, to congratulate
me on having just had a whole genus of flowers of
singular beauty called after me by the French
botanist, J. Decaisne (Prof. de Culture, Musée
d'Histoire Naturelle, Paris) [60]. I was amazed,
for I know next to nothing of botany. The story
was this. A beautiful plant had been sent from
Natal to Europe. It was described at Kew as
Hyacinthus Candicans, but M. Decaisne would not
consent to such a denomination. He pointed out
particulars in the plant that hyacinths have not,
and the absence of other particulars that hyacinths
have, and he renamed it. Why he pitched upon
my name for the purpose I do not know, but suppose
that he may have consulted a list of the South African
medallists of the French Geographical Society, and
finding my name among them, selected it. I have

not the slightest claim to the honour, but accepted its bestowal by him and its ratification by our then greatest botanists, Hooker and Bentham, with amusement. Seedsmen still class it among the hyacinths, saying that they are obliged to have as few separate headings in their catalogues as possible. I append a little picture of *Galtonia Candicans* to this book as a vignette at the bottom of its last page.

Mr. Atkinson (1799–1861) had returned with huge oil paintings from Siberia, which he carried in rolls on camel back, sometimes tandem-fashion. His career was strange. He was originally little more than a quick-witted stone-mason's boy, who afterwards rose, and then hearing that a design was to be competed for at St. Petersburg for some memorial, he drew a design, sent it there, and it was selected. He thereupon moved to Russia, and in some mysterious way obtained the confidence of the Czar Nicholas so completely that Atkinson received what was most unusual, if not unprecedented, a free ukase to travel and paint where he would. Possibly the Czar wished for unbiased and independent evidence as to certain matters in South Siberia, and Atkinson may have acted as a secret agent. He was made much of by persons of the highest rank in Russia, and he was married in the Chapel of the British Embassy to an English lady who had resided in one of the great Russian families as their companion. She accompanied him in his great journey. On their arrival in England they were widely received and welcomed. They took a picturesque but ramshackle small house and garden, called Hawk Cottage, that stood on the old Brompton Road, nearly opposite to where Bina Gardens now are, on a spot that had not then passed into the hands of the builders of streets. They were much visited by members of the highest Russian nobility and by many English friends.

In 1861 Mr. Atkinson died, and his wife applying to the Treasury for some money due to him, was met by the astounding assertion, backed by abundant proof, that she was not legally his wife, inasmuch as he had been married before he went to Russia to a lady who was still living in England. To the natural inquiry why the claim should be now put forward for the first time, considering the publicity under which Mr. Atkinson had lived, the reply was that no news of him had reached the claimant, who occupied a different grade of society, until intelligence had been sent to her by a friend of her husband's death. This tragic termination affected many of us greatly. We recollected that Atkinson had avoided bringing his wife (as we thought she was) to the forefront, and it had been remarked at the time of the publication of his book of travels that he made the scantiest references to her, and never used the word "wife." It was a wonder, and it is so still, how he dared to settle in London and risk a serious criminal charge. Friends gathered round Mrs. Atkinson, as I must still call her, and helped her in many substantial ways. She afterwards returned to Russia.

It was during this time that I made the acquaintance of the then Mr., afterwards Sir John Lubbock, and now Lord Avebury, who was engaged on his

Prehistoric Times, and had attracted the friendship of most of the men of the day who were destined to become famous in science. His week-end invitations were always most instructive and grateful. It is difficult justly to express the value of such opportunities of friendly and unhurried converse. I received great kindness and much warm welcome at his house, and was captivated by the ingenuity of his experiments on ants and bees.

Amongst many friends whose acquaintance I first made at Sir John Lubbock's was Herbert Spencer, then struggling with difficulties connected with his serial publications. They were removed by the unexpected visit of an American gentleman, with a gold watch, who made a brief oration to the effect that Spencer's admirers in America feared the cessation of his publications in pamphlet form owing to financial reasons. That they had consequently subscribed and invested a (handsome) sum in his name in Consols, and had further deputed him—the speaker—to present the gold watch as a token of their esteem. It was a touching and cheering event to Spencer, who always wore the watch. It, moreover, went well, which was not invariably the case with costly presentation watches in those days.

I met Herbert Spencer frequently at the Athenæum, and had many conversations with him there. He was always ready to listen sympathetically to new views and to express his opinion on them, but he disliked to argue. I persuaded him once to go with me to see the Derby, in company with a near relative of mine who was an Oxford clerical don. These two were perhaps as incongruous a pair in some respects as could easily be devised, but they enjoyed each other's company. All went off quite well, except that Spencer would not be roused to enthusiasm by the races. He said that the crowd of men on the grass looked disagreeable, like flies on a plate ; also that the whole event was just like what he had imagined the Derby to be. Still, he evidently liked the excursion, and notwithstanding his asseverations at the time to the contrary, he repeated his experience on at least one subsequent occasion.

For my own part, I especially enjoy the start of the horses, for their coats shine so brightly in the sunshine, the jockeys are so sharp and ready, and the delays due to false starts give opportunities of seeing them well. I don't care much for its conclusion, but I used often after seeing the start to run to the top of the rising ground between the starting point and the stand, and sometimes got a good opera-glass view of much of the finish.

A curious sight caught my attention on one of these occasions. I was on the side of the course that faced the distant stand, and amused myself while waiting in studying the prevalent tint of the sea of faces upon it. At length the horses were off, but it was hot, and I was contented to remain in quiet where I was. When the horses approached the winning-post, the prevalent tint of the faces in the great stand changed notably, and became distinctly more pink under the flush of excitement. I wrote a short notice of the experience in *Nature*, under my initials, but have kept no copy and quite forget the year.

I enjoyed the friendship during more than fifty

years of the Hon. George Brodrick, in his later years Warden of Merton, whose memoirs are probably known to most of my readers. When I first knew him he was reputed one of the foremost of those rising men at Oxford who were contemporaries with my brother-in-law, Arthur Butler, and among whom was Goschen. Brodrick became a distinguished journalist, for many years on the staff of the *Times*. He had a strong taste for geography, partly through being sent in his youth on a long voyage to India and back, for the sake of his health. Becoming a member of the Council of the Royal Geographical Society, he gave important help to the introduction of Geography into the curriculum of his University. He was always a warm friend to me, and I enjoyed not a few brief visits to Merton College when he was established there as its Warden. His eccentricities were all amiable, and gave harmless amusement to his friends; especially his reluctance in accepting the proferred Wardenship of Merton, for which his friends thought he was exactly suited. He, however, considered it to have a serious drawback in depriving him of the possibility of a Parliamentary career, to which most of them considered him unsuited. Moreover, he had twice been an unsuccessful candidate for a seat in Parliament. I do not attempt more in these few lines than to express my grateful remembrance of him, and my appreciation of his many great qualities, including a large capacity for steadfast friendships and a highly religious mind very tolerant of the differing opinions of others.

A grateful intimacy grew up between my wife and myself and Mr. Frederick North of Rougham, in

Norfolk, at that time residing as a widower in his house at Hastings, for which town he was Member of Parliament during many years. His two daughters were then with him, the eldest, Miss Marianne North (1830–1890), widely known for her travels after his death, in order to paint flowers in far distant lands with scientific accuracy. The building in Kew Gardens was devised by her friend J. Fergusson (1808–1886), the writer on architecture, and built to hold her collection ; she presented it to the Gardens. The younger daughter became wife of John Addington Symonds (1840–1893), the well-known critic and writer. My wife and I spent very many happy visits to Hastings Lodge, where the heartiness of reception and the amplitude of real comfort without any attempt at display were remarkable. That valued friendship towards me still continues in the third generation of descent from Mr. North.

I owed to my wife a highly valued intimacy with Mr. and Mrs. Russell Gurney. The clock of the latter, which she left me in her Will, is within two yards of where I am writing this, and I look back to the lifelong friendships of her and her husband with no ordinary affection. The portrait of Mr. Russell Gurney (1804–1878) by Watts, which is in the National Gallery, is extremely like ; it strikes me, if I may venture on any opinion connected with Art, as one of the very best in any of our three great national collections. The portrait of Mrs. Russell Gurney, also by Watts, which is now in the possession of her relatives, is rather forced in pose. It is much to be regretted that no adequate biography has been written of her. The one which is published dwells too exclusively on the devotional side of her character, and fails sadly to bring out her originality, charm, and humour. Like many other persons who are profoundly religious, she too was perfectly tolerant of other beliefs than her own if they were genuine and decorously expressed.

Her endowment of a Chapel of Rest in the Bayswater Road has by no means fulfilled her wishes. Her object was to establish a quiet artistic shelter, where persons desiring a few minutes' withdrawal from the turmoil of life, might enter and commune in quiet with themselves. She obtained a disused chapel, and arranged for its maintenance. Then she took great pains over the designs that were to be painted on the walls in fresco. When these were sufficiently advanced, she, long since a widow and in rapidly declining health, invited many friends to its opening. My wife and I were rather late, and I can see now the sweet welcoming gesture with which she beckoned us up to her on the platform. We never saw her again. She lingered on, unwilling, or unable, to see any even of her oldest friends, and at length died. The Chapel of Rest remained unfinished for some years. It is little used, and can, or could, be entered only at specified hours.

As to Mr. Russell Gurney, who served on many important commissions, he twice refused a judgeship, preferring to retain his post of "Recorder" of the City of London, which is of nearly equal dignity to a judgeship, and did not at that time preclude its holder from sitting in Parliament. He was member for Southampton. I have known no one who struck me as a more just, searching, and yet kindly judge, or whom I would more willingly be tried by if I fell into trouble.

It was to my wife, also, that I owed the friendship of Mr. and Mrs. Robert Hollond of Stanmore. She was exceptionally gifted by nature with grace, sympathy, artistic taste, and many other high qualities. Her portrait, by Scheffer, is in the Tate Gallery. Her face closely corresponded to his imaginary ideal when painting St. Augustine and Monica, so he enjoyed the opportunity of painting Mrs. Hollond's own portrait. She was even more at home in France than in England, and intimate with many distinguished statesmen of the Orleanist party. Her husband's wealth gave her great facilities for cultivating her æsthetic tastes to the full. He was chiefly known to the public at one time as subsidiser of the " Nassau " balloon, which carried him, Green the famous aeronaut, and, I think, Mr., afterwards Lord Justice, James (who was an old friend of his), and two others. They sailed from London to a town in Nassau ; which was at that time by far and away a record distance for a balloon to drift. Numerous memorial pictures of that adventure were in his house.

It was in the middle fifties that my friendship commenced with William Spottiswoode (1825–1883), one of the most capable and true-hearted of men, who became President of the Royal Society, and now lies buried in Westminster Abbey, "at the request alike of the foremost of his countrymen in Church and State, in Science, Art and Literature, and of his own workmen, to whose best interests his life had been devoted." This is the singularly apt inscription on his tombstone. I asked Dean Bradley, then Dean of

Westminster, if he knew who was its author. He replied, "Myself." It is to be regretted that no good biography exists of W. Spottiswoode. Many notices were published at his death, and it gratified me to learn that one which I wrote for the Royal Geographical Society on one aspect of his many-sided character greatly pleased his family and some of his intimate friends.

The main features of his life were that he was the son of the then Queen's Printer, of good Scottish family, and the presumed heir to a considerable fortune. He went to Oxford, where he obtained the University Scholarship in mathematics, and where also intelligence reached him of the entire collapse of his father's fortune through unwise speculation. He braced himself to the occasion, and, after many years of hard work, himself succeeding his father as Queen's Printer, he created a model business on the largest scale, and rehabilitated the lost fortune. In the meantime he had sufficient spare energy to occupy himself day by day with congenial pursuits in literature and science. Among other diversions he loved to travel considerable distances during the few weeks he annually allowed himself for vacation, and to acquire much knowledge of other countries in that way. Enormously worked as he was, he always seemed to have leisure, and he did with thoroughness whatever he undertook.

At this time there was still much ignorance concerning the northern part of the peninsula of Sinai, especially of the plain of El Tih, and he suggested to me that by making judicious preparations its survey might be accomplished within the short space of time that he could afford. I agreed to join him. We worked hard to prepare ourselves, and made a large sketch map, on which notes of every important traveller bearing on the part in which we were interested were entered at the locality they referred to. It was desirable for him to have some experience in surveying, and as I was going to the Isle of Wight, we agreed to practise there. The first and only attempt had an absurd ending. We found a strongly railed field suitable for a commencement, into which we got by climbing the fence, and prepared to unpack, not particularly noticing the cattle in it; but one of them was a bull, who, after the manner of such animals, advanced in so threatening and determined a manner that we had to retreat from the brute as best we could.

This proved to be the end of our joint experiments, for I was taken ill with what seemed at first to be only a very bad sore throat, but which developed into a singular form of quinsy of a dangerous character. My old friends, Mr. Hodgson and Dr. Todd, were unremitting in their attentions, and told me afterwards that they were on the point of having my windpipe opened, as I was nearly suffocating. At last, an abscess which was situated in a gland on the upper surface of the tongue, but far back near its root, broke, and I breathed freely. I was soon able to swallow, and gradually became convalescent, but Mr. Hodgson peremptorily forbade further thoughts of Sinai. I shall have to refer again to W. Spottiswoode.

It has happened to me more than once to be nearly suffocated, and to have been surprised at the absence of that gasping desire for air that one feels when the breath is suddenly checked. A very little seems sufficient to divert attention from that desire, and to leave the sense only of being ill and on the point of swooning. My chief experiences may seem hardly credible ; they were due to a fancy of mine to obtain distinct vision when diving. The convex eyeball stamps a concave lens in the water, whose effect has to be neutralised by a convex lens. This has to be very "strong," because the refractive power of a lens is greatly diminished by immersion in water. My first experiment was in a bath, using the two objectives of my opera-glass in combination, and with some success. I then had spectacles made for me, which I described at the British Association in 1865 [19]. With these I could read the print of a newspaper perfectly under water, when it was held at the exact distance of clear vision, but the range of clear vision was small. I amused myself very frequently with this new hobby, and being most interested in the act of reading, constantly forgot that I was nearly suffocating myself, and was recalled to the fact not by any gasping desire for breath, but purely by a sense of illness, that alarmed me. It disappeared immediately after raising the head out of water and inhaling two or three good whiffs of air.

Mr. Alexander Macmillan asked me in the later fifties to undertake the editorship of a volume to be called *Vacation Tourists* [11], which would be repeated annually if the venture succeeded. His view was that many able young men travelled every summer, each of whom would have enough to say to make a good article, and that a collection of their contributions would suffice for an interesting annual volume. I consented, and found the occupation very agreeable, for it put me into pleasant communication with many whom it was a privilege to know, but excision was often an unwelcome duty. Thus among the many contributions offered for one of the volumes, I had thirteen separate descriptions of sea-sickness. The venture paid its way, but no more, and was discontinued after the third volume.

A total eclipse visible in Spain occurred on July 18, 1860, and the Government lent their magnificent transport the *Himalaya* to those who were selected to observe it, by and under the leadership of the then Astronomer-Royal, Mr., afterwards Sir George, Airy (1801–1892). I applied, and was granted permission to join. We went with great comfort and speed, first to Bilbao, where small parties, of whom mine of four persons was one, were landed. The rest went on to Santander.

Careful preparations had been made in Spain for our comfort, as few of us knew a word of the language, and serious obstructions due to intolerance might otherwise have occurred for want of timely explanation. These excellent arrangements were entirely due to the forethought of Mr. Vignolles, a famous contractor for railways, who was then occupied with those of Spain. One of his many subordinates was allotted as interpreter to each small party ; ours proved to be a most agreeable guide and informant. The position allotted to our party was in the neighbourhood of Logroño, whither we proceeded at once in order to study the neighbourhood and to select a suitable spot. This was quickly found on a picturesque hill called La Guardia, crowned with a convent and village, which lay in the central line of totality, and commanded a grand view of the plain over which the shadow of the coming eclipse would sweep.

Thanks to the diplomacy of our interpreter, we obtained permission to use the flat roof of one of the highest houses, where we established ourselves on the morning of the eventful day. I had nursed with great care an instrument to observe the delicate variations of temperature. It was the invention of Sir John Herschel (1792–1871), who instructed me in its use, but its construction was so fragile that hardly any traveller had as yet been able to take one of them uninjured to its destination. I was no more fortunate than my predecessors, for the long stem of the heavy mercurial bulb broke. It was impossible to feel as unhappy as I ought to have been, because it left me free to gaze at will at the coming great sight.

And a wonderful sight it was, when the pure luminous corona first displayed itself at the moment of totality. It has been one of the great sights of my life. I made rude sketches in the dim light, and afterwards found that the closest representation of the eclipse was to be obtained by blackening paper over a candle and scratching out the lights, on the principle of mezzotints. I published a description of the eclipse in *Vacation Tourists*, with a sketch that has been reproduced more than once, but the curl given to one of the rays of the corona was not credited by most of my fellow-observers. Thus Sir George Airy, when lecturing on the eclipse at the Royal Institution and exhibiting my sketch on the screen, expressed in the most courteous way some reservation as to its acceptance as a true rendering. Photographs of subsequent eclipses have, however, shown that curved rays are a reality.

From Spain I went by diligence to Bordeaux, meeting my wife at the station on her arrival from Paris, and we started for a tour in the Pyrenees and for a stay of some weeks at Luchon. Here I became for the first time bitten with the mania for mountain climbing. As during a few years previously the primary purpose of fences had seemed to be to afford objects for leaping over, so now that of mountains seemed to be for clambering. Mr. Charles Packe, who was an authority on the mountains and botany of the locality, often accompanied me, and the outings were enjoyed excessively. Among other things, I was immensely taken by the sleeping-bag that each French soldier carries who watches the mountain passes through which Spanish smugglers try to steal. It is worn on the back like a heavy knapsack. These bags are made of sheep-skin with the wool inside. On cold days the soldiers sit inside them, pulling the bag up to their waists. They are thus able to keep their posts in trying weather, which smugglers would otherwise have been ready to utilise for their own purposes. I tried the efficiency of one on an interesting night. A heavy storm was gathering, but before the evening closed and before the storm broke, I had time to find a good place on a hill some 1000 feet or more above Luchon, and there to await it inside my bag. Nothing could have been more theatrically grand. The thunder - clouds and the vivid lightning were just above me, accompanied by deluges of rain. Then they descended to my level, and the lightning crackled and crashed about, then all the turmoil sank below, leaving a starlit sky above.

Sleeping-bags were customary in the Pyrenees. Mr. George Bentham told me that when he botanised in the little Republic of Andorre some years previously, there was not a bed in the place, and he was lent a sleeping-bag. They were familiar to Arctic travellers, but had not been thought of by Alpine climbers, so I published my experiences. In consequence, at an amusing dinner of the Alpine Club, of which I was a member for a few years, I was toasted by Mr. Wm. Longman as the greatest "bagman" in Europe. It is very difficult to arrange any sleeping gear that shall satisfy those who rough it rarely. Luxury is out of place. I read in some well-known book that one of the Camerons of Lochiel, when bivouacking with his son in the snow, noticed that the lad had rolled up a snowball to make a pillow. He thereupon rose and kicked it away, saying sternly, " No effeminacy, boy."

Bears were not infrequent. We reached, I think it was Cauteret, after passing a small plantation near the town. During the table d'hôte there was a rush to the windows to see the dead body of a big bear cub which had just been killed at that very plantation. Its mother, who was with it, escaped. I often saw their human-like tracks. They occasionally kill oxen. Once, when near a cattle station, while watching the cattle returning home in file, each in its turn executed a fantastic sort of war-dance as it passed a particular spot, such as I had frequently, but by no means invariably, witnessed in Africa, when a line of my cattle passed over the place where I had shot an ox for food. In this instance the performance was due to a cow having quite recently been killed by a bear. The effect of the smell of blood on oxen and horses is apparently capricious, being sometimes very marked indeed, at other times nil. Horses are frequently terrified by the smell of large wild beasts, but I have helped to skin a lion in full sight of my horse, and rolling the skin up, tied it in a bundle to the back of my saddle, without the horse showing the slightest objection.

My late but passionate love for mountaineering was one cause that subsequently brought me into frequent contact with Professor Tyndall (1820–1893), who was then at his very best physically and mentally. He, I, and Vaughan Hawkins (1833–1908), an eminent classic in his Harrow and Cambridge days and of first rank in mountaineering, made a tour together in Cornwall. We chose our way on Tyndall's principle, that it is easy to find difficult places to climb elsewhere than in the high mountains. Certainly he was skilful at discovering them. One of his freaks sent my heart into my mouth. It was at a gully, strewn deeply with loose stones that led over a sea cliff. Down he dashed, the stones were all set in motion like an avalanche, but somehow he extricated himself in time and got clear to one side of them. At another place an isolated needle or cone of rock was separated from the shore by a narrow strait through which the sea swirled, but which could be leapt at low water. We leapt it, and clambered up, he declaring that it was as difficult a bit of rock-work as he had ever been on. We reached the top and got back successfully, jump and all, to the mainland, where I was glad to feel in safety.   The Irish dash in Tyndall's blood gave a charm to all he did.   He was then fast rising, but had not yet reached the fulness of his subsequent height in popular reputation, which is perhaps the time in the mental development of a man at which his character shows at its brightest.

My wife and I found a frequent travelling-companion in Miss Brandram, afterwards the wife and subsequently the widow of A. MacLennan, the writer on various phases of prehistoric societies, *Marriage by Capture, Totems*, etc.   She was a great friend to both of us ; a companion and kind nurse to my wife when she was ill, an excellent walking companion to myself, and always ready to be of service.   She helped me much in revising some of my earlier writings, especially the last edition of my *Art of Travel*.

During her widowhood Mrs. MacLennan travelled with us again, but at last a disaster occurred at a time when we were living at Cimiez, above Nice.   There is a high-level railway from Nice to Grasse that passes the little station of the Saut de Loup, a waterfall about an hour's walk (I think) from the station, which we wanted much to see.   The footpath runs along a hillside and is perfectly good, but too narrow for two persons to walk abreast.   In more than one place a streamlet cascades over it.   Near its destination the path is crossed by a more considerable streamlet running among stones, that make stepping-stones near enough to the surface to prevent the feet being much wetted while crossing it, and which any one accustomed to mountain walking would trip over without remark.   The pathway was broader at this point, and the stream after crossing it fell into a precipice, at the bottom of which ran the river Loup. Mrs. MacLennan was walking first, and, owing to some strange accident, missed a stone or tripped, and fell heavily on her side, where she lay motionless in the water as though shot dead. I helped her to rise, but she was in great pain. It was difficult to set her on her feet, for the position was not one to stagger safely in, the precipice being much too near.

With great pluck, she went a few steps onward to see the fall, and then the long return walk had to be achieved. She was confined for a long time to bed, and far from fit to travel when she left us. The injury was followed by an internal complaint, of which, after much suffering at her own home, she died.

Few have been more thorough in their friendship to my wife and myself than Sir Rutherford and Lady Alcock and her daughter by a previous marriage, Miss Lowder, now Lady Pelly. I was well acquainted with much of Sir Rutherford's work in China and Japan before I had the pleasure of knowing him personally, because the Foreign Office used to forward those of his dispatches that were of geographical interest to the Royal Geographical Society, where, for want of a better person, they were generally referred to myself. Sir Rutherford's life was eventful; first as an army surgeon in Spain under Sir De Lacy Evans, then Consul in China, then our first Minister in Japan, then Ambassador to China. Lady Alcock seconded him in charge of the well-being of his large staff, with a kindliness that was proverbial. On their return to England they became social favourites from the highest in rank to the

13

lowest, being singularly acceptable through their own attractive qualities, and widely known through reports of their largely unostentatious charitable acts. Sir Rutherford was President of the Royal Geographical Society for the usual term, and we saw much of him and his family at various times, eating our Christmas dinner with them on three or four occasions.

Of many pleasant meetings I will only mention one, when we, in company with Sir Lewis and Lady Pelly, made an interesting tour in the South of France from Royat, by that curious natural formation Montpelier le Vieux, round to Avignon. The valley of the Tarn had recently been made accessible to tourists, and I was particularly desirous of seeing its wonders, so our party stopped at Millau to give me an opportunity of going to the Tarn River for a long day by myself. First some distance had to be travelled by railroad, then some miles by a two-wheeled vehicle across the bare Causses, a high limestone upland, down to the beautifully clear Tarn. Every shower that falls on the Causses percolates through deep "swallows," and finds its way for perhaps 2000 feet vertically through them, issuing from the cliffs as feeders of pure water to the little river.

I was put into a flat-bottomed boat with stalwart boatmen fore and aft, and so dropped down stream. The water was at first so shallow and transparent as to be scarcely visible. The boat seemed to be buoyed in the air above the clean, shingly bottom. So we glided down hour after hour, with vast cliffs on either side clothed sparsely with pre-Rafaelite-looking trees, and with an occasional eagle soaring in the blue sky overhead. Then the river by slow degrees grew

broader, deeper, and swifter, and swirled formidably
in places, requiring much caution in the boatmen ;
the evening closed in while we had still some way
to go.   It was not altogether pleasant, as the punt was
not particularly "stiff," the navigation was difficult,
and it was becoming very dark.   At length the
welcome bridge which betokened our destination
loomed high in front.   The party from Millau had
been there awaiting me till dark, and then left.   I
was fortunate in securing a trap, wherein to drive
the few miles that then separated me from them.

We all went together the next day to Montpelier
le Vieux, so called because its rocks look from a distance
like the turrets of a weird city on a hilltop.   Each rock
stands by itself on a carpet of green verdure.   Crowds
of legends have, of course, clustered round this strange
locality.   Anyhow, it is an ideal place for a picnic in
which to spend the long hours of a sunny day.   The
whole of the south-west corner of France is full of
interest, and the part just mentioned seems quite
unique.

I wish I could more adequately and yet appro-
priately have expressed my affectionate feelings
towards the many friends to whom I have made too
scanty reference in this chapter.

During the year that followed the death of my
wife in 1897, I made a tour with one of her nephews,
a Frank Butler, son of Spencer P. Butler.   He became engaged to an English lady, a niece of Mrs.
MacLennan, while we were touring in Corsica with
her party, and married shortly after.   Henceforward
a niece, Miss Evelyne Biggs, or more strictly speaking
a grandniece of my own, granddaughter of my sister

Lucy, has lived with me as companion, and I have followed a somewhat similar routine of life, except in being no longer advised by the doctor to try cures, the best means of securing health now being to escape a winter in London.

Yearly Medallions.—My fancy had been taken long ago by a custom of certain North American Indians, of naming years, each after some characteristic event that had occurred in it.[1]   It appears that an annual consultation of Indian chiefs was held, at which the more

striking occurrences of the past year were reviewed and one selected as its representative. Thereupon an Indian who was reputed for skill in drawing made a picture or symbol of the event on his buffalo-skin robe. They are as rude in conception and execution as an English child of five years old might draw. Thus the " small-pox year" is symbolically expressed by an elementary

[1] *Photographs of the North American Indians.* By Garrick Mallery, from the Fourth Annual Report of the Museum of Ethnology, Washington, Government Printing Office, 1886.

design of the head, body, and four limbs of a man dotted over with spots. A robe exists (see page 88–89 of the memoir) in which a sequence of seventy-one years is thus recorded in symbols spirally arranged upon it; it was made by a certain Dacota Indian, called Lone Dog.

I adopted this method to illustrate the events of my own life during part of the time while my wife was still living, but they are too rude for publication. I therefore give recent specimens of these medallions drawn by my niece, which refer to two of the years after she had become my companion.

The picture of 1900 is a view on the Nile, and that of 1903 contains the insignia of the late Pope, in memory of a function in Rome at which we were present; also a picture of the breeding-place of sea birds at the Farn Islands, Northumberland, which we visited. The legends round these medallions hardly require explanation, except that An. Photo. stands for Animal Photography. They are—1900, An. Photo., Venice, Greece, Boer War, Egypt. 1903, Rome, Ischia, Farn Isles, Peppard.

A main reason for giving so full a description of such trifling matters is that the Dacota method may be serviceable in more than one way. It suggests an excellent plan for competition in Art schools, where the choice of two or three characteristics of some particular year might be submitted to the students, and prizes given to those who designed the most appropriate medallions.

CHAPTER XIV

GEOGRAPHY AND EAST AFRICA

Burton and Speke—Speke and Grant—Death of Speke—
Livingstone and Stanley—Geographical incidents

THE travels of the successive explorers of Eastern Africa who started from the Zanzibar Coast were watched by geographers with the keenest interest. I was in one way or another somewhat closely connected with the principal actors, and may therefore speak about them with propriety. The information that first drew general attention to this part of Africa was the startling announcement that a snow-topped mountain, Kilimandjaro, had been seen from a distance by the missionaries Krapf and Rebmann on their journeys from Mombas, where they were stationed. Their information was fiercely criticised. It was disbelieved wholly by some, and only partially credited by many others. In addition to this, the missionaries had transmitted reports of a vast Central African lake, based on the collated testimonies of many native travellers. Mr. Erhardt communicated a memoir on this lake to the Royal Geographical Society, and I, who had most to do with their then newly established *Proceedings*, had it with its accompanying map inserted in one of its early numbers. The map was an amazing production and very hypothetical, but the

data from which it was constructed made it clear
that an exploration of those regions would be a
highly promising undertaking. I myself had been
strongly urged to investigate the neighbourhood of
Kilimandjaro, but felt insufficiently restored to health
to undertake the task. An expedition was at length
set on foot in 1856 under the command of Captain
Burton (1821-1890), with J. H. Speke (1827-1864)
as second, for which I myself drafted the instructions.
It accomplished great things, namely, the discovery of
the two lakes, Tanganyika and Victoria Nyanza, but
at the painful cost of a serious breach of friendship
between its leaders. Burton was a man of eccentric
genius and tastes, orientalised in character and
thoroughly Bohemian. He was a born linguist, and
ever busy in collecting minute information as to
manners and habits. Speke, on the other hand, was
a thorough Briton, conventional, solid, and resolute.
Two such characters were naturally unsympathetic.
On reaching Tanganyika, Burton became seriously ill
and temporarily unfitted for travel ; his eyes, too, were
badly inflamed and gave him great trouble. Principally owing to Burton's restless spirit of inquiry, the
existence and position of the lake now known as the
Victoria Nyanza had been ascertained. Burton was
unable to go to it ; therefore Speke went as his deputy,
and so came upon what was suspected by him, and
has proved afterwards to be a headwater of the Nile.
Of course Speke got the credit, for without him the
lake would not have then been reached, but the dis-
appointment to Burton at being superseded in solving
the problem of ages by discovering the source of the
Nile was very bitter and very natural. Burton

brought back, as purely his own work, a most elaborate account of all the tribes he had met by the way, the close accuracy of which has been testified to by succeeding travellers. Only one of his numerous notebooks came under my own careful examination, as already mentioned, and I was astonished at its minuteness. I may mention the occasion, which was this.

The Society for the Propagation of the Gospel were considering the propriety of establishing a mission station at Zanzibar, and desired fuller information about the island than they possessed. In the end they invited me to give a lecture, to which I consented, after talking with Burton, who had been asked and refused, but who very kindly offered me the full use of his original notebook written when in Zanzibar. An elaborate account which he had based on it for publication had been lost. I had no first-hand information about the place, but had known Erhardt and others who knew it well, so was able to compile a respectable description, which was published in the *Mission Field*, June 1, 1861. The notes made by Burton were written in a fine clear hand and most elaborate in detail. He told me that he often used a board with parallel wires, such as are made for the use of the blind, to write notes, unseen, in the night-time.

The next expedition was under Captain Speke, with whom Captain Grant (1827–1892) was associated. They were to take up the quest at the point on the Victoria Nyanza where Speke had reached it, and to travel onwards. This was done, and I may say that the attachment of Grant to

Speke was most remarkable for its loyalty and intensity. They were fine manly fellows, and I can see them now in my mind's eye, as they came to take a final leave, when I knocked two nails into the side of a cupboard as they stood side by side with their backs to it, to mark their respective heights and as a memento of them when away. As is well known, they followed the Nile, not however without a break, from the Lake into Egypt. This break, and the hypothetical placement of the "Mountains of the Moon," whose position Speke saw reason to modify in a second map, gave an opening to criticism of which bitter use was made. Coming down the Nile, Speke and Grant met Captain, afterwards Sir Samuel, Baker (1821–1893) and his large party going up it, and were able to give him timely and valuable information. I do not speak more of Sir Samuel's magnificent work, because it did not fall closely within my own ken, but will conclude what has to be said about Burton and Speke.

In the year 1864 the British Association met at Bath, at which Burton was to read a paper severely criticising Speke's work. Speke was staying in the neighbourhood with a shooting party, and was invited to take part in the discussion. It is the custom that on each morning, a little before the President and Committee of the several Sections of the British Association take their seats, they meet in a separate room to discuss matters that require immediate settlement, and to select the papers that are to be read on the following day. On the present occasion this business had been finished, and Sir James Alexander was urging that the Council of the Association should be requested by the Committee to bring Captain Speke's services to the notice of Government and to ask for their appropriate recognition, when a messenger brought a letter for the President, Sir Roderick Murchison. He motioned to the Secretary, who was seated at his left hand, to read it, while he, the President, continued to attend to Sir James. The countenance of the Secretary clearly showed that the letter contained serious news. Sir James Alexander went on speaking, the letter was in the meantime circulated and read by each in turn, including Captain Burton, who sat opposite to me, and I got it the last, or almost the last of all before the President. It was to say that Speke had accidentally shot himself dead, by drawing his gun after him while getting over a hedge.

Burton had many great and endearing qualities, with others of which perhaps the most curious was his pleasure in dressing himself, so to speak, in wolf's clothing, in order to give an idea that he was worse than he really was. I attended his funeral at the Roman Catholic Cemetery near Sheen. It had been arranged by his widow, Lady Burton, a devoted Catholic, and was crowded with her Catholic friends. I did not see more than three geographers among them, of whom Lord Northbrook, a former President of the Society, was one. From pure isolation, we two kept together the whole time. There were none of Burton's old associates. It was a ceremony quite alien to anything that I could conceive him to care for.

Anyhow, I was glad to be instrumental in procuring a Government Pension of £300 a year for Lady Burton, and in this way. At a meeting of the Council of the Royal Geographical Society, Sir Mountstuart E. Grant Duff, the then President, said that private information had reached him (of which he mentioned some details) that Government would be disposed to grant a pension to Lady Burton if a good case could be made out relating to Burton's services to science, and if the Council of the Society were to back it. Would any one undertake to carry this through? No one answered, so he addressed himself to me personally, asking if I would. I expressed a cordial desire to help, but feeling at the moment too ignorant of the views of competent authorities concerning Burton's linguistic knowledge (on which much emphasis had been laid), and of much else that might with advantage be advanced in his favour, was unable to answer off-hand, but willingly undertook to inquire and report. This I did, asking the opinions of many, with the result that Burton's knowledge of vernacular Arabic and other languages was considered to be unequalled, but not his classical knowledge of them, and that it was better to rest his claims on his wide discursiveness rather than on any one specified performance. I followed this advice, and my Report formed the basis of the proposed application, which in due course gained its end. My own acquaintance with Lady Burton was slight, and my memories of her husband refer chiefly to his unmarried days.

Several of us subscribed to have a public memorial of Speke, and obtained a plot in Kensington Gardens to place it. It now stands in the form of an obelisk, by the side of the broad gravel walk leading northwards from the Albert Memorial. There was much difficulty in selecting an inscription which should not arouse criticism, for there were still those who maintained with Burton that Speke had not discovered the true source of the Nile. Lord Houghton solved the difficulty by simplifying the proposed legend to "Victoria Nyanza and the Nile," which words the obelisk now bears.

Speke, Burton, Grant, Baker, Livingstone, and Stanley are all gone; I wish it could be arranged to make a joint and interesting memorial of our great African explorers in the plot where Speke's obelisk now stands in neglected solitariness. It would not require more than two or three extra yards on either side, parallel to the Grand Walk, and the same in depth, to give room for this, and to allow of the growth of a few hardy plants suggestive of tropical vegetation, with pathways between them. England has done so very much for African geography that she ought to bring the fact home to the national conscience. When Burton died, and again when Stanley died, I made the suggestion that a memorial should be erected by the side of that of Speke, or that appropriate inscriptions should be added, but I heard on good authority that it would be most distasteful to the representatives of both Speke and Grant to do so. Many long years have since passed, and it may be hoped that hard feelings will soften in time and permit what many like myself would consider a laudable and pious act.

I have mentioned the names of Livingstone and Stanley, and here again I have something to say.

The popular opinion has been that Livingstone was left to his fate without adequate care on the part of his countrymen to succour him, and that he was rescued owing to the zeal of the proprietor of an American newspaper and the hardihood of his employee, Mr., afterwards Sir Henry, Stanley.

I was on the Council of the Royal Geographical Society during all the time in question, and can testify to our extreme desire to help Livingstone, but in his later years he had become difficult to meddle with. He had a brusque resentment against anything that might be construed into patronage, feeling, as I understood, that he had been over-much "exploited" by his admirers. There was great fear among those in the Council who knew him better than I did, that he might be annoyed at any attempt to relieve him, and would resent it yet more bitterly than Emin Bey subsequently resented Stanley's compulsory relief. Again, there was no reason to suppose Livingstone to be in serious want. He was thoroughly accustomed to natives of the widely dispersed Bantu race, among whom he probably then was. He travelled without a large party or other encumbrance, so that the favour of even a single chief, such as he might reasonably expect to gain, would amply suffice for his wants. Besides this, he had not cared to write, and there was no knowing where a man like him might be, who had already walked right across Africa and back again. So whenever the question was discussed formally, or otherwise, it seemed better to defer action till some intelligence of his wishes and whereabouts had been received. In the meantime, acting upon his own data and reasonings, the proprietor of the *New York Herald* sent the expedition, whose progress is described in Stanley's book, and which ended so successfully for Livingstone. One wishes that the whole thing could have been effected with less secrecy in the beginning, and less ostentation and comparison of Americans and English to the prejudice of the latter.

When the box of native make that contained Livingstone's remains was brought to England by Cameron, it was deposited in the rooms of the Royal Geographical Society, and a most pathetic sight it was. Many wished to be present at its opening, but Sir Bartle Frere, then the President, determined that no opportunity should be given for journalistic description, and refusing to himself the painful gratification of witnessing it, limited the spectators to very few. Sir William Fergusson, the great operator, was deputed to dissect the arm-bone at the place where the lion had broken it, as means of identification. I forget who were the others. They included some members of Livingstone's family, and Mr. Webb of Newstead Abbey, a great sportsman and friend of Livingstone, familiar with the locality of the injured bone. I think these were all.

The pathos of Livingstone's interment in Westminster Abbey was painfully marred by the use of a conventional coffin and other funeral upholstery. Had he been buried in the box rudely made by natives, that had conveyed his remains from the far interior to the Coast and told its own tale, the ceremony would have been incomparably more touching.

I should have an ungrateful task if I had to speak at length of Stanley's travels down the Congo. His journey was first described at Brighton at 'a large meeting of the Geographical Section of the British Association, of which I was the President. The ex-Emperor and Empress of the French were among the audience. So much mystery had been preserved beforehand about it that none of us had a conception of what was coming, which is quite contrary to usual procedure. Mr. Stanley had other interests than geography. He was essentially a journalist aiming at producing sensational articles, and it was feared from the newspaper letters he had already written that he might utilise the opportunity in ways inappropriate to the British Association. However, the meeting went off without more misadventure than a single interference on my part, but under some tension. I will not enter further into this.

It is highly necessary to the credit of a Society that its Council should, as a rule, and always when there is any misgiving, exact that the papers about to be read should be referred to experts and favourably reported on. The Society gives a pulpit, as it were, to the speaker, and in its turn has a right to exact precautions that these advantages should not be abused. I cannot understand to this day how that strange individual, Rougemont, obtained permission to read his fantastic, perhaps half-hallucinatory paper about the coral reefs and treasures in Australia before the British Association. Putting every other improbability for the moment to one side, the "Art-of-Travel" impossibilities in his story, as in the construction of his raft, would have made me scrutinise with a very wary eye all the rest that he said.

I may mention a ludicrous but discreditable incident at a meeting of the Geographical Section of the British Association, which the timely reference of a paper before it was allowed to be read might perhaps have prevented. It was in Cambridge in 1862. Sir Roderick Murchison had been nominated as President of the Section, but fell ill just before the meeting, and I was nominated and elected in his stead. Mr. W., a Fellow of King's College, had been entrusted with the MSS of a recently deceased Oriental Professor, including a memoir on the inscription upon a stone near Aberdeen. It was well known to antiquarians, and had long puzzled them; the Professor declared it to be Phenician. The title of the Geographical Section then included the already obsolete words "and Philology," so it was technically correct that the paper should be read there. Mr. W. called on me, most desirous, as he said, for the honour of the Association that a paper by so distinguished a University Professor should be read before it. I demurred, saying that it was doubtful whether a single member of the Committee knew a word of Phenician, or were able to discuss its merits. In reply to the question whether that language was really sufficiently well understood to justify a translation, he assured me it was, and mentioned two great works in German, of which I knew nothing, in proof. I still hesitated, but said that if the Committee should agree to accept the communication, I would offer no objection, and they did agree, under the spell of Mr. W.'s eloquence; so the paper was accepted.

When I took the chair the next day, the zeal of Mr. W. was conspicuous in the diagrams he had hung round the walls like a frieze. Each diagram contained a representation of one of the 35 or so characters. Below it was its Hebrew equivalent, and below all was a free translation, in which I noted there were more words than there were letters in the original, and my misgivings grew. The paper proved to be long and tedious, as papers on antiquarian subjects often are, and the audience melted away. At length the reporters could stand it no longer, and most fortunately left also. The audience was then reduced to a mere handful of persons, and when the paper was finished Mr. C. rose, who was a recognised authority on Greek manuscripts, and said that he had no pretensions in respect to a knowledge of Phenician, but as a mere question of resemblance it struck him that the characters (which he pointed out) seemed to him less like the alleged Hebrew equivalents than to the letters forming the Greek word ALEXANDROS. There was no doubt he was right, and the small audience tittered. In the meantime the Secretary, a well-known antiquarian, became more and more excited, and jumped up as soon as Mr. C. had sat down, and exclaimed, "Phenician!" (Contemptuous grunt.) "Greek!" (Another different and equally contemptuous grunt.) "Can you not read 'HIC JACET'?" and I must say his reading seemed to me the least forced of the three. I think all of us felt utterly ashamed. Had the reporters been present, the fun that could have been made by the newspapers out of the incident would have been a disaster to the credit of the Association. The Reports of that

14

meeting in the Journal of the Association have been
so toned down that no one would suspect from
reading them what really took place.

My connection with the Royal Geographical
Society was a long one, and I served for many years
on its Council, but the time came when my deafness
was an insuperable bar to utility. On Sir Clement
Markham becoming President, he very kindly offered
me the vacant post of Trusteeship, which carries with
it a permanent place on the Council, and is not
practically a burden; but I was compelled to decline,
and have taken no direct part in furthering its
interests since that time, but have confined my work
to other pursuits.

I had a hand in many actions of the Society.
In its earlier years there was good cause of complaint as to the method in which the Society was
being worked. Mr. Spottiswoode and myself were
the Joint Hon. Secretaries, and the necessary reform
was only brought about by our simultaneous resignation on the ground that our urgent remonstrances
were shelved by the then President. It was agreed
between us that, to save appearances, Spottiswoode
should continue to act for a short time longer, being
earnestly requested to do so.

In due course a new Assistant Secretary was
appointed, and after some failures to secure a man
capable of worthily filling that important post, we
had the good fortune to find and appoint Mr. H. W.
Bates (1825-1892). He was remarkably well informed
on geographical matters, had been a considerable
traveller in companionship with Alfred Russell
Wallace in South America, and was one of the first

to show that the mimicry of insects was developed as a means of protection. I look back with the greatest pleasure to my long and close association with Mr. Bates in the work of the Royal Geographical Society. His death was a great loss and a great blow to many friends. He and another friend only just dead were exceptionally slow in finding the exact word they wished to use. Yet both of them, in despite of slowness of utterance, succeeded in giving an exact notion of their views in a briefer time than any one else I can think of. Their sentences were a standing lesson to avoid superfluity of words when making explanations.

One new and successful attempt that I set on foot was the intervention of the Royal Geographical Society in geographical education. I began with public schools, having talked the matter well over with W. F. Farrar, then a master at Harrow. He thought the idea quite feasible. Then I had much help from the Hon. G. Brodrick, and encouragement from my brother-in-law, George Butler, then Headmaster of Liverpool College, who shared the belief of Dr. Arnold in the value of geography, if properly taught. That was by no means the general view, which was rather that geography lent itself to cram more easily than any other subject, and that it was hardly possible to set real problems in it, that should compel thought.

The upshot of all was, that the Royal Geographical Society offered an annual gold medal to be competed for by boys belonging to a considerable number of invited schools—in fact to all of the public schools properly so called. The examiners for the medal were annually appointed by the Society. The medal in the first year was won by the present Provost of Glasgow University, Dr. Donald Macalister; that in the second by George Grey Butler, son of my brother-in-law, and for many years Chief Examiner of the Education Office. The medals were continued for some years, but they were said to do incidental harm by tempting the masters of schools of the second rank to divert their best scholars to geography in order to gain *éclat* for the school, thereby interfering with their career in the more generally recognised and bread-winning studies of ordinary education.

The medals were therefore discontinued, and the efforts of the Society were directed to the Universities. I helped in this at first, but Mr. Brodrick and Mr. Douglas Freshfield and others took the matter more thoroughly in hand. After a little while, Mr. MacKinder, now Head of the Department of Economics of the University of London, applied for and gained the post of "Reader" in Geography in the University of Oxford, and he rapidly improved the quality of geographical teaching. General, afterwards Sir Richard Strachey, then President of the Royal Geographical Society, inaugurated the introduction of geography into the University of Cambridge by four lectures. I believe the subject has now gained a firm footing in both Universities. To say the least of it, a thorough knowledge of classical lands, such as can be conveyed by first-rate maps, models, and diagrams, must be helpful to classical students.

CHAPTER XV

BRITISH ASSOCIATION

Its function and merits—My connection with and indebtedness to it—
Sir William Grove

I HAVE been connected with the British Association more or less intimately during many years,
four times as President of a Section or " Department,"
once as deliverer of a Lecture, a member of its Council
almost from my return from South Africa, then from
1863 to 1867 as its General Secretary, and afterwards
as an official member of its Council.

The Association affords what is often the most
appropriate means of ventilating new ideas. It can
create a Committee with or without a grant of money,
giving to its proposer the title either of Chairman or
Secretary, which clothes him with an authority that
an unknown individual would lack, when making
inquiries of public bodies at home or abroad. It
also provides him with colleagues to discuss and
criticise results before they are finally published. A
good example of these advantages may be found in
the Report of the Anthropometric Committee, which
has afforded standard data up to the present time, for
the chief physical characteristics of the inhabitants of
the British Isles. The hard work carried on in its

name was mainly performed by Mr. Roberts, its Secretary, who wrote a book afterwards in which his results were included. He was greatly helped by Sir Rawson Rawson, who was a member of the Committee. The rest of the Committee did little more than discuss subjects and methods, but even that little was helpful. I was its Chairman, but claim no more than an insignificant share in its success.

Again, many years later, in 1888–1889, I was desirous that a proposal of mine should be seriously considered, of awarding marks for physical efficiency in competitive literary examinations. I read my memoir, the Association took it up, and the results of some experiments at Eton and many valuable communications were received in reply, including a careful minute from a high authority of the War Office. These convinced me that although the proposal had strong *a priori* claims to consideration, it did not merit acceptance; so it was dropped.

Many other examples of a similar kind could be quoted, some failing, most succeeding. The British Association in its early days was of still greater value than it is now. At that time locomotion was tedious, and the numerous scientific societies of the present day that issue frequent publications had not come into existence. Local men of science who had been socially overlooked were brought forward to their rightful position by its means. It has frequently happened that an improvement in a town was furthered or even initiated through a visit of the British Association. The papers read there and discussions upon them are not the most important part of its work,

The Reports of the Committees appointed by it are as a rule far more valuable than ordinary memoirs, and so are the Presidential Addresses, but perhaps the most useful function of the British Association lies in causing persons who are occupied in different branches of science, and who rarely meet elsewhere, to be jostled together and to become well acquainted. Its organisation was a wonderful feat, for it was created upon paper, and has required nothing ever since beyond a little easing and extension here and there.

The plan of one meeting is as like that of another as two Roman camps. On entering the reception-room, time seems to have stood still, for the same familiar faces are seen in the same places; the placards that refer to letters, to programmes, to excursions and to the other multifarious business of the Association, are similarly arranged, so after the experience of a single year a member finds himself at home on every future occasion. But the sustained racket of it is great, and I found it too long continued for my own nerves. I had a complete breakdown when I was General Secretary, which compelled me to resign what otherwise was a very pleasant post: it would have been playing with death had I continued to hold it.

My period of office began at the time when the old order of supreme management by a few magnates was giving way to a more democratic government. Its earlier and distinguished members, such as Sabine and Murchison, had naturally so much weight in Council that when they were active and in close touch with their juniors their opinions were sure to prevail. So the duty of a General Secretary in those days was to consult a few of the more eminent persons at first, and again at the close, with the almost complete assurance that whatever names were suggested with their approval, whether as President, Presidents of Sections, or Lecturers, would be accepted by the Council. These consultations with many able men were very instructive. They showed the striking differences between the points of view from which original minds may regard the same topic. Unconventionality seems to be a marked characteristic of such minds; I have noticed it elsewhere and very often.

Among the features of the Association meetings was the "Red Lion" Club, in which clever buffoonery was freely indulged. It was instituted by Edward Forbes (who was rather before my time, and whom I never had the pleasure of knowing). The governing idea was that its members were really lions, acquainted with one another, who had met by chance, during their prowls, in a town where strange proceedings were in progress. The speakers described what they had witnessed, speaking as it were from a superior and leonine pedestal.

I have only attended two of these meetings; in one the buffoonery of Monckton Milnes (afterwards Lord Houghton) was of a first-class order. So also was the humorous sarcasm of Professor W. K. Clifford (1845-1879), the mathematician, also the mimicry of Mr., afterwards Sir, W. Chandler Roberts Austen, an accomplishment that it amazed me to find he possessed. Subsequently, on talking about it, he made the shrewd remark that a useful way of understanding a man's character was to mimic his ways, and that he frequently mimicked new acquaintances in his imagination for that purpose. This seems to me very subtle and true. If we want to raise in our minds a quick sympathy, say, for a friend's tale of grief, we instinctively screw our features into an expression of sorrow, and the required emotion follows almost as a matter of course. It is needless to dwell on the existence of accomplished hypocrites, who screw their faces without the slightest desire to evoke the feeling they appear to express.

My last attempt to utilise the British Association failed owing to my increasing age and infirmities. I wanted to methodise the preservation of records of pedigree stock to serve as data for future inquiries, and wrote memoirs (147, 148) on the subject, in which I showed that photographs of animals, taken under certain simple and feasible conditions, afforded means of calculating their measurements with considerable exactitude, as tested by myself on horses. I took great pains, and was given facilities for photography at one of the great horse shows at the Agricultural Hall. The attempt was perfectly successful in essentials, though several alterations of detail were suggested by that experience, but the effort was far too much for my health. Most of these exhibitions are held during the winter months, and, being now very liable to bronchitis, I found it quite impossible to endure the draughty passages and other discomforts during that season. I could not delegate it to my satisfaction, so was obliged, to my great regret, to abandon all further attempts in that direction, otherwise some useful work might have been done.

The hospitality afforded during the visits of the British Association is always great, but I fear often onerous and unwelcome to the hosts, however carefully their courtesy may conceal such feelings. I have to be grateful for many apparently cordial receptions of this kind. One of the simplest and yet most effective was given at Birmingham by Charles Evans, afterwards Canon of Worcester, but then Headmaster of King Edward's School, where we had been schoolfellows. The building had abundant accommodation, and he got together a very distinguished party. The food provided was plain, but well cooked and plenty of it. A large luncheon table with cold meat was at the disposal of any of the guests who wished to bring friends with him. There was no display, but abundance everywhere, and perfect freedom. Few, except masters of large public schools, could have arranged and carried out such a programme as well and easily as he did.

I have been asked twice to act as President of the Association. On the first occasion my name was formally proposed by the officers of the Association to the Council at which I was then sitting, but I was conscious of my limitations in respect to health, and with many thanks declined, even though some pressure was kindly put on me. On the second occasion, and much more lately, I was actually nominated in my absence, with the offer of most thoughtful arrangements to diminish fatigue, but I had again to decline still more emphatically than before, as my powers of work and endurance had in the meantime become smaller and my deafness had increased.

It is an office that affords an excellent stage from

which to address the public, because the Presidential Address is usually printed more or less in full, and commented on in the leading newspapers, while long extracts from it are given in all of them. It is also an office that carries considerable responsibilities, and one where very useful work may be done by its holder. It requires, however, a more genial speaker at ceremonial meetings than myself, where I simply hate having to come forward. My infirmities have prevented me from attending any of the meetings of the British Association for many past years.

The Addresses of the Presidents of the Association differ much, as might be expected, in interest and importance. One that gained unusual attention, owing to its simplicity and sterling value, was that of Sir William Grove, of whom I will take this occasion to speak.

The late Justice Sir William Grove (1811–1896) is one of those to whom I owe most for sympathy in my inquiries, for helpful criticisms, and for long-continued friendship. His early work as chemist and electrician, his masterly book on the "Correlation of Physical Forces," when the idea was novel that heat, electricity, force, etc., were convertible into one another, and his resolute and successful labours to raise the worth of the Royal Society, promoted him easily into the very first rank of scientific men. At a subsequent time, when he was seriously considering whether or no he should abandon the legal profession, he was unexpectedly promoted to a judgeship, the object of the appointment being to secure a judge capable of dealing with the technicalities of Patent cases. The result, as he told me, and as

I have heard elsewhere, was that not a single Patent case was brought into his Court. Presumably he was dreaded by both sides on account of his searching questions.

It was his practice to rent a large house and shooting during the autumn vacation, and he most hospitably asked my wife and myself to make long visits to him during three autumns. On the first of these an incident occurred which might have ended, but which confirmed, his friendship; namely, the sudden and most severe illness of my wife. The prompt and continuous care shown to her by every member of the family at that time in the house, called for my warmest gratitude. Sir William's second son, who was then a young man, but now a highly distinguished officer, rode several miles to the nearest town, summoned the doctor, and brought back a bag of ice on horseback. Sir William's daughter, Mrs. Hills, nursed her with every possible care for some weeks, until she was sufficiently convalescent to bear removal. Recovery at length ensued, but serious weakness remained, which continued up to her death, nearly forty years later.

One of Sir William Grove's achievements was that of being the main agent, in 1847, of changing the character of the governing body of the Royal Society. It had become too aristocratic, dating from the long presidency of Sir Joseph Banks, and its elections were guided by favour. The struggle between two opposed principles became one between the supporters of different candidates. It was a near contest, but the reform party gained the day. They signalised the memory of their triumph by founding the " Philosophical Club " for the use of the reformers, in distinction to the older Royal Society Club. Both were merely dining clubs that met on the evenings of Royal Society meetings, and they were held on alternate weeks. I, like many others, was a member of both. The members of the Philosophical Club were limited in number to forty-seven, as a reminder of the date of its foundation. This controversy is now quite obsolete, and the two clubs have become amalgamated.

Another very important reform that Sir William Grove carried through on this occasion, was to limit the number of elections to the Royal Society to fifteen in each year, it having been found that fifteen annual elections corresponded to the losses by death ; so the average number of Fellows would thereby remain unchanged. It was the firm opinion of Sir William Grove, which I fully share, that the only feasible way of keeping a standard of qualification from being lowered is to limit the number of selected candidates, for it is scarcely possible to define a standard in words. The question has lately been raised whether fifteen is not too small a number now. On that point I have no up-to-date knowledge that would justify an opinion, but when I served on the Council of the Royal Society many years ago, and the number of candidates averaged little more than fifty, it happened that about twelve out of the fifteen were elected at the first ballot, but there was often considerable delay in fixing upon the remainder. So it seemed that fifteen was a somewhat high number then, but this year there were as many as a hundred candidates. Certainly no one has been elected since

1847 to the Fellowship of the Royal Society who has not done a large amount of sound work, and the credit of the Society has been continuously maintained at a high level.

Many persons imagine in their innocence that when any one appends letters to his name testifying to his being a Fellow of one or more learned societies that he is necessarily a scientific expert. This is true for hardly any other society than the Royal. In all others the letters show little more than that the person who uses them is sufficiently interested in the sciences in question to make it worth his while to pay an annual subscription. I have served on the Councils of many of these societies, and can only recall two cases in which a proposed candidate was *not* elected. In the one, the man had been imprisoned for a grave offence; in the other, he was a wastrel well known to avoid paying his debts.

Many pleasant days have been spent by me under the hospitable roof of Mr. and Mrs. Hills. She was, as already mentioned, a daughter of Sir William Grove, and has been one of my closest friends ever since the terrible illness of my wife mentioned above. Her husband, Judge Hills, died very recently. He was a judge in Alexandria, where he resided during the larger part of the year, but returned every autumn to exercise hospitality in England.

The conversational powers of Sir William Grove were remarkable when he was sufficiently excited to show them to advantage. One evening, before going to a distant meeting of the British Association, he, Professor Huxley, and myself, dined together at the same table at the Athenæum. Never, before or since, have I heard such rapid and continuous conversational sword-play. The sudden thrusts, the quick parries and counter-thrusts, were extraordinarily dexterous. I regret my inability to recall more than this general impression, without any of the actual sentences.

CHAPTER XVI

KEW OBSERVATORY AND METEOROLOGY

General Sir E. Sabine—Sextants and watches—Now merged into National Physical Laboratory — Meteorological Committee, subsequently Council of the Board of Trade—Self-recording instruments, reduction of their tracings—Henry Smith

AN early friendship that exercised great influence in shaping my future scientific life was that of General, afterwards Sir Edward, Sabine, R.A., and President of the Royal Society. At the time of which I am speaking he was its Treasurer; he also held two offices, in both of which I was his successor after some years. They were the Chairmanship of the Kew Observatory and the Secretaryship of the British Association, as already mentioned. General Sabine (1788–1883) devoted himself to the study of magnetism, to its geographical distribution and its periodic and irregular variations. He had joined an Arctic Expedition for the express purpose of making exact magnetical observations in high latitudes, and he had inspired zealous and capable men, at various stations about the globe, to establish a system of continuous and comparable observations. This involved careful examinations of the refined instruments about to be employed, and of instruction in their use. Means for doing all this were established by him at Kew.

The history of the Kew Observatory is far too complicated to be fully described here. It was first instituted owing to the desire of many of the foremost men in physical science, in the early days of the British Association, to have access to a place where physical experiments might be made, and new instruments tested. The Observatory stands in the Old Deer Park, Richmond, adjoining the Kew Gardens. It was originally built for the amusement of George III., while he was more or less insane, and it was begged for by the philosophers and allotted by Government to their use. Its maintenance was defrayed by considerable grants annually voted by the British Association, that mounted at one time to as much as £600. This became far too onerous a charge for their means, so various changes were made in its government and maintenance. At length it fell into the hands of the Royal Society, and was managed by a committee appointed by that body from among its members. It paid its way by charges made for standardising instruments, supplemented by occasional grants. Later on, the interest of a handsome endowment of £10,000 made by Mr. J. P. Gassiott, of whom more presently, placed it in a fairly firm position.

At the time when Sir Edward Sabine caused me to become a member of the Managing Committee, the Kew Observatory had obtained, through his exertions, a high and wide reputation for the exactness of the observations made there, and it had become the place where the outfits of all magnetic observatories, English and foreign, were standardised, and where intending observers were instructed. It was, in fact, the Central

15

Magnetic Observatory of the world. It held an almost equally strong position in respect to the delicate pendulum apparatus by which the force of gravity is measured at different places on the globe, and again with regard to standard thermometers and meteorological instruments generally. Its Managers were eager to extend its operations to any kind of self-paying scientific experiment. Any person desirous of having a new invention tested could get it well done there at a cost that just repaid the trouble, subject, of course, to the permission of the Managing Committee and to the leisure of the staff.

One of the first things that I busied myself about, when I joined it, was to establish means for standardising sextants and other angular instruments. The cheaper kinds of these were unnecessarily bad, and many of the more costly were by no means so good as they should be for their price. I thought at first of utilising heliostats to give sharp points of reference by adjusting minute mirrors at distant points, flashing the sun on to them from larger mirrors at the Observatory, and using the return flashes as the points of reference. One of these small mirrors was fixed to the south obelisk, within a cage which may still be there. This arrangement was so far successful that beautiful stars of light were produced in response to flashes from the Observatory, but the uncertainty of sunshine in our climate showed the method to be of little practical value. Then Messrs. Cooke of York, who were among the foremost makers of large telescopes, devised an arrangement with collimators and artificial light. They made one for Kew, which is contained within a small dark room, and has acted perfectly, to a considerable improvement in the make of the cheaper sextants.

Another thing that I did was to contrive an apparatus by which thermometers could be rapidly and yet very accurately verified, and by which from ten to twenty thousand clinical thermometers are still annually tested. Mr. De la Rue gave me help in devising this. The few pence gained on each of these many thermometers amounted to a respectable sum, and confirmed the solvency of the institution, whose margin of profit over loss was always small and had been precarious. We were thus in a better position to extend our work and to add to our instruments, and we did so.

Another operation which I was among the first, if not the first, to suggest, was the rating of watches. This has been a real success. The performances of watches, when we first took the matter in hand, was by no means proportionate to their cost, more than one highly ornamented and expensive time-keeper failing to obtain a class-place equal to that of others of much inferior pretensions. Now a Kew certificated watch has a special and recognised value, and the makers of valuable watches are far more on their mettle than they used to be.

The influence of the Kew verifications as time went on extended in many other directions, as by testing the performance of telescopes and opera-glasses supplied to the army and navy, in order to ascertain whether their capabilities were up to the specified standard. Mariners' compasses of complicated and delicate construction were also dealt with. A beautiful apparatus devised by Sir Wm. Abney and Major

Leonard Darwin was subsequently set up to test photographic lenses, and to enable appropriate certificates to be given them.

So the institution throve, and was a "going concern," but it was wholly unequal in its scale to the rapidly growing requirements of the day. This feeling found expression in the Anniversary Address to the British Association in 1895, by my cousin Sir Douglas Galton; powerful support was given to his suggestions and efforts, and finally the Kew Committee was merged into the much larger and more important National Physical Observatory, under the directorship of Mr. Glazebrook, which swallowed at a single gulp the whole of our thrifty savings.

I look back with pleasure to my long connection with the Kew Observatory, for its Committee always consisted of very capable men, who gave time without stint to the discussion of the new questions which continually arose, and which could be answered by experts only.

Mr. Gassiott (1797–1877), of whom I have spoken, succeeded Sir Edward Sabine as its Chairman. He was remarkable for solid sense and business acumen, and played a considerable part in the work of the Royal Society. His experiments on electric discharges in quasi-vacuo were very beautiful, and thought highly of at the time. He was a striking instance of the combination of scientific research with the direction of an important business, for he was one of the principal wine merchants, and said to be the largest importer of port wine in London.

Another instance of the same combination was his successor in the same office, Mr. Warren De la

Rue (1815–1889), the famous stationer, whose mechanical ingenuity, artistic taste, and business habits were most valuable. I have served with him on various Councils, where his help and influence were always felt. I shall have shortly again to speak of him. The pretty Kew monogram was his design.

I became Chairman of the Observatory in succession to Mr. De la Rue in 1889, and held that post until 1901, when it ceased to be an independent body. The Observatory has been fortunate in its particularly able Superintendents, Sir Francis Ronalds of electric fame, Dr. Balfour Stewart, subsequently Professor at Owen's College, Manchester, Mr. Whipple, a man of considerable natural gifts, and Dr. Cree, now President of the Physical Society. Many members of their staff were very trustworthy and valuable officials.

Much interest in the laws of the weather had been aroused long previously to 1860, and it was then clearly understood by those who studied them that future progress depended on securing numerous observations made at the same moment, during many years, at stations scattered over a wide area. The popular book of Maury in America and the writings of Admiral FitzRoy drew attention to this need; and Le Verrier, the French astronomer, issued daily charts of the Atlantic, based on such observations as he could obtain from ships and coast stations. But these were so few compared to the area over which they were scattered, and so unequally distributed, that too much guess-work was needed to combine their information into coherent and reasonable systems.

The only fairly well understood feature in those times, of movements of the air, was that of the cyclone, or the huge tropical whirlwind carrying destruction with it. It had been observed that when these whirlwinds occurred in the northern hemisphere they circled in the opposite direction to that of the hands of a clock, round a centre of low barometric pressure, and therefore round an area of uprush of heated and moist air, accompanied, as it would be, with heavy rains. This circling was justly attributed to the spherical shape of the earth in combination with its easterly rotation. An indraught, coming from the direction of the equator, was impressed with an excess of easterly movement, and one from the nearest pole with a deficiency; in other words, the latter had a westerly movement relatively to the place of observation. The observed twist was the necessary result of their coming together. An opposite direction of twist occurred, as would have been expected, in the two hemispheres; in the southern one, the whirlwind circled round the area of uprush in the same direction as the hands of a clock. It was also surmised, that the direction of the wind in ordinary weather was everywhere governed by the same twisting conditions as in the terrible cyclones of the tropics, where it had first been noticed.

I felt greatly disposed to examine more closely into these movements of the air, and it occurred to me that enough help for the purpose might be obtained in Europe from existing observatories, light-houses, and ships in the neighbouring seas. They would enable an experimental map to be made thrice daily for a month, in which the observations should be at stations much closer together than those in the maps of Le Verrier, and yet would embrace a sufficiently large area to exhibit the details of a complete weather system. I took a great deal of pains about this, and finally succeeded in 1862 in obtaining what was wanted.

It was with no small eagerness that I set to work to map out the data. The month began under cyclonic conditions; then, to my intense delight, as that system passed by, it was followed by a condition of affairs the exact opposite to the cyclone, and supplementary to it. The cyclone, as already said, is an uprush of air, associated with a low barometer and clouds, due to the hot and moist air becoming chilled as it rose, and it was fed, as just described, by an indraught with an anti-clock-ways twist in the northern hemisphere. That which I now found, during the latter part of the month in question, was a downrush of air associated with a high barometer and a clear sky, and with an outflow having a clock-ways twist. The one system was clearly supplementary to the other. So in the memoir I contributed on the subject to the Royal Society [16], I called the newly discovered system an "Anti-cyclone." Speaking broadly, the whole of the movements of the lower strata of the air are now looked upon as a combination of cyclones and anti-cyclones, which feed one another. The name established itself at once, and is now familiar.

The present daily weather charts of the *Times*, from data supplied by the Meteorological Office, began to appear at a subsequent date, and I took considerable part in their early construction. I had also made many previous attempts to represent the distribution of the weather in a form suitable for printing with movable types. With the aid of Mr. W. Spottis-woode I had types cut for me of appropriate forms, and casts from them were used in the set of my published charts based on the above-mentioned data (*Meteorographica* (Macmillan), 1863) [17], but these were not a success. Later I tried the plan of cutting curves and arrows in soft material by a drill panta-graph, whence casts might be taken for printing. A drill pantagraph is made like an ordinary one, except that the pencil is replaced by a drill, which is rotated by a string that passes over the joints and does not hinder the movements of its arms. I do not know whether this plan of making the weather maps is still adopted. It was submitted to the *Times* by the Meteorological Council, through their Secretary, and I still have the first trial stereotype that was cast on this principle. I heard that there was trouble at first in finding a suitable soft material better than plaster of Paris and the like, but that this difficulty of detail was soon overcome.

I have already mentioned Admiral R. FitzRoy (1805–1865). He was captain of the surveying ship *The Beagle*, whose name became familiar to the public through Charles Darwin's *Voyage of the "Beagle."* He had always been most zealous in the advancement of weather forecasts and storm warnings. The "cone" was his device. A Meteorological Office was established under his superintendence in 1854, entirely owing to his exertions, but it was on a very small scale. His publications unfortunately failed in scientific solidity, and were occasionally open to serious criticism. I myself ventured to attack them in some particulars which it is needless now to recall.

On his lamented death it was determined to reconstruct the office, and a small Departmental Committee of the Board of Trade was named to consider the question. It consisted of Mr., afterwards Lord, Farrer (1819–1899), who was then the Secretary of the Board, the then Hydrographer, Captain, afterwards Sir Frederick, Evans (1815–1885), and myself. We reported in 1866, and I must here pay a tribute to the singular grasp and thoroughness of Lord Farrer, whose occasional brief notes to me, in the course of the inquiry, were models of clearness combined with cordiality.

The result was the formation of a Meteorological Committee in 1868, of which I was a member, for giving storm warnings to seaports, for procuring data for marine charts of weather, and for maintaining a few standard Observatories with self-recording instruments. An annual grant was made to meet its expenses. This avowedly provisional arrangement worked well for some years, when it was felt that the scope of the Meteorological Committee ought to be somewhat enlarged and its constitution reconsidered. So a second Government Committee was appointed by the Board of Trade and the Treasury jointly, of which I was again a member, and in consequence of their Report the "Meteorological Committee" was changed into the "Meteorological Council," with an enlarged grant. It continued in this form until 1905, a little after I had retired from it owing to increasing deafness. It has subsequently been modified anew, and is now under the Directorship of Dr. W. N. Shaw, with a large governing body, whose meetings are much less frequent than those of the Council had been, and interfere less in details.

My long connection with the able men with whom I co-operated for nearly forty years on the Meteorological Committee and Council has given very great pleasure to me, and I had the satisfaction in its earlier days, when new instruments and methods were frequently called for, of being able to do my full share of the work. I will mention only one or two things about which I was much occupied, as examples. Part of our action was to maintain a few well-equipped self-recording Observatories—that is to say, where the instruments wrote down their own movements, photographically or otherwise. For instance, a sheet of photographic paper was moved slowly by clock-work in front of a barometer. The barometer stood in front of a slit in a screen, with a lamp on the other side. The light of the lamp passed freely through the empty portion of the glass tube on to the sensitive paper, but was shut off by the mercury. Hour lines were automatically marked upon the paper. The result was technically called a photographic "tracing," which showed at each moment of time how the barometer then stood. An analogous contrivance was adapted to every one of the other instruments.

All the instrumental data were recorded by these tracings, but they were much too cumbrous in form and size for easy comparison. The question then arose whether it would not be possible to reduce these voluminous documents and print them in a compendious yearly volume. If so, the tracings would require very much more reduction in breadth than in height, for the photographic mark made by the recorder was so broad that the scale of the tracing had to be proportionately wide open; otherwise the neighbouring irregularities would blur together. A sharp line drawn along the middle of the tracings might, however, be much compressed laterally and yet show all the irregularities distinctly. I designed a compound drill pantagraph for the purpose, which reduced the tracings in height independently of the reduction in length. One part of the machine worked the drill forward and backwards, the other part moved the plate from side to side upon which it worked. The result was to express the tracings by fine grooves cut into a piece of soft metal. These were again reduced by an ordinary pantagraph. The whole process required thinking out in numerous details, but it proved quite a success. It is described in the annual Report of the Meteorological Office for 1869.

Squares of zinc, one for each day, were grooved by the drill pantagraph so as to show every one of the data without confusion. They referred to Wind Velocity and Direction, Barometric Height, Rainfall, Dry and Wet Thermometer, together with a line to show the amount of Humidity in the air, which was mechanically calculated from the combined traces of the two thermometers. These squares were placed beneath a large and beautifully designed German pantagraph, whose pointer was directed along the grooves in the zinc, while the diamond point of the scribe scratched the varnish on a copper plate, which was then etched by acid. The result was to produce quarto copper plates, each containing the whole of the instrumental data for each of the seven stations for five consecutive days. The original tracings are reduced to the ratio of 6 : 1 in horizontal and 2 : 1 in vertical measure. This work was steadily pursued for twelve years, which is long enough to include a complete cycle of solar sun-spots. The illustration is a facsimile of the upper two lines of one page, from which the fourth and fifth days have been removed, for want of space.

It surprises me that meteorologists have not made much more use than they have of these comprehensive volumes. But there is no foretelling what aspect of meteorology will be taken up by the very few earnest and capable men who work at it. Each of them wants voluminous data arranged in the form most convenient for his own particular inquiry.

I take this opportunity of mentioning another attempt of mine which was not brought into practice but may hereafter be useful ; at all events, it is of interest. The object was to gain some knowledge of the upper currents of the air, such as are now being obtained by small balloons or kites, which carry self-recording instruments. It seemed to me that the cloud made by a bursting shell fired high in the air over the sea, at a little frequented part of the coast, as that of West Ireland, when no vessel was within the possibility of damage from falling fragments, ought to give what was needed. The first questions to be answered were as to the height to which a shell of appropriate size could be sent, the visibility of the result, and the cost of each

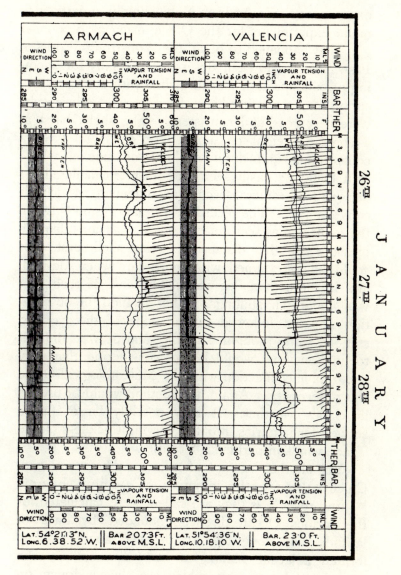

ARMACH

VALENCIA

26TH

JANUARY

27TH

28TH

LAT. 54°21.3' N. BAR. 207·3 FT.
LONG. 6.38.52. W. ABOVE M.S.L.

LAT. 51°54.36' N. BAR. 23·0 FT.
LONG. 10.18.10 W. ABOVE M.S.L.

experiment. Sir Andrew Noble kindly undertook to make experiments for the Office, using a 10-pounder gun that happened to be at the Armstrong Works at Elswick. It had been designed especially for shooting at balloons, and was furnished with the necessary spring for preventing harm from recoil. The results were very good and consistent. The shells burst at a constant height of about 9000 feet, and gave a conspicuous and durable cloud of smoke, whose drift could be easily seen and its rate calculated. I designed a camera-obscura arrangement to do this conveniently. The recorded interval of time between the explosion as seen and as heard, was an adequate measure of the distance of the shell-burst. It could be ascertained with more care when desired, and in more than one way. The cost of each shot was about ten shillings. This method of observation was not followed up, as none of the existing stations were thought suitable, and it was difficult to find one that would be so, considering that easy telegraphic connection with the Meteorological Office was a necessity. Again, the method would be useless in cloudy weather. It may possibly be of future service for inquiries into the varying thickness of the Trade winds in particular localities.

Yet another attempt of mine may be mentioned. Chiefly through the initiative of Admiral Fitzroy, " Wind roses," as they are called, were calculated for the various Ocean districts, bounded by lines of latitude and longitude 10 degrees apart. They formed adjacent rectangles or "squares" in the maps used by seamen, which are always drawn on " Mercator's projection." The "rose" consists of divergent spikes directed towards each of the sixteen primary points of the compass, whose several lengths are proportional to the frequency of winds in their direction.   A shade or other sign shows the proportion of the winds above a specified strength.   Consequently the roses afford means for judging which of two competing courses receives, on the average, the greater share of favourable winds.   But it is no easy matter to calculate by mother-wit the relative efficiency of the winds as expressed by roses, upon the run of a ship along any particular course.   Almost every wind can be utilised to some degree ; we want to know the aggregate effect in the required direction of the average of the winds from all the sixteen primary points.   I showed how this could be found mechanically for any ship whose sailing qualities were known, and suggested that "passage roses" should be calculated for a typical vessel wherever wind roses existed.   I think this would have been taken in hand, had not steam begun to largely supersede sails, and was doing so at a rapidly increasing rate.

I was rather scandalised by finding how little was known to nautical men of the sailing qualities of their own ships, along each of the sixteen points of the compass, assuming a moderate sea, and a moderate wind blowing steadily from one direction.   I think, if I had a yacht, that this would be the first point I should wish to ascertain in respect to her performances.

When the Meteorological Council was established, its first President was that most accomplished classical scholar, as well as mathematician, Professor Henry

Smith (1826–1883) of Oxford, to whose memory the highest tributes have been paid, notably by Sir Mountstuart E. Grant Duff. It was delightful to watch his facility in dealing with difficulties, whether of administration or expression. The Chairman usually has to remain in the Office after the meetings are closed to write letters connected with what has just been transacted. The Secretary, Mr. Robert Scott, was of course present at those times, and he told me of a peculiarity of Henry Smith that I should never have guessed, namely, that when an important letter had to be written, it was his habit to begin by filling a half-sheet and then tearing it up to begin afresh. I myself am very familiar with the way in which the mind settles itself while writing the address and date and the " Dear Sir," but should have thought from the exceptional rapidity of the ordinary working of Henry Smith's mind that he would have been the last person to need a long pause to give his ideas time to crystallise.

Notwithstanding his multifarious duties and interests, he worked hard at the inquiries of the moment. In one of these I was closely associated with him, namely, in an attempt to analyse the extremely complex system of ocean currents round the Cape and up the West Coast of South Africa. They admit of being identified and distinguished partly by their direction and partly by their temperature. Volumes of cold water coming from the direction of the South Pole sometimes plunge far below the surface and reappear in the midst of an otherwise unbroken surface current.

It was a great shock and grief to us all when,

without previous forewarning, intelligence reached us of Henry Smith's death, after a brief but singularly painful illness in 1883.

We all looked to General, afterwards Sir Richard, Strachey (1817–1908) to succeed him, which he did. He too has died only two days before I write these lines. A prominent place ought to be given to him in my "Memories," for we have been connected in our pursuits very frequently and in very different ways. He was one of the hardest and most unobtrusive of workers, who exercised a powerful influence in many great matters, especially in India, but shrank from publicity and ostentation. Like most master minds, he had a characteristic way of looking at things that is hard to describe. It often led to his taking an unpopular side in discussions, though by treating the question very clearly from his own point of view he caused his opinion to be at last accepted. He has been a steadfast friend to me throughout my life. I cannot refrain from quoting the official letter he wrote as Chairman of the Meteorological Council, when I resigned my seat, it is so gracefully and kindly expressed.

"METEOROLOGICAL OFFICE
May 9, 1901

"DEAR MR. GALTON,—The new body of Directors of the Office held their first meeting on Wednesday, 24th April. In the letter from the Royal Society notifying their appointment, there was a paragraph intimating that the resignation of your seat on the Council had been accepted.

"It was only natural that the first act of the new body should be to recall the long period during which you have occupied a seat either on the original

16

Meteorological Committee or the Council, and to endorse, with the emphasis arising from their full knowledge of your work, the appreciation which the President and Council of the Royal Society recorded in their letter.

"It therefore becomes a duty, by which I am no little honoured, to convey to you the feeling of the Council upon the termination of your official services as a Member of the body on which we have so long worked together.   This task I undertake with a full sense of the difficulty of adequately expressing the extent to which the work of the Meteorological Office is indebted for its success and utility to your services, which have extended over thirty-four years.

"It is no exaggeration to say that almost every room in the Office and all its records give unmistakable evidence of the active share you have always taken in the direction of the operations of the Office. The Council feel that the same high order of intelligence and inventive faculty has characterised your scientific work in Meteorology that has been so conspicuous in many other directions, and has long become known and appreciated in all centres of intellectual activity.

"With the Office entering upon a new phase of its service to the public, it is impossible for the Council not to feel that the work of the past thirty-four years has only opened the way, as all good work does, for further development.   I am confident that you will still be interested in the success of the undertaking in which you have had so great a share, and the Council will value in the future, as they have done in the past, any suggestion you may make about the work of the Office.

Believe me, very faithfully yours,
(Sgd.)   RICHARD STRACHEY, *Chairman*"

It is needless to say more than that I was greatly touched by this letter. I was also so much impressed with its literary skill, that on calling shortly after on Sir Richard I begged him, as a matter about which I felt curious on purely literary grounds, to tell me its origin. He said that it was really his own writing, though based on a draft prepared at the Office, and added, "And it is all strictly true." Persons are to be envied who can express their feelings so gracefully as in that letter.

CHAPTER XVII

ANTHROPOMETRIC LABORATORIES

Laboratory at the International Health Exhibition—That in the Science
Gallery, South Kensington — New instruments — Finger-prints
adopted by the Home Office—Letter from M. Alphonse Bertillon

M Y inquiries into hereditary genius, of which
I shall speak in a later chapter, were sufficiently advanced before the year 1865 to show the
pressing necessity of obtaining a multitude of exact
measurements relating to every measurable faculty
of body or mind, for two generations at least, on
which to theorise. I therefore set myself to work
in many directions towards achieving this object, in
some cases for immediate use, in others to bear fruit
hereafter.

The first attempt was to stimulate schools to weigh
and measure, which was successful at Marlborough
College, through the aid of the then Headmaster,
Dr. Farrar, afterwards Archdeacon of Westminster,
and later still Dean of Canterbury, who was enthusi-
astic about all improvements. Subsequently, I wrote
an article in the *Fortnightly Review*, March 1882,
beginning with, " When shall we have Anthropometric
Laboratories, where a man may from time to time
get himself and his children weighed, measured, and
rightly photographed, and have each of their bodily

sincerely yours

Francis Galton

faculties tested, by the best methods known to modern science?" I went on to describe what could be done in this way by existing methods, and what more it was desirable to have.

When the International Exhibition of 1884 was under consideration, I offered to equip and maintain a Laboratory there, if a suitable place were given, the woodwork set up, and the security of it taken off my hands. This was done, and I arranged a long narrow enclosure with trellis-work, in front and at its ends. A table ran alongside the trellis-work on which the instruments were placed and where the applicants were tested, and a passage was left between the table and the wall. This gave a quasi-privacy, while it enabled outsiders to see a little of what was going on inside. A doorkeeper stationed at one end admitted a single applicant at a time, who had to pay threepence. The superintendent took him through the tests in turn, and dismissed him at the other end with his schedule filled up. Sometimes I helped him; then two persons could be tested together, the one a little in advance of the other. The arrangement worked smoothly, and the Laboratory was seldom unemployed.

The measurements dealt with Keenness of Sight and of Hearing; Colour Sense, Judgment of Eye; Breathing Power; Reaction Time; Strength of Pull and of Squeeze; Force of Blow; Span of Arms; Height, both standing and sitting; and Weight. The ease of working the instruments that were used was so great that an applicant could be measured in all these respects, a card containing the results furnished him, and a duplicate made and kept for statistical purposes, at the total cost of the threepenny fee, already described, for admission. That just defrayed the working expenses.

It is by no means easy to select suitable instruments for such a purpose. They must be strong, easily legible, and very simple, the stupidity and wrong-headedness of many men and women being so great as to be scarcely credible. I used at first the instrument commonly employed for testing the force of a blow. It was a stout deal rod running freely in a tube, with a buffer at one end to be hit with the fist and pressing against a spring at the other. An index was pushed by the rod as far as it entered the tube in opposition to the spring. I found no difficulty whatever in testing myself with it, but before long a man had punched it so much on one side, instead of hitting straight out, that he broke the stout deal rod. It was replaced by an oaken one, but this too was broken, and some wrists were sprained.

I afterwards contrived, and used in a subsequent Laboratory, a pretty arrangement that gave the swiftness, though not the force of the blow, with absolute safety, and which could be used for other limbs than the arm. The hand held a thread, the other end of which was tied to an elastic band, capable of pulling it back faster than any human hand could follow ; so the hand always *retarded* its movement. Its speed was shown by the height to which a bead, actuated by the string (it is needless to explain details), was tossed up in front of a scale. This never failed, and was perfectly easy to manipulate.

The observations made in this Laboratory were of great use to me later on. Four hundred complete sets are published in the *Anthropometric Inst. Journal* 1884 [81], and afford good material for future use in many ways.

Among other instruments that I contrived then or subsequently, were small whistles with a screw plug, for determining the highest audible note, the limit of which varies much in different persons and at different ages. A parcel of schoolboys might interchange very shrill and loud whistles quite inaudibly to an elderly master. I found them to produce marked effects on cats, and made many experiments at a house where I often stayed, in which my bedroom window overlooked a garden much frequented by them. My plan was to watch near the open window, and when a cat appeared and had become quite unsuspicious and absorbed, to sound one of these notes inaudible to most elderly persons. The cat was round in a minute. I noticed the quickness and precision with which these animals direct their eyes to the source of sound. It is not so with dogs.

I contrived a hollow cane made like a walking stick, having a removable whistle at its lower end, with an exposed indiarubber tube under its curved handle. Whenever I squeezed the tube against the handle, air was pushed through the whistle. I tried it at nearly all the cages in the Zoological Gardens, but with little result of interest, except that it certainly annoyed some of the lions. I have often met with persons who perceived no purely audible sound when very high notes were sounded, but who experienced a peculiar feeling of discomfort which I have occasionally felt myself. This, I think, was the case with some of the lions, who turned away and angrily rubbed their ears with their paws, just as the persons of whom I have spoken often did with their hands.

It was difficult to find a simple machine that would register the length of Reaction Time—that is, the interval between a Stimulus and the Response to it, say between a sharp sound and the pressure of a responding finger on a key. I first used one of Exner's earlier instruments, but it took too much time, so I subsequently made one with a pendulum. The tap that released the pendulum from a raised position made the required sound,—otherwise it made a quiet sight-signal, whichever was wished,—and the responding finger caused an elastic thread parallel to the pendulum and swinging with it to be clutched and held fast, in front of a scale, graduated to $\frac{1}{100}$ths of a second. This acted well; there was no jar from seizing the elastic thread, and the adjustments gave no trouble.

For testing the Muscular Sense, I used cartridges packed evenly with cotton wool and with shot, so as to be exactly alike on the outsides but of different weights. The weights ran in a regular geometric series, and were broken up into sets of three. Each set lay in a grooved square of wood, in any order; the test was to arrange them by the sense of their heaviness, in their proper order, as shown by the inscriptions at one end of each. This method acted quickly, because it was easy to judge by the sometimes hesitating, sometimes decided manner in which a particular set was handled, whether or no the differences were clearly perceived, and to substitute others in turn more appropriate to the acuteness of sense of the person tested.

One hears so much about the extraordinary sensitivity of the blind, that I was glad of an opportunity of testing a large number of children in an asylum. The nature of the test was fully explained to them, and that the most successful ones were to receive a sweetmeat.   It was evident that all did their best, but their performances fell distinctly short of those of ordinary persons.   I found afterwards a marked correlation between at least this form of sensitiveness and general ability.

After the Health Exhibition was closed in 1885, it seemed a pity that the Laboratory should also come to an end, so I asked for and was given a room in the Science Galleries of the South Kensington Museum.   I maintained a Laboratory there during about six years, and found an excellent man, Sergeant Randal, for its Superintendent.   Useful data were obtained from this Laboratory, but I found that it ought to be either in the hands of a trained scientific superintendent, who would be competent to undertake much more refined measurements than mine were intended for, or else that a great many more persons than I could tempt to attend should be roughly measured.

Some few notabilities came, among whom I would especially mention Mr. Gladstone, whose measurements proved very acceptable to Mr. Brock the sculptor, in making a posthumous statue of him for Liverpool.   Mr. Gladstone was amusingly insistent about the size of his head, saying that hatters often told him that he had an Aberdeenshire head—"a fact which you may be sure I do not forget to tell my Scotch constituents."   It was a beautifully shaped head, though low, but after all it was not so very large in circumference. Of those persons whom I have mentioned in the foregoing chapters, the heads of William Spottiswoode and Mr. Gassiott were larger round; Professor Sharpey's was the largest of all. A slight want of symmetry on which Mr. Gladstone laid stress was no peculiarity at all, for the heads of normal persons are rarely quite symmetrical.

The "Measurement of Resemblance" between portraits is a subject on which I have been engaged off and on during late years, and which I hope to take up again. The best of my ideas at present is to prepare a strip of card one inch broad and printed with numerals of various standard sizes from 1 to 9. Then to mount the portraits on slides actuated by strings, and to station them at such distances that the interval between the pupils of the eyes and the mouth in each portrait shall be apparently the same as the breadth of the strip. Then to interpose a wedge of tinted glass in front of an eye-hole, and to slide it until the portraits become indistinguishable. In that position to read off the smallest of the standard numbers that is simultaneously legible. I have made many experiments, differing in particulars, and described one of them in *Nature*, October 4, 1906 [176], which seems to me not so good as the one briefly outlined above.

The chief value to me of the Laboratory during the latter part of the time of its existence, and the reason why I continued it so long, lay in the convenience it afforded for obtaining and testing the value of finger-prints. My interest in them arose through a request to give a Friday evening lecture at the Royal Institution (which was delivered May 25, 1888) on what is briefly called "Bertillonage"; that is, on the system devised by M. Alphonse Bertillon for identifying persons by the measurements of their bodily dimensions. The subject was attracting much interest at the time, and had received a great deal of off-hand newspaper praise. There was, however, a want of fulness in the published accounts of it, while the principle upon which extraordinarily large statistical claims to its quasi-certainty had been founded was manifestly incorrect, so further information was desirable. The incorrectness lay in treating the measures of different dimensions of the same person as if they were *independent* variables, which they are not. For example, a tall man is much more likely to have a long arm, foot, or finger than a short one. The chances against mistake had been overrated enormously owing to this error; still, the system was most ingenious and very interesting.

I made the acquaintance of M. Bertillon during a short visit to Paris, and had the opportunity of seeing his system at work. Nothing could exceed the deftness of his assistants in measuring the criminals; their methods were prompt and accurate, and all the accompanying arrangements excellently organised. But I had not means of testing its efficiency with closeness, which would have required more time and interference with current work than was permissible. I was nevertheless prepared to give an account at the Royal Institution of what I had seen, but, being desirous of introducing original work of my own, I gave to my lecture the more general title of "Personal Identification and Description" [107], on which larger subject there was much new to be said.

When thinking over the matter, the fact occurred to my recollection that thumb-marks had not infrequently been spoken and written about, so I inquired into their alleged use, especially by the Chinese. I also wrote a letter to *Nature* asking for information, which had the important effect of drawing a response from Sir William Herschel, who, as a Commissioner in India, had actually used them in his district, for many years, as a means of preventing personation. But the system fell into disuse after his departure. Sir William gave me every assistance, by forwarding to me both old and modern finger-prints of himself and of others of his family, and in showing his way of making the impressions.

I took up the study very seriously, thinking that finger-prints might prove to be of high anthropological significance, but I may say at once that they are not. I have examined large numbers of persons of different races to our own, as Jews, Basques, Red Indians, East Indians of various origins, Negroes, and a fair number of Chinese. Also persons of very different characters and temperaments, as students of science, students of art, Quakers, notabilities of various kinds, and a considerable number of idiots at Earlswood Asylum, without finding any pattern that was characteristic of any of them. But as I continued working at finger-prints, their importance as a means of identification became more and more obvious, and since my theoretical work on Heredity, Correlation, etc., of which I shall speak further, had not yet "taken on," there was spare time for inquiry into finger-prints.

I described the results in the above-mentioned lecture so far as they had then been obtained, and subsequently in a more advanced shape in a memoir read before the Royal Society in 1891 [117]. It was argued in it that these patterns had a theoretical significance, which has not, I think, even yet been adequately appreciated, which bears on discontinuity in evolution. I showed that the different classes of patterns in finger-prints might be justly compared to different genera. As, however, they had been formed without any aid from natural selection, I concluded that natural selection had no monopoly in moulding genera, but that internal conditions must be quite as important.

I have always believed that the number of positions of stability in every genus must be limited, from which moderate deviations, but not great ones, are possible without causing destruction. There are limits which, if they can be overpassed without disaster, would require a new position of stability in the organisation. Comparatively few intermediate finger-patterns are found between a "loop" and a "whorl," these representing two different and well-marked genera or positions of stability.

The modern division of views concerning the immediate causes of evolution, whether it be due to the slow accumulation of small factors or else by the sudden mutations of de Vries, are paralleled by those held by the physicists of the fifties on the method by which a glacier adapts itself to its bed, just as if it were a viscous body, which it certainly is not in the ordinary sense of the word. Professor Tyndall ascribed its adaptation of form to a succession of internal crunches and re-freezings ; in other words, to successive conditions of stability.

It became gradually clear that three facts had to be established before it would be possible to advocate the use of finger-prints for criminal or other investigations. First, it must be proved, not assumed, that the pattern of a finger-print is constant through-out life. Secondly, that the variety of patterns is really very great. Thirdly, that they admit of being so classified, or "lexiconised," that when a set of them is submitted to an expert, it would be possible for him to tell, by reference to a suitable dictionary, or its equivalent, whether a similar set had been already registered. These things I did, but they required much labour.

A Committee was appointed by the Home Office to inquire into the different systems of identification that had been adopted or proposed for use with criminals. They visited my Laboratory, and thoroughly inspected what I had to show. It was a great pleasure to work with and for such sympathetic and keen inquirers, but I regretted all the time that my methods were hardly ripe for inspection ; still, they were fairly adequate. The result was a Report strongly in favour of their adoption, of which the part that bears on finger-prints is reprinted in my *Finger Print Directory* [131].

I had communicated with M. Alphonse Bertillon, suggesting that he should consider the introduction of finger-prints into his own system, but the idea did not commend itself to him. Afterwards I sent

him further information on what had been more
recently done, to which he answered, on June 15, 1891,
that he was much disposed to add my method to his
own, especially for persons under age, but he feared
practical difficulties, such as in cleaning the fingers
after printing from them.   Also it was a question
whether his assistants, who were but little educated,
would be zealous enough to learn a new method.
He ended by asking me, on the next occasion when
I happened to pass through Paris, to give a morning
to his Depot to experimentalise on the criminals
there.   It has been stated more than once that the
finger-print system was initiated by M. Bertillon, so
I have mentioned these historical details, and give
his untranslated letter in a footnote.[1]   The omitted
portion refers to quite another matter, in which he
was then assisting me.

I have said that my method was not so fully
elaborated as I should have wished when the
Committee examined it, so I worked hard at it afterwards, and published the results in 1895 in the book
already mentioned, bearing the title of *Finger Print
Directory*, using the term "Directory" in the same sense
as in the familiar phrase of "Post Office Directory."
It was an unlucky choice of a word, for its equivalent
in French means a Board of Directors, so its title

[1] *Extract from letter of M. Alphonse Bertillon*, 15 *Juin* 1891 :
" Je vous remercie de votre nouvel envoi relativement aux *impressions
digitales*. Je suis fort disposé à ajouter votre procédé au signalement
anthropométrique surtout pour les enfants. Mais je redoute quelques
difficultés pratiques pour le nettoyage des doigts après l'impression
faite, etc. Puis mes agents si peu instruits mettront-ils le zèle nécessaire
pour apprendre votre méthode? Je crois que vous traversez souvent
Paris, pourriez vous à votre prochain voyage, me consacrer une matinée
au Dépot, pour un essayage sur la vile multitude?"

may have misled. This book contained a method of classification far in advance of what I had published before, and is in most essential points the same as that in present use in Scotland Yard.

Sir Edward, then Mr. Henry, when in office in India, came to my Laboratory to learn the finger-print process, and he introduced it first into Bengal, and afterwards throughout India. The Bertillon system did not work at all well there, because measurements had to be taken at many different local centres where accuracy could not be guaranteed. Then Mr. Henry was dispatched to the Cape, where great difficulty had arisen about identification, and he introduced finger-prints there also. After this he was called to England, and soon selected to hold his present important post. From what I have seen during the few visits I have paid to Scotland Yard, the finger-print system answers excellently, and can deal easily with many thousands of sets—certainly with twenty thousand.

I hardly know over how large a part of the world this system is now in use to the exclusion of other methods. It is so in England, India, and Argentina. It is used in connection with measurements in Brazil, Egypt, and many other countries.

It is necessary for its successful employment that the clerks at the central Bureau should be thoroughly acquainted with their work. There is much for them to learn as to the uniform classification of many small groups of often recurring patterns, and in realising what is and what is not essential to identification. Certain changes in the print may wholly depend on the greater or less pressure of the finger. The impression is usually made by what may be described as the crests of the mountain ridges of the pattern ; a strong pressure will show the connecting *cols* as well, so the latter are unimportant. Decipherment is a peculiar art. Gross differences are conspicuous enough to an untrained eye, but even in these a novice may sometimes contrive to make mistakes when an imperfect impression is submitted to him. On the other hand, the art of taking good prints is very easy, and may be learnt in a single lesson by any intelligent and handy man.

Much has been written, but the last word has not been said, on the rationale of these curious papillary ridges ; why in one man and in one finger they form whorls and in another loops. I may mention a characteristic anecdote of Herbert Spencer in connection with this. He asked me to show him my Laboratory and to take his prints, which I did. Then I spoke of the failure to discover the origin of these patterns, and how the fingers of unborn children had been dissected to ascertain their earliest stages, and so forth. Spencer remarked that this was beginning in the wrong way ; that I ought to consider the purpose the ridges had to fulfil, and to work backwards. Here, he said, it was obvious that the delicate mouths of the sudorific glands required the protection given to them by the ridges on either side of them, and therefrom he elaborated a consistent and ingenious hypothesis at great length.

I replied that his arguments were beautiful and deserved to be true, but it happened that the mouths of the ducts did not run in the valleys between the crests, but along the crests of the ridges themselves. He

17

burst into a good-humoured and uproarious laugh, and told me the famous story which I have heard from each of the other two who were present on the occurrence. Huxley was one of them. Spencer, during a pause in conversation at dinner at the Athenæum, said, "You would little think it, but I once wrote a tragedy." Huxley answered promptly, "I know the catastrophe." Spencer declared it was impossible, for he had never spoken about it before then. Huxley insisted. Spencer asked what it was. Huxley replied, "A beautiful theory, killed by a nasty, ugly little fact."

CHAPTER XVIII

COMPOSITE PORTRAITS AND STEREOSCOPIC MAPS

Sir Edmund Du Cane and criminal characteristics—Principle of composites—Analytical photography—Stereoscopic photographs of models of mountainous districts

MY first idea of composite portraiture arose through a request by Sir Edmund Du Cane, R.E., then H.M. Inspector of Prisons, to examine the photographs of criminals, in order to discover and to define the types of features, if there be any, that are associated with different kinds of criminality. The popular ideas were known to be very inaccurate, and he thought the subject worthy of scientific study. I gladly offered to do what I could, and he gave me full opportunities of seeing prisons and of studying a large number of photographs of criminals, which were of course to be used confidentially.

At first, for obtaining pictorial averages I combined pairs of portraits with a stereoscope, with more or less success. Then I recollected an often observed effect with magic lanthorns, when two lanthorns converge on the same screen, and while the one is throwing its image, the operator slowly withdraws the light from it and throws it on to the next one. The first image yields slowly to the second, with little sense of discordance in the parts that at all resemble one another. It was obviously possible to photograph superposed images on a screen by the simultaneous use of two or more lanthorns. What was common to all of the images would then appear vigorous, while individual differences would be too faint for notice. There would, however, be great difficulty in accurately superposing them without the aid of expensive apparatus. Then the idea occurred to me that no lanthorns were needed for the purpose, but that the pictures themselves might be severally adjusted in the same place, and be photographed successively on the same plate, allowing a fractional part of the total time of exposure to each portrait.

My earlier experiments were with the full-face photographs of criminals. I selected three which were not greatly unlike, and were of the same size, as judged by measuring the vertical distance between the pupils of the eyes and the parting of the lips. Out of a thin card I cut a window of the size of the portrait, and fastened two threads over it, one vertical, the other crossways. Lastly I made a pin-hole in the card on either side of the window. Thus provided, I laid each portrait in turn on the table, and adjusted the card until the cross line passed over the pupils of the eyes, and the vertical line bisected the interval. Then I pricked through the two pin-holes the paper on which the portrait was. I could thus hang all three portraits one behind the other on two pins that projected from a board, with the assurance that the principal features of each face would occupy an identical position in front of a fixed camera. I photographed them in turns. The camera was uncapped during one-third of the normal time of exposure while the first portrait was in front of it. Capping it again, I took away the front portrait and exposed the second, then uncapping the camera I took the second portrait; and similarly the third. The result was particularly promising; it was difficult to believe that the composite was not a simple portrait. I tested the truth of the result by placing the photographs in different order, and by many other ways. Then I extended its application. The method of composite portraiture was first published in *Nature*, 1878, and more fully in the *Journ. Anthrop. Inst*, 1879 [51], also in the Journal of the Photographic Society, at which I exhibited it, and elsewhere. The method is republished in *Human Faculty* [76].

I gladly acknowledge my indebtedness to Sir Edmund Du Cane not only for helping me with material for these experiments, but for having, as he told me, suggested the inclusion of my finger-print system in the instructions to the Committee of Identification, described in the last chapter. He was an extremely accomplished man, with high and humane views, and sympathised with not a few of the subjects on which I have been engaged.

I have successfully made many composites both of races and of families. The composites are always more refined and ideal-looking than any one of their components, but I found that persons did not like being mixed up with their brothers and sisters in a common portrait. It seems a curious and rather silly feeling, but there can be no doubt of its existence. I see no other reason why composite portraiture should not be much employed for obtaining family types. Composites might be made of brothers and sisters, parents and grandparents, together with a composite of the race, each in their due proportions, according to the Ancestral Law (see chapter on Heredity). The result would be very instructive, but the difficulty of obtaining the material is now overwhelming. Male and female portraits blend well together, with an epicene result.

With the help of Dr. Mahomed and the permission of the authorities of Guy's Hospital, I took many photographs of consumptive patients and made composites of them, which are published in the Guy's Hospital Reports, vol. xxv. They show two contrasted types, the one fine and attenuated, the other coarse and blunted. Dr. Mahomed was a very promising physician, on the eve of becoming well known, when he caught a fever of the same description, I am told, as that on which he had become an authority, and died of it in his newly purchased house.

I could not make good composites of lunatics; their features are apt to be so irregular in different ways that it was impossible to blend them. I took a photographer with me to Hanwell, where it was arranged that the patients should sit two at a time on a bench. One of them was to be led forward and posted in front of the camera, while his place on the bench was filled by the second patient moving up into it, whose previous place was to be occupied by a third patient. It happened that the second of the pair who were the first to occupy the bench considered himself to be a very mighty man, I forget whom, but let us say Alexander the Great. He boiled with internal fury at not being given precedence, and when the photographer had his head well under the velvet cloth, with his body bent, in the familiar attitude of photographers while focusing, Alexander the Great slid swiftly to his rear and administered a really good bite to the unprotected hinder end of the poor photographer, whose scared face emerging from under the velvet cloth rises vividly in my memory as I write this. The photographer guarded his rear afterwards by posting himself in a corner of the room.

Many years later, I tried to perform the exact opposite to composite photography, namely, to annul all that was typical in a portrait and to preserve its peculiarities. I called it "Analytical Photography," and explained it in *Nature*, 1900, and in the *Photo. Soc. Jour.*, 1900–1901. It depends on the fact that a positive and a negative glass plate, *both in half or still fainter tones*, when held face to face neutralise the peculiarities of one another, so the effect of their combination is to produce a uniform grey. My plan was to fix a *negative* composite in front of a *positive* portrait of one of its elements, all in half tones, with the result that the composite abstracted all the typical portion of the portrait while its peculiarities were isolated and remained. "Alice in Wonderland" would have described it as the "grin without the Cheshire Cat." I succeeded, but the result did not give an intelligible idea of the peculiarities, the non-essentials being as strongly marked as the essentials, and the whole making a jumble; so I went no farther with this process.

In 1882 I published an illustrated memoir in *Nature* on the conventional way in which artists had hitherto represented a galloping horse. Mr. Muybridge had, by means of beautiful photographs of twenty momentary successive attitudes, recently shown, beyond possibility of cavil, that the conventional representation was totally untrue to fact. I asked myself the question why observant artists had agreed for so long a time in drawing galloping horses with their four legs extended simultaneously, and why their representation had never been objected to. It occurred to me that composites of successive attitudes that were too momentary to be distinguished might answer the question, which it did. When all of the twenty attitudes are combined in a single picture, the result is certainly suggestive of the conventional representation, though in a very confused way. Then, finding by my own observation that it was difficult to watch all four legs at the same time, also seeing that according to the photographs of Mr. Muybridge, the two fore legs were extended during one quarter of a complete motion, and that during another quarter the two hind legs were similarly extended, I made composites of these groups separately. Then, cutting them in half and uniting the front half of the former to the hind half of the latter, a very fair equivalent was obtained to the conventional attitude. I inferred that the brain ignored one-half of all it saw in the gallop, as too confused to be noticed ; that it divided the other half in two parts, each alike in one particular, and combined the two halves into a monstrous whole.

This is a convenient place to speak of the method of stereoscopic maps, which I devised so long ago as 1863. It was published together with specimens made for me by my cousin, long since dead, R. Cameron Galton, in the *Proceedings* of the Royal Geographical Society [18] of that year. I cannot fully understand why stereoscopes do not hold a higher position in popular estimation than they do ; it may be partly due to two causes—to the fact that the two eyes are unequally operative in a larger proportion of persons than might be supposed, and to the cost and unwieldiness of the usual stereoscope. Compound lenses give better and wider images than plain ones, but for common purposes I find that plain ones, mounted as in an eyeglass, serve quite well enough. Those I generally use are cheap things, mounted in a strip of wood.

I wished to obtain a map that should have the effect of a model, so suitable models were procured and photographed stereoscopically. The result was a perfect success. An unexpected result occurred when a pure white plaster cast was treated in this way, for it wholly failed to give the required appearance of a solid, but if grains of dust were sprinkled over it, much more if names were written on it, the stereoscopic effect appeared in its full strength. Good models, and therefore stereoscopic maps made from them, give a far better idea of a mountainous country than any ordinary map can do, however cleverly it may be shaded. Map-makers might well pay some attention to stereoscopic maps and to providing cheap eyeglasses with which to view them.

CHAPTER XIX

HUMAN FACULTY

Measurement of mental powers—Centiles—Number forms—Visions of sane persons—Experiments on self—Classification by judgment—Sandow—Weight of cattle—First and second prizes—Arithmetic by smell—Influences of gesture, voice, etc.

AFTER I had become satisfied of the inheritance of all the mental qualities into which I had inquired, and that heredity was a far more powerful agent in human development than nurture, I wished to explore the range of human faculty in various directions in order to ascertain the degree to which breeding might, at least theoretically, modify the human race. I took the moderate and reasonable standpoint that whatever quality had appeared in man and in whatever intensity, it admitted of being bred for and reproduced on a large scale. Consequently a new race might be created possessing on the *average* an equal degree of quality and intensity as in the exceptional case. Relative infertility might of course stand in the way, but otherwise everything seemed to show that races of highly gifted artists, saints, mathematicians, administrators, mechanicians, contented labourers, musicians, militants, and so forth, might be theoretically called into existence, the average excellence of each race in its particular line

being equal to that of its most highly gifted representative at the present moment.

I desired to plan a laboratory in which Human
Faculty might be measured so far as possible, and, after
much inquiry and trouble, drew up and sent a printed
circular to experts, showing in outline what seemed
to me feasible, and drawing attention to desiderata.
Useful replies reached me from many quarters.

There was no one to whose intelligent co-operation
I then owed more than Professor Croom Robertson
(1842–1892) of University College. His genius and
temperament were of the most attractive Scottish type
—exact, sane, and very genial. He was well known
by his work on Hobbes, and as the founder and Editor
of the periodical *Mind*, in which his critical notices of
current philosophical literature were soon recognised
as of especial weight. He was a thorough friend,
whose death left a void in my own life that has never
been wholly filled.

The leading ideas of such a laboratory as I had
in view, were that its measurements should effectually
"sample" a man with reasonable completeness. It
should measure *absolutely* where it was possible,
otherwise *relatively* among his class fellows, the
quality of each selected faculty. The next step
would be to estimate the combined effect of these
separately measured faculties in any given proportion,
and ultimately to ascertain the degree with which the
measurement of sample faculties in youth justifies a
prophecy of future success in life, using the word
"success" in its most liberal meaning.

The method of centiles (or of per-centiles as
I originally called it) was devised to give greater pre-

cision to the meaning of "class-place." The familiar
phrases of top of his class, near the top, half-way down
it, and the like, express a great deal, but they express
much more if used in connection with the size of the
class. A useful way of reducing classes of all sizes
to a common one is as follows. The names of the
individuals are entered in the order of their class-
places in a long column, beginning with the highest.
The names are separated by lines which resemble the
rungs of a ladder, and will here be called rungs for
distinction. The interval between the lowest and
highest rungs is divided along the sides of the ladder
into equal parts to form a scale, usually one of 100
parts. In this the lowest rung stands at 0° and the
highest at 100°. Such divisions are called centiles.
If the divisions are not in hundredths, but otherwise
as tenths, eighths, or quarters, they are still called by
words ending in "—ile," as decile, octile, and quartile.
The marks corresponding to the class-places at each
centile, decile, octile, or quartile, are independent of
the size of the class, except in that small degree to
which all statistical deductions are liable when derived
from different samples of the same store of material.

The diagram opposite explains the process. For
reasons of space it is adapted here to a class of only
twelve individuals, but it is applicable equally well to
classes however large, and the larger the better.

The method of centiles affords a convenient and
compact way of comparing the amounts of specified
faculties in different individals. All this is an
old tale now, but I had to take a great deal of
trouble before it was clearly thought out and well
tested.

Names.	Marks or Measures.	Class-Place.	Divisions of Scale.	
			Quarters.	Hundredths (Centiles).
				$0°$
		1st		
		2nd		
		3rd		
		4th	— Lower quartile —	$25°$
		5th		
		6th		
		7th	— Middle quartile — (Median)	$50°$
		8th		
		9th		
		10th	— Upper quartile —	$75°$
		11th		
		12th		
				$100°$

As it may interest persons to know how they would stand among the visitants to a large London Exhibition, I give a brief extract on next page from my published table (*Nature*, January 8, 1885), [86], concerning those measured at the International Health Exhibition.

Suppose the reader to be a male adult, and the strength of his pull as with a bow to be 78 lbs., he will learn that his class-place in that particular is at the seventieth centile. In other words, that of those measured at the above Exhibition about[1] 70 per cent. were weaker and 30 per cent. stronger.

This little table contains excellent material for comparing the powers of the two sexes.

From Measurements made at the Anthropometric Laboratory in the International Health Exhibition of 1884.

Subject of Measurement.	Unit of Measure.	Sex.	Centiles.				
			10°	30°	50°	70°	90°
Height standing, without shoes	Inches	M.	64·5	66·5	67·9	69·2	71·3
		F.	59·9	62·1	63·3	64·6	66·4
Span of arms . .	Inches	M.	66·1	68·2	69·9	71·4	73·6
		F.	59·5	61·7	63·0	64·5	66·7
Weight in indoor clothing .	Pounds	M.	125	135	143	150	165
		F.	105	114	122	132	142
Breathing capacity .	Cubic inches	M.	177	199	219	236	277
		F.	102	124	138	151	177
Strength of pull with a bow	Pounds	M.	60	68	74	78	89
		F.	32	36	40	44	51

One of my many inquiries related to what I called "Number Forms"; it originated in this way. Mr. George Bidder, Q.C., son of the engineer who in his youth was the famous "calculating boy" (1806–1878), and who inherited and transmitted much of his father's remarkable powers, wrote in a postscript of a letter to me in response to other inquiries, that he himself habitually saw numbers in his mind's eye,

[1] The word "about" is a slight reservation due to each class man, being one-half place short of his nominal class-place. In a class of 100, the topmost occupies the post of ½, and the lowest that of 99½. There are 101 divisions or "rungs" from 0° to 100° inclusive, but only 100 persons. The existence of this half place may be neglected by the ordinary reader, though an expert would lay stress upon it.

arranged in a peculiar form, of which he sent a drawing. It began with the face of a clock, numbered I. to XII., and then tailed off, much like the tail of a kite, into an undulating curve, having 20, 30, 40, etc., at each bend. This prompted me to ask others whom I met whether he or she saw anything of the kind, and I received affirmative replies from a few girls.

I then went to my Club and successively asked the same question of every friend whom I saw, but invariably met with a more or less contemptuous negative. Nothing daunted, I inquired further, and soon found a goodly number of distinguished persons who perceived these curious forms, no two of them alike. After prolonged questioning in many directions I gathered enough material for a memoir, and being determined to publish it in a way that could not be pooh-poohed, I selected six well-known friends out of those who said that they saw them, and having assured myself that they would speak to the veracity of their several diagrams, I invited them all to a good dinner, and took them to the meeting of the Anthropological Institute on March 9, 1880, where the diagrams were hung up. These were G. Bidder, Col. Yule, Rev. G. Henslow, Prof. Schuster, J. Roget, and Mr. Wood Smith. They acted faithfully up to their assurances, and so the fact of the existence of Number-Forms was solidly established. Their remarks are published in the *Journal of the Anthropological Institute* [63]. I possessed a collection of most curious forms, not a few of them appearing in three dimensions and drawn in perspective; many of them were coloured.

Before quitting this subject I may be allowed to tell a tale thereon. I had to deliver a lecture at the British Association, in which these Number-Forms were to be spoken of, and did a rash thing. It was that after describing their character and frequency, I said, " Now, will every person in this large meeting who is conscious of seeing a Number-Form, hold up his hand?" There was a dead silence; those who should have responded were too shy to move, and not a hand was raised. I suddenly bethought myself of a tale that had not long since appeared in the *Times*, as told by a German soldier to his comrades over a bivouac fire, to account for a want of solidarity in the French resistance. It was this, and I told it with some variations to the meeting :—

" The Chief Rabbi of Dantzig was a wealthy and hospitable man. (I repeat what I read, and beg pardon if the tale was applied to the wrong person.) One day his house caught fire and even the contents of his good cellar suffered. The Jews took counsel what to do for their beloved Rabbi. First a handsome subscription was proposed, but overruled; then another idea was mooted, then another, each less costly than the preceding; and at the last it was agreed that every Jew should visit the house on a day to be fixed, and bring with him a bottle of Eau de Vie de Dantzig (the original said " wine "). That after an appropriate speech of greeting to the Rabbi, he should descend into the cellar and empty his bottle into a vat prepared for the purpose. The day came, the Chief Rabbi prepared a sumptuous collation, and listened with delight to the flattering addresses of his guests; then, when the ceremony was concluded,

he went down to the cellar with his family, all of
them brimful of kindly feelings, to taste the result.
He turned the tap, a beautifully clear fluid ran into
his glass; he lifted it with gratitude to his lips, when
suddenly his countenance fell; he sipped a second
time and exploded in wrath, for the fluid was pure
water. The fact was that each Jew had said to
himself, 'What matters it whether I put in a spirit
which costs money, or water which costs nothing?
My own contribution will make no sensible difference
to the total result.' As every Jew acted on this
principle, the result was pure water.

"Now each of you who perceive Number-Forms
has acted in a similar way, so there has been no
response to my request; but I cannot let the matter
drop, therefore I call on Professor S——, whom I see
on the platform, and who, I know, perceives these
Forms, to hold up his hand, and I trust then that
you who have hitherto abstained through shyness
will do so likewise."

The appeal succeeded; up went Professor S——'s
hand, and up went a multitude of scattered hands all
about the body of the hall.

In 1881 I gave one of the Friday Evening
Lectures at the Royal Institution on the Visions of
Sane Persons [65], in which I dwelt on the far
greater frequency than was supposed, of hallucinations
and illusions among individuals in normal health, as
ascertained through numerous inquiries verbally or
by letter. It very often happened that the verbal
reply to my question took a form like this, " No, no;
I've never had any hallucination"; then, after a pause,

18

"Well, there certainly was one curious thing," etc. etc.

One afternoon at tea-time, before a meeting of the Royal Society, Sir Risdon Bennett (1809-1891), a well-known physician, President of the College of Physicians in 1876, and a Fellow of the Royal Society, drew me apart and told me of a strange experience he had had very recently. He was writing in his study separated by a thin wall from the passage, when he heard the well-known postman's knock, followed by the entrance into his study of a man dressed in a fantastic medieval costume, perfectly distinct in every particular, buttons and all, who, after a brief time, faded and disappeared. Sir Risdon said that he felt in perfect health; his pulse and breathing were normal, and so forth, but he was naturally alarmed at the prospect of some impending brain disorder. Nothing, however, of the sort had followed. The same appearance recurred; he thought the postman's knock somehow originated the hallucination.

I begged him to publish the curious case fully with his name attached, as it would then become a classical example, but he hesitated; however, he did ultimately publish it at some length in a medical paper, but signed only with his initials. I wholly forget its date. If any reader interested in these things should come across the paper, these imperfect but vivid recollections of mine may corroborate such impressions as he would have of its veracity, for I heard the story at length, very shortly after the event, told me with painstaking and scientific exactness, and in tones that clearly indicated the narrator's earnest desire to be minutely correct. I purposely omit many details, doubting the accuracy of my own memory in those respects. There can be no impropriety now in publishing the name hitherto withheld.

I gave in the lecture many examples of guiding "stars" and the like, and referred to the fact that the visionary temperament has manifested itself largely at certain historical times, and under certain conditions of national life, and endeavoured to account for this by the following considerations :—

That the visionary tendency is much more common among sane people than is generally suspected.

In early life it seems to be a hard lesson for an imaginative child to distinguish between the real and the visionary world. If the fantasies are habitually laughed at and otherwise discouraged, the child soon acquires the power of distinguishing them; any incongruity or nonconformity is quickly noted, the fact of its being a vision is found out; it is discredited, and no further attended to. In this way the natural tendency to see visions is blunted by repression. Therefore, when popular opinion is of a matter-of-fact kind, the seers of visions keep quiet; they do not like to be thought fanciful or mad, and they hide their experiences, which only come to light through inquiries such as those I have been making. But let the tide of opinion change and grow favourable to supernaturalism, then the seers of visions come to the front. It is not that a faculty previously non-existent has been suddenly evoked, but that a faculty long smothered in secret has been suddenly allowed freedom to express itself, and it may be to run into extravagance owing to the removal of reasonable safeguards.

The following experiments on Human Faculty are worth recording; they have not been published before. In the days of my youth I felt at one time a passionate desire to subjugate the body by the spirit, and among other disciplines determined that my will should replace automatism by hastening or retarding automatic acts. Every breath was submitted to this process, with the result that the normal power of breathing was dangerously interfered with. It seemed as though I should suffocate if I ceased to will. I had a terrible half-hour; at length by slow and irregular steps the lost power returned. My dread was hardly fanciful, for heart-failure is the suspension of the automatic faculty of the heart to beat.

A later experiment was to gain some idea of the commoner feelings in Insanity. The method tried was to invest everything I met, whether human, animal, or inanimate, with the imaginary attributes of a spy. Having arranged plans, I started on my morning's walk from Rutland Gate, and found the experiment only too successful. By the time I had walked one and a half miles, and reached the cab-stand in Piccadilly at the east end of the Green Park, every horse on the stand seemed watching me, either with pricked ears or disguising its espionage. Hours passed before this uncanny sensation wore off, and I feel that I could only too easily re-establish it.

The third and last experiment of which I will speak was to gain an insight into the abject feelings of barbarians and others concerning the power of images which they know to be of human handiwork. I had visited a large collection of idols gathered by missionaries from many lands, and wondered how each of those absurd and ill-made monstrosities could have obtained the hold it had over the imaginations of its worshippers. I wished, if possible, to enter into those feelings. It was difficult to find a suitable object for trial, because it ought to be in itself quite unfitted to arouse devout feelings. I fixed on a comic picture, it was that of Punch, and made believe in its possession of divine attributes. I addressed it with much quasi-reverence as possessing a mighty power to reward or punish the behaviour of men towards it, and found little difficulty in ignoring the impossibilities of what I professed. The experiment gradually succeeded; I began to feel and long retained for the picture a large share of the feelings that a barbarian entertains towards his idol, and learnt to appreciate the enormous potency they might have over him.

I will mention here a rather weird effect that compiling these " Memories " has produced on me. By much dwelling upon them they became refurbished and so vivid as to appear as sharp and definite as things of to-day. The consequence has been an occasional obliteration of the sense of Time, and to replace it by the idea of a permanent panorama, painted throughout with equal vividness, in which the point to which attention is temporarily directed becomes for that time the Present. The panorama seems to extend unseen behind a veil which hides the Future, but is slowly rolling aside and disclosing it. That part of the panorama which is veiled is supposed to exist as vividly coloured as the rest, though latent. In short, this experience has given me an occasional feeling that there are no realities corresponding to Past, Present, and Future, but that the entire Cosmos is one perpetual Now. Philosophers have often held this creed intellectually, but I suspect that few have felt the possible truth of it so vividly as it has occasionally appeared to my imagination through dwelling on these "Memories."

Many mental processes admit of being roughly measured. For instance, the degree to which people are bored, by counting the number of their Fidgets. I not infrequently tried this method at the meetings of the Royal Geographical Society, for even there dull memoirs are occasionally read. A gallery in the meeting room is supported by iron columns. The portion of the audience as seen from the platform who are bounded by two of these columns, and who sit on two or three of the benches, are a convenient sample to deal with. They can be watched simultaneously, and the number of movements in the group per minute can be easily counted and the average number per man calculated. I have often amused myself with noticing the increase in that number as the audience becomes tired. The use of a watch attracts attention, so I reckon time by the number of my breathings, of which there are fifteen in a minute. They are not counted mentally, but are punctuated by pressing with fifteen fingers successively. The counting is reserved for the fidgets. These observations should be confined to persons of middle age. Children are rarely still, while elderly philosophers will sometimes remain rigid for minutes together.

I will now revert to the problem with which I started, of measuring by Classification, and will give a few instances of its employment. Some years ago I attended a meeting in the Albert Hall, at which prizes of much value were to be awarded to the best made men in Sandow's gymnastic classes, as estimated by three examiners, of whom Sir A. Conan Doyle was one, while Sandow himself acted as referee.

I regret to have destroyed or mislaid the notes I made, so the following description of the very instructive ceremony may be inaccurate in small details.

The prizes were three, of an aggregate value of not far from £1000, and given by Mr. Sandow. He had made a tour to his many centres of gymnastic teaching in England, and picked out from each of them the man or men who were most likely to stand well in the competition. The day arrived; I got a good seat, and was prepared with an opera glass. The competitors marched into the arena; they were about eighty in number, and they were in ranks of ten abreast. They were stripped to the waist, but calico cloths coloured something like a leopard skin were thrown over their shoulders. So they marched round the arena, then the front row discarded their leopard skins, and jumped each man on to one of a row of pedestals arranged in front of the organ. The electric light was thrown on them. The three examiners walked in front and behind, taking notes and interchanging views. The man who was selected as the best of this batch went to one side; the others rejoined their companions. The same proceeding was gone through with the second row, and so on successively to the end. Then the selected ones came forward and stood on the pedestals as before, and were examined still more minutely, if possible. Finally, the first, second, and third man in order of their estimated merit were marched to the middle of the hall to the tune of the "Conquering Hero," and received their costly prizes in the form of athletic groups in gold, silver, or bronze.

The point that especially interested me was that I had done my best to form just decisions of my own, and that I had already selected those who came second and third as among the best three. But I had wrongly classed the first prizeman. However, after the judges had made their award I recognised the superior justness of their estimate to my own. The power of classifying men correctly, by mere inspection, seemed to me much greater after this experience than before.

A little more than a year ago, I happened to be at Plymouth, and was interested in a Cattle exhibition, where a visitor could purchase a stamped and numbered ticket for sixpence, which qualified him to become a candidate in a weight-judging competition. An ox was selected, and each of about eight hundred candidates wrote his name and address on his ticket, together with his estimate of what the beast would weigh when killed and "dressed" by the butcher. The most successful of them gained prizes. The result of these estimates was analogous, under reservation, to the votes given by a democracy, and it seemed likely to be instructive to learn how votes were distributed on this occasion, and the value of the result. So I procured a loan of the cards after the ceremony was past, and worked them out in a memoir published in *Nature* [177-8]. It appeared that in this instance the *vox populi* was correct to within 1 per cent. of the real value ; it was 1207 pounds instead of 1198 pounds, and the individual estimates were distributed in such a way that it was an equal chance whether one of them selected at random fell within or without the limits of -3.7 per cent., or $+2.4$ per cent. of the middlemost value of the whole.

The result seems more creditable to the trust-worthiness of a democratic judgment than might have been expected. But the proportion of the voters who were practised in judging weights undoubtedly surpassed that of the voters in ordinary elections who are versed in politics.

I endeavoured in the memoirs just mentioned, to show the appropriateness of utilising the *Median* vote in Councils and in Juries, whenever they have to consider money questions. Each juryman has his own view of what the sum should be. I will suppose each of them to be written down. The best interpretation of their collective view is to my mind *certainly not* the average, because the wider the deviation of an individual member from the average of the rest, the more largely would it effect the result. In short, unwisdom is given greater weight than wisdom. In all cases in which one vote is supposed to have one value, the median value *must* be the truest representative of the whole, because any other value would be negatived if put to the vote. If it were more than the median, more than half of the voters would think it too much; if less, too little. My idea is that the median ought to be ascertained, which could be very quickly done by the foreman, aided by one or two others of the Jury, and be put forward as a substantial proposal, after reading the various figures from which it was derived.

This is a convenient place for speaking of an

analogous problem that interested me a few years previously [159]. I have had more than once to assist in determining how a given sum allotted for prizes ought to be divided between the first and second men when only two prizes are given. The same problem has to be solved by the judges of cattle shows, and it is, if a little generalised, of very wide application. I attacked it both theoretically and practically, and got the same results both ways. When the number of candidates is known, and the distribution of merit follows the well-known Gaussian law, the calculation is easy enough, but when the number of candidates is not known it is a different matter; moreover, the Gaussian law may not apply to the case, though it will probably do so pretty closely. So I calculated what the ratios would be in classes of different numbers and according to the Gaussian law. The ratio in question is that between the excess of the first performance over the third, and the excess of the second performance over the third. The third being the highest that gets no prize at all, forms the starting-point of the calculation. When the numbers of candidates were either 3, 5, 10, 20, 50, 100, 1,000, 10,000, or 100,000, I found, to my surprise, that the ratio was much the same. The appropriate portion of the total of one hundred pounds which should be allotted to the first prize proved to be seventy-five pounds, leaving twenty-five or one-third of its amount for the second prize. Even when the number of candidates were at the minimum of 3, the first prize would be £67; if 5, it would be £71; if 10, it would be £73; and if 100,000, it would be £75 (to the nearest whole figures).

Then, through the courtesy of Mr. Muir, the Chief Examiner at the Education Office, I was allowed to examine a large number of results from the Civil Service Examinations, and found that the average value of the first prize should be £74. Taking groups of 50 cases, each group gave that value pretty closely, no one differing as much as £4 from it.

The subject has since been generalised and discussed in *Biometrika* with far more mathematical skill than I possess, by both Professor Karl Pearson and Mr. W. F. Sheppard (a former Senior Wrangler), with practically the same result, so that if only two prizes are to be given, whatever be the character of the competition, and whatever the number of candidates, the first prize should in round numbers be three times the value of the second.

Professor Max Müller had, in a work dated 1886 or 1887, laid an exaggerated stress, as I considered, on language as a means of thought, upon which I wrote some remarks in *Nature* [98], entitled "Thought without Words," which led to a short newspaper controversy, June 2, between us two. My point was that I myself thought hardest when making no mental use of words. Professor Max Müller's definitions of what he considered "words" seemed to me to vary, and therefore to be elusive, so I did not and will not pursue the matter farther.

It led, however, to the idea of an experiment that seemed worth making, which I described [128] as "Arithmetic by Smell." When we propose to add, and *hear* the spoken words "two" and "three," we instantly through long habit *say* "five." Or if we *see* those figures, we have a mental image, and *write* 5. Surely, Sound and Sight-symbols are not the only Sense-symbols by which arithmetic could be performed.

Leaving aside Colour, Touch, and Taste, I determined to try Smells. The scents chiefly used were peppermint, camphor, carbolic acid, ammonia, and aniseed. Each scent was poured profusely on cotton wool loosely packed in a brass tube, with a nozzle at one end. The other end was pushed tightly into a caoutchouc tube, whose free end was stopped with a cork. A squeeze of the tube caused a whiff of scented air to pass through the nozzle. When the squeeze was relaxed, fresh air was sucked in and became scented by the way. I taught myself to associate two whiffs of peppermint with one of camphor, three of peppermint with one of carbolic acid, and so on. Next, I practised small sums in addition with the scents themselves, afterwards with the mere imagination of them. I banished without difficulty all visual and auditory associations, and finally succeeded perfectly. Thus I fully convinced myself of the possibility of doing sums in simple addition with considerable speed and accuracy, solely by imagined scents. I did not care to give further time to this, as I only wanted to prove a possibility, but did make a few experiments with Taste, that promised equally well, using salt, sugar, quinine, and citric acid.

I have once in my life experienced the influence of Personal Ascendancy in that high degree which some great personalities have exercised, and the occasion of which I speak was the more striking owing to the absence of concurrent pomp. It was on Garibaldi's arrival in London, where he was hailed as a hero. I was standing in Trafalgar Square when he reached it, driving up Parliament Street. His vehicle was a shabby open carriage, stuffed with Italians, regardless of style in dress; Garibaldi alone was standing. I had not been in a greatly excited or exalted mood, but the simplicity, goodness, and nobility impressed on every lineament of Garibaldi's face and person quite overcame me. I realised then what I never did before or after, something of the impression that Jesus seems to have exercised on multitudes on more than one occasion. I am grateful to that experience for revealing to me the hero-worshipping potentialities of my nature.

When the late Mr. Spurgeon first made his reputation, I went, as many others did, to hear him. I was in the gallery of his "Tabernacle," which was said to hold 11,000 persons, and in which certainly 9000 were then present, as roughly counted by myself. The men had their hats on, and conversation was unchecked. Suddenly there was a slight stir that travelled through the crowd, and the almost childlike features of the young preacher came into view as he rose from below and mounted the platform. He simply raised his hand; there was a simultaneous removal of hats and a great hush, and then the words began. It was a marvellous instance of the commanding power of a simple gesture.

One more instance, and I have done. It occurred towards the close of my undergraduate days at

Cambridge at a festival which I will not particularise further than to say it was partly solemn at first, and broadened into good fellowship without any excess. Songs were sung, and J. Mitchell Kemble, the subject of Tennyson's early "Ode to J. M. K.,"[1] gave time to the chorus of one of the songs by raising his arm and moving his glass. By those most simple gestures, he drove us all into an enthusiasm, comparable with that to which negroes are occasionally driven by an accurately timed tom-tom. In one of Bulwer's novels, the performer in a barn exercises equal power over his audience by the movements of a stick.

The human senses, when rythmically stimulated in certain exact cadences, are capable of eliciting overwhelming emotions not yet sufficiently investigated.

[1] Nephew of the two great actors, John Philip Kemble and of Mrs. Siddons ; brother of Adelaide and of Fanny Kemble, and having at least four other near relations who were noted actors.

CHAPTER XX

HEREDITY

THE publication in 1859 of the *Origin of Species*
by Charles Darwin made a marked epoch in
my own mental development, as it did in that of
human thought generally. Its effect was to demolish
a multitude of dogmatic barriers by a single stroke,
and to arouse a spirit of rebellion against all ancient
authorities whose positive and unauthenticated state-
ments were contradicted by modern science.

I doubt, however, whether any instance has
occurred in which the perversity of the educated
classes in misunderstanding what they attempted to
discuss was more painfully conspicuous. The meaning of the simple phrase "Natural Selection" was
distorted in curiously ingenious ways, and Darwinism
was attacked, both in the press and pulpit, by persons
who were manifestly ignorant of what they talked
about. This is a striking instance of the obstructions
through which new ideas have to force their way.
Plain facts are apprehended in a moment, but the
introduction of a new Idea is quite another matter, for
it requires an alteration in the attitude and balance of

the mind which may be a very repugnant and even painful process.   On my part, however, I felt little difficulty in connection with the *Origin of Species*, but devoured its contents and assimilated them as fast as they were devoured, a fact which perhaps may be ascribed to an hereditary bent of mind that both its illustrious author and myself have inherited from our common grandfather, Dr. Erasmus Darwin.

I was encouraged by the new views to pursue many inquiries which had long interested me, and which clustered round the central topics of Heredity and the possible improvement of the Human Race. The current views on Heredity were at that time so vague and contradictory that it is difficult to summarise them briefly.   Speaking generally, most authors agreed that all bodily and some mental qualities were inherited by brutes, but they refused to believe the same of man.   Moreover, theologians made a sharp distinction between the body and mind of man, on purely dogmatic grounds.   A few passages may undoubtedly be found in the works of eminent authors that are exceptions to this broad generalisation, for the subject of human heredity had never been squarely faced, and opinions were lax and contradictory.   It seems hardly credible now that even the word heredity was then considered fanciful and unusual.   I was chaffed by a cultured friend for adopting it from the French.

I had been immensely impressed by many obvious cases of heredity among the Cambridge men who were at the University about my own time.   The Classical Class List was first established in 1824, consequently the number of " Senior Classics " up to 1864 inclusive was 41, that is to say, the names of

the 41 very first men in Classics at Cambridge in
each of these 41 years were known and published.
It will be sufficient as an example to give the names
of 7 of these Senior Classics, all of whom had a
father, brother, or son whose success was as notable
as their own (I count a Senior Wrangler as equal
to a Senior Classic). They are: 3 Kennedys,
2 Lushingtons, 1 Wordsworth, and 1 Butler. This
fact alone would justify a serious attempt to inquire
into Hereditary Ability, and I soon found the power
of heredity to be as fully displayed in every other
direction towards which I turned. The Myttons
mentioned in Chapter VIII. were an unquestionable
instance of a very peculiar hereditary temperament.

After many months of hard work, I wrote, in 1865,
two preliminary papers in *Macmillan's Magazine*,
entitled "Hereditary Talent and Character" [20].
These contain the germs of many of my subsequent
memoirs, the contents of which went to the making
of the following books: *Hereditary Genius*, 1869;
English Men of Science, 1874; *Human Faculty*,
1883; *Natural Inheritance*, 1889; and to my quite
recent writings on Eugenics. On re-reading these
articles, I must say that, considering the novel
conditions under which they were composed, and
notwithstanding some crudeness here and there, I am
surprised at their justness and comprehensiveness.
It has fortunately been my usual habit (sometimes
omitted) of keeping copies of my various memoirs,
which are now bound in volumes. There are considerably more than a hundred and seventy publications in all, as will be gathered from the not wholly
complete list in the Appendix, and I am pleased to

19

find myself still in accord with nearly every one of those recently re-read or referred to.

Hereditary Genius [22] made its mark at the time, though subjected to much criticism, no small part of which was captious or shallow, and therefore unimportant. The verdict which I most eagerly waited for was that of Charles Darwin, whom I ranked far above all other authorities on such a matter. His letter, given below, made me most happy.

" DOWN, BECKENHAM, KENT, S.E.
3rd December

" MY DEAR GALTON,—I have only read about 50 pages of your book (to Judges), but I must exhale myself, else something will go wrong in my inside. I do not think I ever in all my life read anything more interesting and original — and how well and clearly you put every point ! George,[1] who has finished the book, and who expressed himself in just the same terms, tells me that the earlier chapters are nothing in interest to the later ones ! It will take me some time to get to these latter chapters, as it is read aloud to me by my wife, who is also much interested. You have made a convert of an opponent in one sense, for I have always maintained that, excepting fools, men did not differ much in intellect, only in zeal and hard work ; and I still think this is an *eminently* important difference. I congratulate you on producing what I am convinced will prove a memorable work. I look forward with intense interest to each reading, but it sets me thinking so much that I find it very hard work ; but that is wholly the fault of my brain and not of your beautifully clear style.—Yours most sincerely,

(Signed)   " CH. DARWIN "

[1] Now Professor Sir George H. Darwin, K.C.B., F.R.S., etc,

The rejoinder that might be made to his remark about hard work, is that character, *including the aptitude for work*, is heritable like every other faculty.

I had been overworked, and unable to give as close attention as desirable while correcting the proofs, so mistakes were to be feared. Happily there were not many, but one was absurd, and I was justly punished. It was due to some extraordinary commingling of notes on the families of Jane Austen and of Austin the jurist. In my normal state of health the mistake could not have been overlooked, but there it was. I was at that time a member of the Committee of the Athenæum Club, among whose members there happened to be a representative of each of the above families, who "gave it me hot," though most decorously.

I had much pleasant correspondence at a later date with Alphonse de Candolle, son of the still greater botanist of that name. He had written a very interesting book, *Histoire des Sciences et des Savants depuis deux Siècles*, in which he analysed the conditions that caused nations, and especially the Swiss, to be more prolific in works of science at one time than another, and I thought that a somewhat similar investigation might be made with advantage into the history of English men of science.

It was a daring undertaking, to ask as I did, in 1874, every Fellow of the Royal Society who had filled some important post, to answer a multitude of Questions needful for my purpose, a few of which touched on religion and other delicate matters. Of course they were sent on the distinct understanding that the answers would be used for statistical purposes only.   I took advice on the subject, notably of Herbert Spencer, and I think (though I cannot say for certain) from Dr. W. Farr also.   Dr. W. Farr (1807–83) was the head of the Registration Department in Somerset House.   I frequently consulted him, and always to my advantage, for he was highly gifted and cultured.   He was most sympathetic, and keenly appreciated what might be called the poetical side of statistics, as shown by his Annual Reports and other publications.

The size of my circular was alarming.   Though naturally very shy, I do occasional acts, like other shy persons, of an unusually bold description, and this was one.   After an uneasy night, I prepared myself on the following afternoon, and not for the first time before interviews that were likely to be unpleasant, by what is said to have been the usual practice of Buffon before writing anything exceptional, namely, by dressing myself in my best clothes.

I can confidently recommend this plan to shy men as giving a sensible addition to their own self-respect, and as somewhat increasing the respect of others.   In this attire I went to a meeting of the Royal Society, prepared to be howled at ; but no ! my victims, taken as a whole, tolerated the action, and some even approved of it.

Much experience of sending circular questions has convinced me of the impossibility of foretelling whether a particular person will receive them kindly or not.   Some are unexpectedly touchy.   In this very case, a man of high scientific distinction, with whom I was well acquainted, who was of good social position, of whose family many details were already known to me, all of which were honourable, and whose biography has since disclosed no skeleton in the cupboard, was almost furious at being questioned. On the other hand, a Cabinet Minister, whom I knew but slightly, gave me full and very interesting information without demur.

The results of the inquiry showed how largely the aptitude for science was an inborn and not an acquired gift, and therefore apt to be hereditary. But, in not a few instances, the person who replied was a "sport," being the only one of his family who had any care for science, and who had persevered in spite of opposition. The paternal influence generally superseded the maternal in early life, though the mother was usually spoken of with much love, and very often described as particularly able. This seemed to afford evidence that the virile, independent cast of mind is more suitable to scientific research than the feminine, which is apt to be biased by the emotions and to obey authority. But I have said my say long since in the book *English Men of Science* [36], and must not reiterate.

The dearth of information about the Transmission of Qualities among all the members of a family during two, three, or more generations, induced me in 1884–85 to offer a sum of £500 in prizes to those who most successfully filled up an elaborate list of questions concerning their own families. The questions were contained in a thin quarto volume of several pages, printed and procurable at Macmillan's, cost price, which referred to the Grandparents, Parents, Brothers, Sisters, and Children, with spaces for more distant relatives. A promise was given, and scrupulously kept, that they should be used for statistical purposes only. My offer had a goodly response, and the names of the prize-winners were duly published in the newspapers. I was much indebted, when devising the programme and other prefatory details, both to Professor Allman (1812–1898), the biologist, and to my old friend at King's College, Mr. (afterwards Sir) John Simon. The material afforded by the answers proved of considerable importance, and formed the basis of much of my future work. I had it extracted in a statistical form, in considerable detail, which was of much value to Professor Karl Pearson at the outset of his inquiries, before he had been able to collect better and much more numerous data of his own. It will be convenient to defer speaking of the results of all this until the last chapter.

I had long tried to gain some insight into the relative powers of Nature and Nurture, in order that due allowance might be made for Environment, neither too much nor too little, but without finding an adequate method of obtaining it. At length it occurred to me that the after-history of those twins who had been closely alike as children, and were afterwards parted, or who had been originally unlike and afterwards reared together, would supply much of what was wanted. So I inquired in all directions for appropriate cases, and at length obtained a fair supply, on which an article in *Frazer's Magazine*, Nov. 1875,[1] was written. The evidence was overwhelming that the power of Nature was far stronger than that of

---

[1] It was revised and added to in the *Journal of the Anthropological Institute*, 1875 [43], and then incorporated into *Human Faculty*, 1883 (which is now republished in an exceedingly cheap form in "Everyman's Library").

Nurture, when the Nurtures of the persons compared were not exceedingly different. It appeared that when twins who had been closely alike had afterwards grown dissimilar, the date of divergence was usually referred to a time when one of them had a serious illness, sufficient to modify his constitution.

Many years later I was so harassed with the old question of Determinism, which would leave every human action under the control of Heredity and Environment, that I made a series of observations on the actions of my own mind in relation to Free Will. I employ the word not merely as meaning " unhindered " but in the *special* sense of an *uncaused* and *creative* action. It was carried on almost continuously for six weeks, and off and on for many subsequent months [55]. The procedure was this. Whenever I caught myself in an act of what seemed to be " Free Will " in the above sense, I checked myself and tried hard to recollect what had happened before, made rapid notes, and then wrote a full account of the case. To my surprise, I found, after some days' work, that the occasions were rare on which there seemed room for the exercise of Free Will as defined above. I subsequently reckoned that they did not occur oftener than once a day. Motives for all the other events could be traced backwards in succession, by orderly and continuous steps, until they led into a tangle of familiar paths. It was curious to watch the increase of power given by practice, of recalling mental actions which being usually overlooked give the false idea that much has been performed through a creative act, or by inspiration, which is really due to straightforward causation. The subject is too complex to be more fully gone into here ; I must refer to the Memoir itself.   The general result of the inquiry was to support the views of those who hold that man is little more than a conscious machine, the slave of heredity and environment, the larger part, perhaps all, of whose actions are therefore predictable.   As regards such residuum as may not be automatic but creative, and which a Being, however wise and well-informed, could not possibly foresee, I have nothing to say, but I found that the more carefully I inquired, whether it was into hereditary similarities of conduct, into the life-histories of twins, or introspectively into the actions of my own mind, the smaller seemed the room left for this possible residuum.

Many possibilities suggested themselves after reading Darwin's " Provisional theory of Pangenesis." One was that the breed of a race might be sensibly affected by the transfusion of blood from another variety.   According to Darwin's theory, every element of the body throws off gemmules, each of which can reproduce itself, and a combination of these gemmules forms a sexual element.   If so, I argued, the blood which conveys these gemmules to the places where they are developed, whether to repair an injured part or to the sexual organs, must be full of them.   They would presumably live in the blood for a considerable time.   Therefore, if the blood of an animal of one species were largely replaced by that of another, some effect ought to be produced on its subsequent offspring.   For example, the dash of bull-dog tenacity that is now given to a breed of greyhounds by a single cross with a bull-dog, the first generation corresponding to a mulatto, the second to a quadroon, the third to an octoroon, and so on, might be given at once by transfusion. Bleeding is the simplest of operations, and I knew that transfusion had been performed on a large scale ; therefore I set about making minute inquiries.

These took a long time, and required much consideration. At length I determined upon trying the experiment on the well-known breed of rabbits called silver greys, of which pure breeds were obtainable, and to exchange much of their blood for that of the common lop-eared rabbit; afterwards to breed from pairs of silver greys in each of which alien blood had been largely transfused. This was done in 1871 on a considerable scale. I soon succeeded in establishing a vigorous cross-circulation that lasted several minutes between rabbits of different breeds, as described in the *Proceedings of the Royal Society*, 1871 [25]. The experiments were thorough, and misfortunes very rare. It was astonishing to see how quickly the rabbits recovered after the effect of the anæsthetic had passed away. It often happened that their spirits and sexual aptitudes were in no way dashed by an operation which only a few minutes before had changed nearly one half of the blood that was in their bodies. Out of a stock of three silver grey bucks and four silver grey does, whose blood had been thus largely adulterated, and of three common bucks and four common does whose blood had been similarly altered, I bred eighty-eight rabbits in thirteen litters without any evidence of alteration of breed. All this is described in detail in the Memoir.

I was indebted to expert friends for making these

delicate operations, my own part was confined to inserting cannulæ and the like.   At first Dr. Murie did all the dexterous and difficult work.   He had been a traveller in company with Consul Petherick, far up the White Nile, and was then Prosector at the Zoological Gardens.   I called on him to discuss the matter.   A dead cobra was lying on his table, and on my remarking that I had never properly seen a poison fang, he coolly opened the creature's mouth, pressed firmly at exactly the right spot, and out started that most delicate and wicked-looking thing, with a drop of venom exuding from it, just in front of his nail.   I thought that a man who was so confident of his anatomical knowledge and of his nerve as to dare such an act, must be an especially suitable person to conduct my experiments, and was fortunate enough to secure his co-operation.

I continued the experiments for another generation of rabbits beyond those described in the *Proc. Royal Society*, with equally negative results.   Mr. Romanes subsequently repeated the experiments with my instruments, and they corroborated my own.   So this point seems settled.

The laws of Heredity are concerned only with deviations from the Median, which have to be translated from whatever they were measured by, whether in feet, pounds weight, intervals of time, or any other absolute standard, into what might be called "Statistical Units."   Their office is to make the variabilities of totally different classes, such as horses, men, mice, plants, proficiency in classics, etc. etc., comparable on equal terms.   The statistical unit of each series is derived from the series itself. There is more than one kind of them, but they are all mutually convertible, just as measures recorded in feet are convertible into inches. The most convenient unit for purpose of explanation, though not for calculation, is the half difference between the marks or measures corresponding to the lower or to the upper quantities respectively.[1]

Deviations expressed in statistical units are usually found to conform with much closeness to the results of a certain theoretical law, discovered by Gauss, the great mathematician, and properly called by his name, though more familiarly known as the Normal Law. It supposes all variability to be due to different and equally probable combinations of a multitude of small independent causes. The relative frequency of different amounts of these, reckoned in statistical units, can thence be computed. It is done by refined methods based on the same general principles as those by which sequences of different lengths, in successive throws of dice, are determined.

Results of the computation are shown in the bottom line of the following small table :—

Centiles and Corresponding Deviation from the Median.

Centiles .	10th	20th	30th	40th	50th	60th	70th	80th	90th
Deviations .	− 1·90	− 1·25	− 0·78	− 0·38	− 0	+ 0·38	+ 0·78	+ 1·25	+ 1·90

[1] This unit is known by the uncouth and not easily justified name of "Probable Error," which I suppose is intended to express the fact that the number of deviations or "Errors" in the two outer fourths of the series is the same as those in the two middle fourths ; and therefore the probability is equal that an unknown error will fall into either of these two great halves, the outer or the inner.

The deviation at the 25th is − 1, that at the 75th is + 1 ; so the difference between them is 2, and the half difference is 1.

As these lines are being written, the circumstances under which I first clearly grasped the important generalisation that the laws of Heredity were solely concerned with deviations expressed in statistical units, are vividly recalled to my memory. It was in the grounds of Naworth Castle, where an invitation had been given to ramble freely. A temporary shower drove me to seek refuge in a reddish recess in the rock by the side of the pathway. There the idea flashed across me, and I forgot everything else for a moment in my great delight.

The following question had been much in my mind. How is it possible for a population to remain alike in its features, as a whole, during many successive generations, if the *average* produce of each couple resemble their parents? Their children are not alike, but vary : therefore some would be taller, some shorter than their average height ; so among the issue of a gigantic couple there would be usually some children more gigantic still. Conversely as to very small couples. But from what I could thus far find, parents had issue less exceptional than themselves. I was very desirous of ascertaining the facts of the case. After much consideration and many inquiries, I determined, in 1885, on experimenting with sweet peas, which were suggested to me both by Sir Joseph Hooker and by Mr. Darwin. Their merits are threefold. They have so little tendency to become cross-fertilised that seedsmen do not hesitate to grow differently coloured plants in neighbouring beds ; all the seeds in their pods are of the same size, that is to say, there is no little pea at the end as in the pod of the common pea, and they are very hardy and prolific. I procured a large number of seeds from the same bin, and selected seven weights, calling them K (the largest), L, M, N, O, P, and Q (the smallest), forming an arithmetic series. Curiously, their lengths, found by measuring ten of a kind in a row, also formed an arithmetic series, owing, I suppose, to the larger and plumper seeds being more spherical and therefore taking less room for their weight than the others. Ten peas of each of these seven descriptions, seventy in all, formed what I called a "set."

I persuaded friends living in various parts of the country, each to plant a set for me. The uniform method to be followed was to prepare seven parallel beds, each 1½ feet wide and 5 feet long, to dibble ten holes in each at equal distances apart, and 1 inch in depth, and to put one seed in each hole. The beds were then to be bushed over to keep off the birds. As the seeds became ripe they were to be gathered and put into bags which I sent, lettered respectively from K to Q ; the same letters having been stuck at both ends of the beds. Finally, when the crop was coming to an end, the whole foliage of each row was to be torn up, tied together, and sent to me. All this was done, and further minute instructions, which I need not describe here, were attended to carefully. The result clearly proved *Regression* ; the mean Filial deviation was only one-third that of the parental one, and the experiments all concurred. The formula that expresses the descent from one generation of a people to the next, showed that the generations would be identical if this kind of *Regression* was allowed for.[1]

In 1886 I contributed two papers [91, 92] to the Royal Society on Family Likeness, having by that time got my methods for measuring heredity into satisfactory shape. I had given much time and thought to Tables of Correlations, to display the frequency of cases in which the various deviations say in stature, of an adult person, measured along the top, were associated with the various deviations of stature in his mid-parent, measured along the side. (I had long used the convenient word " mid-parent " to express the average of the two parents, after the stature or other character of the mother had been changed into its male equivalent.) But I could not see my way to express the results of the complete table in a single formula. At length, one morning, while waiting at a roadside station near Ramsgate for a train, and poring over the diagram in my notebook, it struck me that the lines of equal frequency ran in concentric ellipses. The cases were too few for certainty, but my eye, being accustomed to such things, satisfied me that I was approaching the solution. More careful drawing strongly corroborated the first impression.

All the formulæ of Conic Sections having long since gone out of my head, I went on my return to London to the Royal Institution to read them up. Professor, now Sir James, Dewar, came in, and probably noticing signs of despair in my face, asked me what I was about ; then said, "Why do you bother over

[1] See Pres. Address, Section H, Brit. Assoc. Aberdeen, 1885 [87].

this? My brother-in-law, J. Hamilton Dickson of Peterhouse, loves problems and wants new ones. Send it to him." I did so, under the form of a problem in mechanics, and he most cordially helped me by working it out, as proposed, on the basis of the usually accepted and generally justifiable Gaussian Law of Error. So I begged him to allow his solution to be given as an appendix to my paper [91], where it will be found.

It had appeared from observation, and it was fully confirmed by this theory, that such a thing existed as an " Index of Correlation "; that is to say, a fraction, now commonly written r, that connects with close approximation every value of deviation on the part of the subject, with the *average* of all the associated deviations of the Relative as already described. Therefore the closeness of any specified kinship admits of being found and expressed by a single term. If a particular individual deviates so much, the *average* of the deviations of all his brothers will be a definite fraction of that amount; similarly as to sons, parents, first cousins, etc. Where there is no relationship at all, r becomes equal to 0; when it is so close that Subject and Relative are identical in value, then $r = 1$. Therefore the value of r lies in every case somewhere between the extreme limits of 0 and 1. Much more could be added, but not without using technical language, which would be inappropriate here.

The problem as described above is by no means difficult to a fair mathematician. Mr. J. H. Dickson set it to a class of his higher students, most of whom answered it. It has since been remarked that this same mechanical problem had been solved still more comprehensively by a French mathematician. Professor Karl Pearson subsequently extended its application to variables not governed by the Gaussian Law, and the exact determination of the Index of Correlation by his refined method has now become the object of most biometric work.

I have received much help at various times from Mathematical friends. On one occasion, being impressed with the probability (owing to Weber's and Fechner's Laws) that the true mean value of many of the qualities with which I dealt would be the Geometric and not the Arithmetic Mean, I asked Mr. Donald Macalister, of whom I have already spoken, to work out the results. He, as a schoolboy, was the first to gain the prize medal of the Royal Geographical Society, then became the Senior Wrangler of his year at Cambridge, subsequently Chairman of the Medical Council, and is now Provost of Glasgow University. His memoir is supplementary to mine on the "Geometric Mean," *Proceedings of the Royal Society*, 1879 [53].

My first serious interest in the Gaussian Law of Error was due to the inspiration of William Spottiswoode, who had used it long ago in a Geographical memoir for discussing the probability of the elevations of certain mountain chains being due to a common cause. He explained to me the far-reaching application of that extraordinarily beautiful law, which I fully apprehended. I had also the pleasure of making the acquaintance of Quetelet, who was the first to apply it to human measurements, in its elementary binomial form, which I used in my *Hereditary Genius*.

The mathematician who most frequently helped me later on was the Rev. H. W. Watson, who moreover worked out for me the curious question of the " Probability of the Extinction of Families" [40]. It appeared in 1875 in the *Proceedings of the Royal Society* as a joint paper, at his desire ; but all the hard work was his : I only gave the first idea and the data. He helped me greatly in my first struggles with certain applications of the Gaussian Law, which, for some reasons that I could never clearly perceive, seemed for a long time to be comprehended with difficulty by mathematicians, including himself. They were unnecessarily alarmed lest the well-known rules of Inverse Probability should be unconsciously violated, which they never were. I could give a striking case of this, but abstain because it would seem deprecia-tory of a man whose mathematical powers and ability were far in excess of my own. Still, he was quite wrong. The primary objects of the Gaussian Law of Error were exactly opposed, in one sense, to those to which I applied them. They were to get rid of, or to provide a just allowance for errors. But these errors or deviations were the very things I wanted to preserve and to know about. This was the reason that one eminent living mathematician gave me.

The patience of some of my mathematical friends was tried in endeavouring to explain what I myself saw very clearly as a geometrical problem, but could not express in the analytical forms to which they were accustomed, and which they persisted in misapplying. It was a gain to me when I had at last won over Mr. Watson, who put my views into a more suitable shape. H. W. Watson was Second Wrangler of his

20

year, and had the reputation among his college fellows of extraordinary subtlety and insight as a mathematician. He was perhaps a little too nice and critical about his own work, losing time in over-polishing, so that the amount of what he produced was lessened. He wrote on the *Kinetic Theory of Gases*.

I may mention two anecdotes about him. He had been a good Alpine climber and met with various incidents. One was that he and a friend, F. Vaughan Hawkins, set off at a good pace to vanquish some new but not difficult peak, and passed on their way a somewhat plodding party of German philosophers bound on the same errand. One of Watson's shoes had shown previous signs of damage, but he thought he could manage to get on for a day or two longer if he now and then covered it with an indiarubber galosh that he then took with him for such emergencies. It was a cumbrous addition, but succeeded fairly, and he and his friend reached the top long before the Germans, whom they thought no more about. However, shortly after, a Swiss-German newspaper gave a somewhat grandiose account of the ascent of the mountain in question by Professors This and That, in which it was remarked that the Professors would have been the very first to reach its summit had not two jealous Englishmen provided themselves with "Gummi Schuhe" and so were able to outstrip them.

The other anecdote refers to the circumstances under which Watson became Rector of a valuable living, that of Berkswell, near Coventry. I repeat the tale to the best of my remembrance as he told it me, but doubtless with mistakes in a few details. He was a Master at Harrow when some scrape had occurred, and a boy in whom he was interested was judged guilty and sent up to be flogged. The boy protested his innocence so vehemently, that although appearances were sadly against him, Watson was ready to believe what he said, and took unusual pains to investigate the matter. The result was that the boy was completely exculpated. A few years after, the boy's father bought the property at Berkswell in which the gift of the living was included. It happened to be then vacant, and the new proprietor found he must either nominate some one at once, or the nomination would lapse, and fall (I think) to the Bishop. He knew of no suitable clergyman. Then the boy called out, "Give it to Mr. Watson," which the father, knowing the story, did.

I thought that some data which were needed might be obtained by breeding insects, without too great expenditure of time and money, and it ended in my selecting for the purpose, under the advice of Mr. Merrifield, a particular kind of Moth, the "Selenia illustraria," which breeds twice a year and is hardy. Mr. Merrifield most kindly undertook to conduct the experiments for me, and his methods were beautifully simple and suitable. They are described in the *Transactions of the Entomological Society*, 1887 [100]. Another friend also undertook a set. I will not describe any of the results at length, because they failed owing to rapidly diminishing fertility in successive generations, and through the large disturbing effects of small differences in environment. All the moths in the first generation were photographed neatly on octavo pages by a friend, Miss Reynolds, and a very great deal of trouble was taken about them, but all in vain. The only consolation that I have is that the experiences gained by Mr. Merrifield enabled him to pursue other experiments on moths with great success, which have led to his increased reputation as an entomologist.

Later still it seemed most desirable to obtain data that would throw light on the *Average* contribution of each Ancestor to the total heritage of the offspring in a mixed population. This is a purely statistical question, the same answer to which would be given on more than one theoretical hypothesis of heredity, whether it be Pangenetic, Mendelian, or other.

I must stop for a moment to pay a tribute to the memory of Mendel, with whom I sentimentally feel myself connected, owing to our having been born in the same year 1822. His careful and long-continued experiments show how much can be performed by those who, like him and Charles Darwin, never or hardly ever leave their homes, and again how much might be done in a fixed laboratory after a uniform tradition of work had been established. Mendel clearly showed that there were such things as alternative atomic characters of equal potency in descent. How far characters generally may be due to simple, or to molecular characters more or less correlated together, has yet to be discovered.

I had thought of experimenting with mice, as cheap to rear and very prolific, and had taken some steps to that end, when I became aware of the large collections of Basset Hounds belonging to the late Sir

Everard Millais. He offered me every facility. The Basset Hound records referring to his own and other breeds had been carefully kept, and the Stud Book he lent me contained accounts of nearly 1000 animals, of which I was able to utilise 817. All were descended from parents of known colours; in 567 of them the colours of all four grandparents were also known. Wherever the printed Stud Book was deficient, Sir Everard Millais supplied the want in MS from the original records. My inquiry was into the heredity of two alternative colours, one containing no black, the other containing it; their technical names were lemon-white and tri-colour (black, lemon, white) respectively. I was assured that no difficulty was felt in determining the category to which each individual belonged. These data were fully discussed in a memoir, published (1897) in the *Proceedings of the Royal Society* [139], on what is now termed the "Ancestral Law," namely, that the *average* contribution of each parent is $\frac{1}{4}$, of each grandparent $\frac{1}{16}$, and so on. Or, in other words, that of the two parents taken together is $\frac{1}{2}$, of the four grandparents together $\frac{1}{4}$, and so on. My data were not as numerous as is desirable, still the results were closely congruous, and seem to be a near approximation to the truth. The conclusions have been much discussed and criticised, and they have been modified by Professor Karl Pearson; but they have not been seriously shaken, so far as I know.

CHAPTER XXI

RACE IMPROVEMENT

Eugenics—Passages from my early writings—Original sin—Breeding
dogs for intelligence—Great extension of my work by Professor Karl
Pearson—Eugenics laboratory—Duty towards race improvement

THE subject of Race Improvement, or Eugenics,
with which I have much occupied myself
during the last few years, is a pursuit of no recent
interest.   I published my views as long ago as 1865,
in two articles written in *Macmillan's Magazine* [20],
while preparing materials for my book, *Hereditary
Genius*.   But I did not then realise, as now, the
powerful influence of Small Causes upon statistical
results.   I was too much disposed to think of marriage
under some regulation, and not enough of the effects
of self-interest and of social and religious sentiment.
Popular feeling was not then ripe to accept even the
elementary truths of hereditary talent and character,
upon which the possibility of Race Improvement
depends.   Still less was it prepared to consider dis-
passionately any proposals for practical action.   So
I laid the subject wholly to one side for many years.
Now I see my way better, and an appreciative audience
is at last to be had, though it be small.

As in most other cases of novel views, the wrong-
headedness of objectors to Eugenics has been curious.

The most common misrepresentations now are that its methods must be altogether those of compulsory unions, as in breeding animals. It is not so. I think that stern compulsion ought to be exerted to prevent the free propagation of the stock of those who are seriously afflicted by lunacy, feeble - mindedness, habitual criminality, and pauperism, but that is quite different from compulsory marriage. How to restrain ill-omened marriages is a question by itself, whether it should be effected by seclusion, or in other ways yet to be devised that are consistent with a humane and well-informed public opinion. I cannot doubt that our democracy will ultimately refuse consent to that liberty of propagating children which is now allowed to the undesirable classes, but the populace has yet to be taught the true state of these things. A democracy cannot endure unless it be composed of able citizens; therefore it must in self-defence withstand the free introduction of degenerate stock.

What I desire is that the importance of eugenic marriages should be reckoned at its just value, neither too high nor too low, and that Eugenics should form one of the many considerations by which marriages are promoted or hindered, as they are by social position, adequate fortune, and similarity of creed. I can believe hereafter that it will be felt as derogatory to a person of exceptionally good stock to marry into an inferior one as it is for a person of high Austrian rank to marry one who has not sixteen heraldic quarterings. I also hope that social recognition of an appropriate kind will be given to healthy, capable, and large families, and that social influence will be exerted towards the encouragement of eugenic marriages.

Confusion is often made between statistical and individual results. It sometimes seems to be held seriously that if the effect of a particular union cannot be accurately foretold, the application of the rules of Eugenics is vain. This is not the case. Statistics give us assurance concerning the fate of such or such a *percentage* of a large number of people which, when translated into other terms, is the probability of each of them being affected by it. From the statesman's point of view, where lives are pawns in the game and personal favour is excluded, this information is sufficient. It tells how large a number of undesirables or of desirables can be introduced or not into a population by such and such measures. Whether their names be A, B, or C, or else X, Y, or Z, is of no importance to the " Statistician,"—a term that is more or less equivalent to that of " Statesman."

In accordance with one principal purpose of these pages, which is to show the fundamental coherence of most of my many inquiries, I will quote several passages from the above-mentioned articles written in 1865. They expressed then, as clearly as I can do now, the leading principles of Eugenics. They will each be followed by a remark as to how I should wish to modify them.

" The power of man over animal life, in producing whatever varieties of form he pleases, is enormously great. It would seem as though the physical structure of future generations was almost as plastic as clay, under the control of the breeder's will. It is my desire to show, more pointedly than, so far as I am aware, has been attempted before, that mental qualities are equally under control."

Then follows a discussion of inherited abilities, of the same character as that which was afterwards developed more fully in *Hereditary Genius*. If I were to re-write the above passage, it would be modified by limiting the power of the breeder to perpetuating and intensifying qualities which have *already appeared* in the race. The possibility would at the same time be recognised of the unforeseen appearance of "sports" or "mutations" of a kind not hitherto observed, but which for all that may become hereditary. Such in past times may have been the electric organs of certain eels and rays, the illuminating capacity of glow-worms, fire-flies, and inhabitants of deep waters, the venom in certain snakes, and the power of speech in man.

After some pages of remarks, the latter of them on the physical attributes of very able men, the article continues :—

"Most notabilities have been great eaters and excellent digesters, on literally the same principle that the furnace which can raise more steam than is usual for one of its size must burn more freely and well than is common. Most great men are vigorous animals with exuberant powers and an extreme devotion to a cause. There is no reason to suppose that in breeding for the highest order of intellect we should produce a sterile or a feeble race."

I should now alter the last sentence to "There is no reason to doubt that a very high order of intellect might be bred with little, if any, sacrifice of fertility or vigour."

"Many forms of civilisation have been peculiarly unfavourable to the hereditary transmission of rare talent. None of them were more prejudicial to it than that of the Middle Ages, when almost every youth of genius was attracted into the Church and enrolled in the rank of a celibate clergy."

This argument was largely developed in *Hereditary Genius*.

"Another great hindrance to it is a costly tone of society, like that of our own, where it becomes a folly for a rising man to encumber himself with domestic expenses, which custom exacts, and which are larger than his resources are able to meet. Here also genius is celibate, at least during the best period of manhood.

"A spirit of clique is not bad. I understand that in Germany it is very much the custom for professors to marry the [sisters] or daughters of other professors, and I have some reason to believe, but am anxious for fuller information before I can feel sure of it, that the enormous intellectual digestion of German literary men, which far exceeds that of the corresponding class of our own countrymen, may, in some considerable degree, be due to this practice."

I have not even yet obtained the information desired in the last paragraph, the correspondents who partly promised to give it not having done so. As many members of our House of Lords marry the daughters of millionaires, it is quite conceivable that our Senate may in time become characterised by a more than common share of shrewd business capacity, possibly also by a lower standard of commercial probity than at present.

"So far as beauty is concerned . . . it is not so very long ago in England that it was thought quite natural that the strongest lance at the tournament should win the fairest or the noblest lady. The lady was the prize to be tilted for. She rarely objected to the arrangement, because her vanity was gratified by the *éclat* of the proceeding. Now history is justly charged with a tendency to repeat itself. We may therefore reasonably look forward to the possibility, I do not say the probability, of some such practice of competition. What an extraordinary effect might be produced on our race if its object was to unite in marriage those who possessed the finest and most suitable natures, mental, moral, and physical!"

The last paragraph must of course be interpreted in the semi-jocular sense in which it was written.

I may here speak of some attempts by myself, made hitherto in too desultory a way, to obtain materials for a "Beauty-Map" of the British Isles. Whenever I have occasion to classify the persons I meet into three classes, "good, medium, bad," I use a needle mounted as a pricker, wherewith to prick holes, unseen, in a piece of paper, torn rudely into a cross with a long leg. I use its upper end for "good," the cross-arm for "medium," the lower end for "bad." The prick-holes keep distinct, and are easily read off at leisure. The object, place, and date are written on the paper. I used this plan for my beauty data, classifying the girls I passed in streets or elsewhere as attractive, indifferent, or repellent. Of course this was a purely individual estimate, but it was consistent, judging from the conformity of different attempts in the same population. I found London to rank highest for beauty ; Aberdeen lowest.

In another article, after some further discussion, I say :—

" I hence conclude that the improvement of the breed of mankind is no insuperable difficulty. If everybody were to agree on the improvement of the race of man being a matter of the very utmost importance, and if the theory of the hereditary transmission of qualities in men was as thoroughly understood as it is in the case of our domestic animals, I see no absurdity in supposing that, in some way or other, the improvement would be carried into effect.

" Most persons seem to have an idea that a new element, specially fashioned in heaven, and not transmitted by simple descent, is introduced into the body of every new-born infant. It is impossible this should be true, unless there exists some property or quality in man that is not transmissible by descent. But the terms *talent* and *character* are exhaustive ; they include the whole of man's spiritual nature, so far as we are able to understand it. No other class of qualities is known to exist, that we might suppose to have been interpolated from on high."

The article concludes as follows :—

" It is a common theme of moralists of many creeds, that man is born with an imperfect nature. He has lofty aspirations, but there is a weakness in his disposition that incapacitates him from carrying his nobler purposes into effect. He sees that some particular course of action is his duty, and should be his delight ; but his inclinations are fickle and base, and do not conform to his better judgment. The whole moral nature of man is tainted with sin, which prevents him from doing the things he knows to be right.

" I venture to offer an explanation of this apparent anomaly which seems perfectly satisfactory from a scientific point of view. It is neither more nor less than that the development of our nature, under Darwin's law of Natural Selection, has not yet over-taken the development of our religious civilisation. Man was barbarous but yesterday, and therefore it is not to be expected that the natural aptitudes of his race should already have become moulded into accordance with his very recent advance. We men of the present centuries are like animals suddenly trans-planted among new conditions of climate and of food ; our instincts fail us under the altered circumstances.

" My theory is confirmed by the fact that the members of old civilisations are far less sensible than those newly converted from barbarism, of their nature being inadequate to their moral needs. The conscience of a negro is aghast at his own wild impulsive nature, and is easily stirred by a preacher ; but it is scarcely possible to ruffle the self-complacency of a steady-going Chinaman.

" The sense of Original Sin would show, according to my theory, not that man was fallen from a high estate, but that he was rapidly rising from a low one. It would therefore confirm the conclusion that has been arrived at by every independent line of ethno-logical research, that our forefathers were utter savages . . . and that after myriads of years of barbarism our race has but very recently grown to be civilised and religious."

The above paragraphs appeared also in *Hereditary Genius*.

These views published by me forty-five years ago are still up to date, owing to the slow advance of the popular mind in its appreciation of the force of heredity. My fault in other parts of these articles was a tendency to overrate the speed with which a great improvement of the race of mankind might, theoretically, be effected. I had not then made out the law of Regression. With this qualification the above extracts express my present views.

Before concluding with these magazine articles, I will make yet another extract in reference to a subject which a friend urged upon me quite recently as a worthy subject of experiment, namely, the breeding of animals for intelligence. The following extract shows that I considered it long ago. I have frequently since thought of making an attempt to carry it out, but it would have occupied more time and money than I could have spared. As it is just possible that the idea may now catch the fancy of some one, and induce him to make a trial, I reprint the passage here :—

"So far as I am aware, no animals have ever been bred for general intelligence. Special aptitudes are thoroughly controlled by the breeder. He breeds Dogs that point, that retrieve, that fondle or that bite ; but no one has ever yet attempted to breed for high general intellect, irrespective of all other qualifications. It would be a most interesting subject for an attempt.

We hear constantly of prodigies of dogs, whose very intelligence makes them of little value as slaves. When they are wanted, they are apt to be absent on their own errands. They are too critical of their master's conduct. For instance, an intelligent dog shows marked contempt for an unsuccessful sports-man. He will follow nobody along a road that leads to a well-known tedious errand. He does not readily forgive a man who wounds his self-esteem. He is often a dexterous thief and a sad hypocrite. For these reasons an over-intelligent dog is not an object of particular desire, and therefore I suppose no one has ever thought of encouraging a breed of wise dogs. But it would be a most interesting occupation for a country philosopher to pick up the cleverest dogs he could hear of, and mate them together, generation after generation—breeding purely for intellectual power, and disregarding shape, size, and every other quality."

The phrase "regardless of every other quality" is too strong, some regard should be paid to the physique and to the character of the dogs.

Perhaps twenty females, ten males, and a fluctu-ating population of puppies would be enough for an experiment. The cost of this would not be very great, and would be sensibly diminished in time by money derived from the sale of pups.

The idea of the improvement of the human race was again mooted in 1884, and the term Eugenics was then first applied to it in my *Human Faculty*. Afterwards it was strongly emphasised in my "Huxley Lecture" before the Anthropological Institute in 1901 [161], on the "Possible Improvement of the Human

Breed under the existing conditions of Law and Sentiment."

Great steps towards estimating the values of the influences concerned in effecting it had been made in the meantime by Professor Karl Pearson. He took up my work on Correlation [104], vastly extending its theory, and adding largely to the data. I had gone no further than to obtain simple results based on the Gaussian law of distribution ; he worked out those results with great mathematical skill and elaboration. He also generalised them so as to deal with other laws of distribution than the Gaussian.

Moreover, Professor Karl Pearson established a Biometric Laboratory in University College, where accurate computations are made, and whence a quarterly publication, *Biometrika*, is issued. It was established by him and Professor Weldon, whose untimely death has been a deep sorrow to many friends and a serious loss to the science of heredity. I also was nominally connected with *Biometrika* as " Consulting Editor."

The ground had thus become more or less prepared for further advance ; so, after talking over the matter with the authorities of the University of London, and obtaining their ready concurrence, I supplied sufficient funds to allow of a small establishment for the furtherance of Eugenics. The University provided rooms, and gave the sanction of their name and various facilities, and I provided the salaries for a Research Fellow and for a Research Scholar. The Eugenics Laboratory of the University of London is now situated in University College, in connection with Professor Karl Pearson's biometric laboratory, and I am glad to say he has consented to take it, for the present at least, under his very able superintendence ; as I am too old and infirm now to be able to look properly after it. Valuable memoirs are being published by the Laboratory from time to time, and the young institution promises to be a permanent success.

The authorities of the newly established Sociological Society were disposed to take up the subject of Race Improvement, so I gave lectures at two of their meetings in 1904 and 1905, which are published in Vols I. and II. of the *Sociological Papers* [169]. The subjects were on, " Eugenics, its Scope and Aims," " Restrictions in Marriage," " Studies in National Eugenics," and " Eugenics as a Factor in Religion." Eugenics is officially defined in the Minutes of the University of London as "the study of agencies under social control that may improve or impair the racial qualities of future generations, either physically or mentally."

Skilful and cautious statistical treatment is needed in most of the many inquiries upon whose results the methods of Eugenics will rest. A full account of the inquiries is necessarily technical and dry, but the results are not, and a " Eugenics Education Society " has been recently established to popularise those results. At the request of its Committee I have lately joined it as Hon. President, and hope to aid its work so far as the small powers that an advanced age still leaves intact may permit.

A true philanthropist concerns himself not only with society as a whole, but also with as many of the individuals who compose it as the range of his affections can include. If a man devotes himself solely to the good of a nation as a whole, his tastes must be impersonal and his conclusions so far heartless, deserving the ill title of "dismal" with which Carlyle labelled statistics. If, on the other hand, he attends only to certain individuals in whom he happens to take an interest, he becomes guided by favouritism and is oblivious of the rights of others and of the futurity of the race. Charity refers to the individual; Statesmanship to the nation; Eugenics cares for both.

It is known that a considerable part of the huge stream of British charity furthers by indirect and unsuspected ways the production of the Unfit; it is most desirable that money and other attention bestowed on harmful forms of charity should be diverted to the production and well-being of the Fit. For clearness of explanation we may divide newly married couples into three classes, with respect to the probable civic worth of their offspring. There would be a small class of "desirables," a large class of "passables," of whom nothing more will be said here, and a small class of "undesirables." It would clearly be advantageous to the country if social and moral support as well as timely material help were extended to the desirables, and not monopolised as it is now apt to be by the undesirables.

I take Eugenics very seriously, feeling that its principles ought to become one of the dominant motives in a civilised nation, much as if they were one of its religious tenets. I have often expressed myself in this sense, and will conclude this book by briefly reiterating my views.

Individuals appear to me as partial detachments from the infinite ocean of Being, and this world as a stage on which Evolution takes place, principally hitherto by means of Natural Selection, which achieves the good of the whole with scant regard to that of the individual.

Man is gifted with pity and other kindly feelings; he has also the power of preventing many kinds of suffering. I conceive it to fall well within his province to replace Natural Selection by other processes that are more merciful and not less effective.

This is precisely the aim of Eugenics. Its first object is to check the birth-rate of the Unfit, instead of allowing them to come into being, though doomed in large numbers to perish prematurely. The second object is the improvement of the race by furthering the productivity of the Fit by early marriages and healthful rearing of their children. Natural Selection rests upon excessive production and wholesale destruction; Eugenics on bringing no more individuals into the world than can be properly cared for, and those only of the best stock.

GALTONIA CANDICANS

APPENDIX

PRINCIPAL AWARDS AND DEGREES

INDEX